Southerners and Other Americans

Southerners and Other Americans

GRADY McWHINEY

Basic Books, Inc., Publishers
NEW YORK

PREFACE

Early in the nineteenth century a young New Englander, Henry C. Knight, visited the South and commented upon how "peculiar" the speech he heard was to "a northern ear." Both the sounds and their meaning seemed foreign to him. "The Virginians use clever for intelligent; whereas we use it for a kind of negative character of weak intellect," wrote Knight. "What . . . we call afternoon, they call evening. . . . *Tote* . . . is much used; implying both suspension and locomotion. They say—to grow a crop, for, to raise a crop; he was raised, for, he was educated; mad for angry. . . ." Both Virginians and Kentuckians "tuck a *t* at the end of such words as onct, twict, skifft," observed Knight; the "word *great* is sometimes used to signify *little;* as, that lady has a great foot, meaning, without irony, a little foot"; and "the epithet *mighty* is quite popular with old and young, as, for instance, mighty weak."

Differences other than accents and speech habits have separated Southerners and Northerners throughout most of American history, but there has never been agreement on the extent or the depth of these variations. Thomas Jefferson thought that they were vast. He characterized Southerners as hotheaded, indolent, unstable, and unjust; Northerners as cool tempered, sober, persistent, and upright. Alexis de Tocqueville noted differences, but he concluded: "The observer who examines . . . the United States . . . will readily discover that their inhabitants . . . constitute a single people; . . . more truly a united society than some nations of Europe which live under the same legislation and the same prince."

Historians have carried on the argument. At one extreme—Francis B. Simkins who stressed, especially in *The Everlasting South* (1963), that section's incongruity with the rest of the nation and the distinctness of southern culture; at the other extreme—such historians as Charles G. Sellers, Jr., who insisted in *The Southerner as American* (1960) that a common Americanism has united Southerners and Northerners throughout their history and "that the traditional emphasis on the South's differentness and on the conflict between Southernism and Americanism is wrong historically."

Just how much Southerners and Northerners differed and the consequences of their unconformity has long fascinated me. In the following essays, written over the past twenty years, I have tried to analyze some of the historical relationships between Southerners and other Americans as well as between groups and classes of Southerners.

My research suggests that at times regional differences have been exaggerated; at other times they have been distorted. So have certain differences and similarities among Southerners. Too often writers have lumped large numbers of people together into poorly defined groups and generalized about their attitudes and characteristics. Acts or statements by a few became the basis for conclusions about many. Any generalization—even the most insightful and suggestive—is subject to criticism. But there is a vast difference between a tentative thesis, admittedly speculative and meant to challenge, and a conclusion arrived at by following preconceptions or applying prescribed dogma.

Included here are studies on party politics in antebellum Alabama, the political fate of the freedmen, and the Socialist vote in Louisiana in 1912, which indicate that the politics of consensus and convenience has been pervasive in the South as well as elsewhere in the country. Except perhaps on the question of slavery, Americans of all regions have generally made common cause wherever their advantage lay. Most people seem to be apolitical most of the time. Usually they leave politics to the politicians and go about the ordinary pursuits permitted by their occupations and life-styles. The political behavior that appears to form national patterns in response to deep philosophical questions is frequently only the "accident" of largely local combinations of economic and social interests that can be incorporated into national platforms.

Though most of the essays in this volume treat of political and social affairs, a few concentrate upon military subjects—sensitive topics, partly because many myths are associated with them. It has been claimed that warfare is one of the few activities in which Southerners excel. Such a generalization is easier to refute than to dispel; it clings to the popular mind like gun smoke to a breezeless battlefield. Nevertheless, I have tried to clear some of the air by examining generalizations about the social and military roles of certain Southerners and other Americans. A study of Old Army officers gave me an opportunity to assess the impact of standardized education and expectations on some of the most intimate values men possess. Though military education at West Point modified certain aspects of behavior, it left attitudes on sex, women, and marriage as diverse as it found them. Other essays reveal the influence of a Southerner upon the military thinking of the Union's most successful general, how those two symbols of sectionalism—Abraham Lincoln and Jefferson

Davis—acted in the "first shot" crisis, why Davis selected certain military leaders, and to what extent he and they were responsible for the Confederacy's defeat.

Myths about slavery, plantations, poor whites, secession, the Civil War, Reconstruction, black-white relations, and a host of other topics envelop the South. Southerners as well as Northerners have been the willing captives of certain legends. Some have been nurtured by science or social science and some by monistic ideology; other myths were deliberately cultivated and perpetuated to support white supremacy or the political dominance of certain groups. Whatever the reason, the result has been a distortion of much of the thinking and writing about the South. Often it is pictured as the most out-of-step part of the nation, the deformity that has long prevented Americans from living up to their own self-image of the world's nicest and most beautiful people. For more than a century people have been trying to reform the South, and much of this reformist spirit is evident in writing about the section. Authors had to get right with prevailing opinion; those who failed to damn white Southerners or to denounce Dixie's backwardness, meanness, and racism were usually dismissed as apologists for the South. Yet some of the writers who attacked the southern version of Americanism were surprisingly ignorant of the circumstances they attempted to describe. Nor has the danger of distortion passed. In recent years the growing separation between blacks and whites has added suspicion and hostility to the already difficult task of understanding what motivated the people of both races.

The testing of generalizations and stereotypes has always delighted me. Attacking myths, I believe, is one of a historian's most enjoyable activities. It could be argued that such pursuits have some useful purpose, for people certainly can understand each other better when their minds are uncluttered by falsehoods. But hunting myths is also what historians do, for good or ill, simply because that is the way they were trained, and because they have a taste for discovering what really happened. In such studies as "The Ghostly Legend of the Ku Klux Klan," "Reconstruction and Americanism," and "The Meaning of Emancipation," I attempted to correct some errors that had crept into our thinking about races and sections. Blacks were less credulous than some historians had supposed, and white Northerners—when it was advantageous—exploited Negroes as readily as did white Southerners. Once again, the evidence indicates that differences between races and sections were no more pronounced than similarities.

The South, a victim of myth and history, may well continue to seem strangely unlike the rest of America. In the aftermath of the civil rights movement, as I suggest in the concluding essay on black history, the black power banner has replaced the bloody shirt. While the memory of slavery still evokes strong feelings, the South surely will retain a half-mythical uniqueness often defined by exaggerated accusations and uncritical rationalizations. Writers may continue to distort the South's past, but they should at least recognize that there is now and has always been much variation among Southerners—that the South has generally been as devoted as the rest of the country to such pervasive American values as capitalism, economic and social mobility, materialism, democracy and republicanism, evangelical religion, patriotic nationalism, consensus politics, and utilitarianism. Moreover, there is considerable evidence that today there is as much race and class prejudice and perhaps more hypocrisy in northern cities and suburbs than in the South.

Of course the South is different. There are sounds and sights and scents below the Potomac found nowhere else. Life there seems slower paced. Pollution is much in evidence, yet the air often appears fresher, the water clearer, than in most other comparably populated areas of the country. It is still easier to get a hearty breakfast in the South than in most other places; people generally are more courteous, more friendly. If all this is a nostalgic impression of one who was born in the South but has lived outside the region most of his adult life, it is nevertheless a very strong impression. The South, whether blossoming or sweltering, may differ from the rest of the country more sensually than economically or politically, more in style than in substance.

But style is too important to discount. Southernness does not necessarily mean separateness, but it does suggest that the people of the South have been, and are, other Americans.

GRADY MCWHINEY
Wayne State University

ACKNOWLEDGMENTS

During the two decades that I have been studying and writing about the South, I have become indebted to many people. My first real interest in the region's history developed while I was an undergraduate at Centenary College. The man who introduced me to the subject was W. Darrell Overdyke, without whose encouragement I probably would not have gone to graduate school.

At Louisiana State University, where I received a master's degree, several people influenced my thinking about the South. Francis B. Simkins, who did so much more for me than direct my master's thesis, had the most profound impact upon me. I also learned much from other professors—especially T. Harry Williams, who excited my interest in the Civil War—and from Charles P. Roland and Otis Singletary, who were then more advanced graduate students.

Had Simkins remained at LSU, I doubtless would have stayed on, for I had become devoted to him both as a teacher and as a friend. I could not follow him because the college to which he was going offered no doctoral program. Moreover, he argued that I should study outside the South. He recalled his own experiences as a country boy from South Carolina studying at Columbia University; there, he suggested, was the place for me to lose some of my provincialism. He wrote, in his inimitable style, to Harold Syrett, then a Columbia professor, asking him to take me in hand.

That letter and the associations that followed from it shaped my future. Syrett was most cordial when I called at his office; he told me that a brilliant young assistant professor was offering his first Ph.D. seminar and that there might be a place for me in it. A call to the professor arranged an interview for me, and subsequently I was admitted to the seminar. That is how I became one of David Herbert Donald's students.

Being a Donald student was then, and it has continued to be, an invaluable experience. No one has ever taught me more. Those of us who made it through his first seminar—Ari Hoogenboom, Stanley P. Hirshson, Irwin Unger, and myself—learned from each other, but not nearly so much as we learned from David Donald. He was a taskmaster who wrote more on the margin and back of seminar papers than his students wrote on the front. He terrified us all; each time we turned in a paper we feared that it would be our last, that he would drop us from the seminar. But his teaching techniques worked with us. A little fear stimulated our desire to improve and probably was just what most of us needed. He always mixed encouragement and sometimes even praise with devastating criticism. If you could profit from criticism, he would give his time without stint. He was always accessible to his students and concerned with their welfare. For twenty years I have been the recipient of his help, kindness, patience, and understanding. He directed my doctoral dissertation and has read critically most of what I have written. I continue to admire and to learn from him.

It is impossible to list here all the people who have tried in various ways to help me understand the South, but I must acknowledge a few of them. My old friend Ari Hoogenboom read and offered advice on nearly all of the essays in this volume. Other friends who have read one or more of the essays and made valuable suggestions are Ray A. Billington, Robert R. Dykstra, Don E. Fehrenbacher, June I. Gow, William Gum, Holman Hamilton, Stanley P. Hirshson, John T. Hubbell, Perry D. Jamieson, Henry A. Kmen, William E. Leuchtenberg, E. B. Long, Penelope K. Majeske, Howard H. Quint, Charles P. Roland, Herbert H. Rowen, Charles G. Sellers, Jr., David A. Shannon, Kenneth M. Stampp, W. Patrick Strauss, Irwin Unger, V. Jacque Voegeli, Robert C. Walton, Bell I. Wiley, and T. Harry Williams.

I am indebted to the original publishers for permission to reprint the following essays:

"Were the Whigs a Class Party in Alabama?" which first appeared in the *Journal of Southern History* 23 (1957): 510–22. Copyright 1957 by the Southern Historical Association. Reprinted by permission of the Managing Editor.

"The Confederacy's First Shot," which originally was published in *Civil War History* 14 (1968): 5–14.

"Who Whipped Whom?" which appeared in *Civil War History* 11 (1965): 5–26.

"Reconstruction and Americanism," which was first published in Charles G. Sellers, Jr., ed., *The Southerner as American* (Chapel Hill: University of North Carolina Press, 1960), pp. 89–103.

"The Ghostly Legend of the Ku Klux Klan," written in collaboration with Francis B. Simkins, which was first published in the *Negro History Bulletin* 14 (1951): 109–12.

"Rustic Radicalism," which originally appeared under a somewhat expanded title in the *Journal of Southern History* 20 (1954): 315–36. Copyright 1954 by the Southern Historical Association. Reprinted by permission of the Managing Editor.

GM

CONTENTS

Southerners
and Other
Americans

CHAPTER I

Late Antebellum Americans

One of the great myths of American history is that when the Civil War began Southerners were fundamentally different from Northerners. Many writers—before and after the war—have fostered this myth. Their exaggeration of southern nationalism, "Cavalier and Yankee" stereotypes, and the differences between the economies of the North and the South have convinced generations that in 1861 the two sections were basically divergent and antagonistic. Off and on for over a hundred years Americans have been told that the Civil War was "irrepressible," the result of an inevitable clash between diametrically opposed civilizations—one democratic, industrial, and progressive; the other aristocratic, agricultural, and static. At the war's outset soldiers on both sides—victims of this same propaganda—thought that Northerners and Southerners were basically different people. Rebels had been taught that Yankees were vulgar, materialistic, brutal, and deceitful. Yankees, on the other hand, considered Rebels ignorant, arrogant, dirty, brutal, and untrustworthy. Each side denounced the other as cowards and drunkards. It was a surprise to many soldiers to discover, as the war progressed, how much they had in common with their enemies. In 1864 a Union private wrote of fraternization with Confederates in Georgia: "We made a bargain with them that we would not fire on them if they would not fire on us, and they were as good as their word. It seems too bad that we have to fight men that we like. Now these Southern soldiers seem just like our own boys. . . ."

Writers, intent upon showing the Civil War era's conflicts and controversies, have tended to magnify the differences between Northerners and Southerners out of all proportion. In 1861 the United States did not contain, as some people have suggested, two civilizations. Many Southerners were more similar to certain Northerners than to other Southerners; southern highlanders and Louisiana Cajuns, for example, shared little in common with other inhabitants of the South. Tennesseeans and Ohioans might actually be more alike than Tennesseeans and Mississippians, but that depended upon whether the Tennesseeans lived in the eastern, middle, or western part of their state and on whether the Ohioans lived in the northern or southern part of their state. Variations existed nearly everywhere in the United States. Each state and section had a wide range of types. Most areas had citizens who were rich or poor, religious or irreligious, boastful or modest, indolent or energetic, honest or dishonest. Some white Northerners defended slavery; some white Southerners opposed it. White people generally considered black people their inferiors, but often whites and blacks alike looked down on "poor white trash." Certain slaves were freer than certain free whites. The vast majority of white men—even in the South—owned no slaves, but some black men owned other blacks. Lumberjacks, farmers, merchants, and fishermen shared common interests whether they lived in Michigan or North Carolina; so did a wide range of other people.

Besides exaggerating sectional differences, observers have too often ignored or minimized the common elements of the antebellum American experience. By focusing upon the importance of slavery, the secession controversy, and the Civil War—undeniably some of the most compelling and dramatic events of the nineteenth century—they have obscured certain fundamental patterns of social history. They also have overlooked the importance of occupations, which were more significant than sections in determining an American's life style. A man's social location was a much more revealing index to his place in pre–Civil War America than was his geographical location. The overwhelming reality of the time was a fantastic rate of economic expansion, and what people did for a living—as well as where they did it—determined their share in that expansion. Though people of the same vocation held varied attitudes, occupational categories created subcultures that influenced behavior and helped shape social, economic, and political attitudes.

The absence of rigid sectionalism before 1860 was nowhere more apparent than in politics. In 1850 no single party or group controlled American politics. The president was a Whig, but thirteen more Democrats than Whigs sat in Congress. Even so, the balance of power in the House of Representatives, where Democrats outnumbered Whigs by only three, rested with nine members of the Free-Soil party. Since 1841, after twelve years of domination by Jacksonians, American politics had been relatively fluid, without a consistent majority party. From 1841 to 1850 no party controlled both the presidency and Congress for more than two years.

Nor did either major party rely exclusively upon one social class or section of the country for support. Whiggery more than Democracy appealed to persons of established family and wealth, but the Whig party also attracted men of humble background like David Crockett and Abraham Lincoln. To insist that most Whigs were wealthy aristocrats, as some writers have done, suggests an uncritical acceptance of Democratic propaganda. Successful American parties are never homogeneous; they cut across class and regional lines, appeal to as many diverse interests as possible, and almost always have both a liberal and a conservative wing. These axioms were as true in the fifties as they are today, for the primary aim of American parties and political leaders is to win elections and to stay in office. To accomplish this end they appeal to and "represent" more voters than their opponents; all else is subverted to the struggle for office and its privileges of power and patronage. Naturally men of wealth were Democrats just as men of wealth were Whigs. But meshed in each organization were planters and small farmers, bankers and debtors, manufacturers and mechanics, city and country folk, Northerners and Southerners. No one can say precisely what motives bound these various men together—self-interest, idealism, the influence of friends or relatives, the charisma of some leader.

Disunity was impossible so long as these alliances held firm, for both major parties cut across sectional lines. Each had strong organizations in nearly every state. Even in the South political contests were usually close and neither party enjoyed a decisive advantage. For nearly thirty years the South voted for the winning presidential candidate, Whig or Democrat. The South simply followed the general political and party patterns of the rest of the country, though certain southern states sometimes deviated from the national norm. South Carolina, Tennessee, and Kentucky frequently supported unsuccessful candidates. In the eight presidential elections between 1824 and 1852, South Carolina backed losers five times; Tennessee and Kentucky voted for defeated candidates four times. In contrast, the slave states of Mississippi, North Carolina, and Georgia supported losers only twice in these same eight elections, and Louisiana voted for winners seven times. Only one northern state had a better record of picking winners; New York supported all eight winners. Several northern states voted for more losers than victors. Vermont backed a winner twice; Massachusetts three times. Ohio and New Jersey voted for the victorious candidate in only half of the elections.

National voting patterns indicate no real sectional unity before the fifties. Alabama and Illinois were on the same side in all eight presidential elections between 1824 and 1852; Illinois and Massachusetts were never on the same side in any of these elections. Alabama and Pennsylvania supported the same candidates in six elections; Pennsylvania and Massachusetts supported the same candidates twice. Tennessee and Ohio were on the same side more often than New York and New Jersey. Louisiana and Indiana voted alike six times; Louisiana and South Carolina only three times. North and South Carolina backed the same men in only three contests, but North Carolina and New York were on the same side in six elections. Between 1840 and 1848, when the Whigs and the Democrats were most evenly matched, Whig presidential candidates carried a total of twenty southern states; Democratic candidates won eighteen southern states.

In the fifties, of course, political parties divided, and new parties emerged. After the Compromise of 1850 "conscience" Whigs and anti-slavery Democrats began to act together. Righteous mobs of Northerners, outraged by the fugitive slave act, defied federal law to rescue captured Negroes. Sentiment became so strong that some northern states passed "personal liberty laws" to protect escaped slaves. These laws were justified on states' rights grounds. Gradually the old national parties lost supporters; multiple interest politics simply gave way to idealism, intolerance, and local interest. In the South the old parties split into secessionist and unionist camps. In the North many former Whigs and Democrats joined the Republican party, which was completely sectional in its appeal. This rift in the national parties undermined political compromise, elected a minority president in 1860, and resulted in the secession of the states of the lower South.

It cannot be denied that there were real differences between the sections in the late antebellum period. Many Southerners believed that everyone else in the country was out of step. "Why," asked a young Georgian, "are strangers so critical of us?" The answer, of course, was the South's devotion to slavery. Nowhere in the western world was the "peculiar institution" defended more strongly. To the abolitionist, slavery was a nightmare of terror and oppression, but to the apologist it was a happy system of reciprocal relationships and mutual respect. There were, in fact, at least three proslavery positions. Dr. Josiah Nott and his racist supporters offered "scientific" evidence that the Negro was subhuman and therefore should be held perpetually in bondage. The religionists, who probably represented the views of a majority of slaveholders, rejected the racist thesis as incompatible with the Christian doctrine of mankind's unity; they considered slavery a transition between barbarism and civilization to be ended in the distant future when plantation life had prepared the Negro for freedom. The feudalists, like the religionists, championed a personalized and familial view of slavery. They too believed that the Negro was human, but they argued that slavery benefited both master and slave. The feudalists wanted the institution to remain static, a bulwark against undesired social change. All advocates agreed that if slavery as it existed in the fifties was not a positive good, it was necessary as a labor system and a social control system.

Thus Southerners defended slavery because they considered it profitable and because they feared that its abolition would create more problems than it would solve. There is no easy answer to the endless debate over whether or not slavery was profitable, for the institution was as complex and as difficult to characterize as capitalism. A few Southerners damned slavery as uneconomical, but more people owned more slaves in the fifties than ever before. Slaves appeared to be an excellent investment; they could perform a variety of tasks, including the reproduction of slaves who might be added to the owner's labor force or sold in a steadily rising market. Though less than a fourth of all free Southerners owned slaves, nonslaveholders had practical, thoroughly American reasons for defending the "peculiar institution." Slave ownership represented wealth and success, and those who had none hoped to acquire human chattel some day. Even in the upcountry, where slaves constituted a small percentage of the population, small farmers often defended slavery. The Scotch-Irish and German settlers of Burke County, North Carolina, for example, were realists who had known hard labor and poverty. Their respect for property was almost fanatical, and they labored assiduously to acquire wealth. Slavery was an established institution that they accepted readily without qualms. To them legality was synonymous with morality; they were slaveholders without a guilty conscience. Some slaveowners did object to slavery on moral grounds, but just how many is difficult to determine. The overwhelming majority of planters and farmers throughout the South probably agreed that their own economic opportunity depended upon the maintenance of Negro bondage. A farmer could make a start—grow a little cotton on a few acres—without slaves, but to cultivate a great estate he needed a large gang of slaves. He knew that he had a chance to become wealthy because cotton was a democratic crop. Unlike most other staples, it allowed a man with little capital to begin on a small scale, but it placed no limits on his expansion. Thus cotton and slavery complemented each other; together they provided the opportunity for many white men to become rich.

In 1850 over half of the South's 74,000 cotton plantations were in Alabama, Mississippi, and Georgia. There, as well as on the sugar estates of south Louisiana and the rice plantations of South Carolina and Georgia, lived the richest masters and the overwhelming majority of slaves. A slave's life was shaped by many factors: his own personality and intelligence, his job, where he lived, his master's character. Generally slaves received better treatment if they lived on a small farm rather than on a large plantation, or in the upper rather than in the lower South. Slaves who were skilled artisans usually enjoyed more freedom than members of a field gang. House servants might be indulged or brutalized as the master pleased, but most suffering took place in the large plantation's slave camps remote from the master's home. Slaves were worked hardest on the big cotton estates and in the rice and sugarcane fields, where absentee owners sometimes demanded profits at any cost.

The acquisitive spirit permeated southern life in the fifties. Southerners sometimes believed themselves untouched by the American business ethic, but they were as devoted as Northerners to the profit motive. Nearly every ambitious Southerner wanted to be a planter. "Cotton planting is the most lucrative business that can be followed," wrote one man. "Some planters net $50,000 from a single crop."

Perhaps cotton was too democratic. "The farmers in this country live in a miserable manner," wrote a visitor to the deep South. "They think only of making money and their log houses are hardly fit to live in. If the price of cotton stays up, everybody will starve. No one will raise corn for man or beast." Too many planters had come to depend upon cotton as a certain way to wealth. It was not. During the fifties overproduction and increased competition for markets drove the price of cotton down. Some attempts were made to stabilize declining prices by crop diversification, direct trade with Europe, and legislation to check the migration of slaves westward. None was successful. Most planters simply planted more cotton to maintain or to increase their income, thus depressing prices further. Few planters admitted that overproduction and declining prices caused their difficulties; it was easier to blame the tariff, the greedy merchants, the North.

Southerners were not the only people in the country who complained; indeed, discontent was already an American characteristic. Citizens in every part of the nation were forever complaining about this or that or things in general. This did not mean that the average American in the fifties was discouraged or oppressed. On the contrary, he boasted of his freedom and opportunity. But complaining had simply become a habit.

Farmers complained as much as anyone, yet in the late antebellum period no group of Americans enjoyed higher status or more political power. The fifties were golden years for agriculturists, northern and southern. They and their commercial allies controlled the country, which was overwhelmingly rural—nearly 85 percent of the American people lived on farms. American farmers generally were prosperous and confident, so affluent in fact that they began to build pretentious houses and to buy manufactured goods from the East as well as luxury items from abroad. Many a sodbuster, goaded by wife and daughters, imported lace from France and pianos from Germany. Why not? Farms were doubling in value, and farm produce sold well. The railroads, which followed the farmer westward, speeded his staples to market. In the East and abroad there was an increasing demand for farm goods; during the fifties American grain exports more than doubled. Of the 113 million acres under cultivation in 1850, fully 31 million were planted in corn. The nation's most versatile crop, it could be eaten by the farmer's family, shelled and shipped to market, ground into meal, fed to farm animals, or made into whiskey. The 1850 corn crop alone was worth over $296 million. After corn, the most important staples were wheat and cotton. Both would become much more valuable during the fifties; in fact, by 1860 the United States grew seven-eighths of all the world's cotton. Small wonder the farmer was confident and cocksure.

So much land was available in America that almost every man owned the acreage he tilled. The average farm was 203 acres, but some men held vast estates. Stephen Duncan of Mississippi owned eight large plantations and over a thousand slaves; in 1850 his income from the sale of sugar and cotton—after deducting factor's commission, transportation costs, insurance, and other expenses—was nearly $170,000. Estates of over 20,000 acres were common even in the Middle West. Michael Sullivant, who owned 80,000 acres in Illinois, employed over a hundred laborers.

Because in the fifties the future seemed to be his, the farmer bought more land and more machines; he speculated confidently in land, and he indulged his own and his family's tastes for "store-bought" finery. The glitter of his pre–Civil War prosperity blinded him to the economic difficulties ahead—to the dislocations of civil war, to inflation followed by depression, to an inadequate credit system, to discriminatory freight rates. Within three decades the farmer would lose his aplomb; he would also have some serious doubts about the economy that had brought him to the edge of disaster. But in the late antebellum period no one suspected that the Farmer's Age was about to end. The agriculturalist believed that his prosperity was boundless, for the United States was clearly a land of unlimited riches.

Yet not all farmers were equally prosperous in the fifties. Some merely struggled along; others had to move or starve. The best opportunities, as always, attracted the most interest, and men hurried to possess fertile soil. The most populous states at the beginning of the fifties were New York, Pennsylvania, Ohio, Virginia, and Tennessee. Each had a million or more inhabitants and, except for Virginia, all had experienced a population increase of 25 percent or more since 1840. But their growth was modest compared to the population increase in the West. In 1820 73 percent of the American people lived east of the Allegheny Mountains; in 1850 only 55 percent resided east of the mountains. In the decade of the forties no less than seven western states had population increases of 45 percent or more, and five new states with a total of nearly 900,000 citizens had entered the Union.

Wisconsin was typical of these western states. A territory with 30,000 inhabitants in 1840, it boasted a population of 300,000 in 1850. No place in the country seemed to offer such promise. Land was fertile and cheap; government tracts sold for as little as $1.25 per acre. There were so many buyers the land office in Milwaukee often sold $200,000 worth of real estate a week. City lots increased in value fivefold between 1845 and 1850. Wages were high and taxes were low; 160 acres of good land was taxed only $8 a year.

Relatively inexpensive transportation to the West also helped attract hordes of immigrants. A trip through the Erie Canal, from Albany to Buffalo, New York, cost only $7.50, with meals; less comfortable accommodations were available for as little as $2, but the traveler had to provide his own food. One immigrant recalled that breakfast on an Erie Canal boat consisted of "Baked Potatoes, all Hot Bread and Butter, new Milk, smoked Ham, Tea or Coffee, preserved fruits, Biscuits & Jam." He also described the dinner table as "Loaded with Plenty of the good things of this life—enough to tempt the appetite of a Epicure and no stint." During the night, while the traveler slept, his boots were polished by "a Darkey." From Buffalo through the Great Lakes, steamships carried passengers to Milwaukee in four days at the amazingly low cost of $10, scarcely more than the price of a four-day stay in a good hotel. These lake steamers were elegant as well as fast. "The vessel is equipped in every possible way for the convenience of the passengers," wrote one voyager; "there is, for example, a barber shop. There is also a band, and both the food and the service, provided by Negro servants, are as good as can be found anywhere."

Besides Milwaukee, the major debarkation point for lake travelers was Chicago, America's eighteenth city in 1850 with a population of 29,963. Trains as well as steamers surged in and out of that city; the McCormick plant manufactured agricultural implements of every description, and real estate salesmen did a brisk business. "Every one in the place seemed in a hurry, and a kind of restless activity prevailed which I had seen no where else in the West, except in Cincinnati," wrote a stranger. Through Chicago in the fifties passed streams of western migrants. Most of them, as one observer reported, were "wild, rough, almost savage looking men form North Germany, Denmark and Sweden—their faces covered with grizzly beards, and their teeth clenched upon a pipe stem. They were followed by stout, well-formed, able-bodied wives and healthy children. Neither cold nor storm stopped them in their journey to the promised land."

Not every migrant found what he sought. "I have not been able to get into any kind of business yet," complained a man from Oregon Territory. "Tailoring is not worth anything. The country is so full of people wanting employment that it is hard for any to get anything to do and wages have fallen a considerable since we came. Flour is now worth $15 per hundred pounds and potatoes $2.50 per bushel. Ann and the girls take in washing and make pies to sell. We get 25 cents for washing large things; 12½ for small; we have done about $5.50 worth this week."

Thousands of people had rushed to the California gold fields, but few became rich. By 1850 gold was no longer easy to find, and living costs were high—$21 a week for board in one mining camp. "The mines are fast failing," wrote a man who stated that the average miner cleared less than $3 a day. "The stories that you read about the great amount of money taken out here, are all gammon, nine times out of ten. They are fabricated by the traders to induce people to come to this country. Be not deceived. I would advise no one to come here who can live where he is. If he were here, by making a slave of himself and living a dog's life, he might make some more than at home, but not enough to compensate him for the sacrifices he must make."

Yet determination and hope for a better life caused some men to endure hardship and disappointment. From Sacramento an Ohioan wrote his wife in 1850: "what the Devil the men will do that is crossing the Plains & coming by water to California this season God only knows for California will be Devilishly dug over this Summer. I am getting thundering tired of it myself laying on the hard ground every night & have a stone for my pillow, cooking my own bread & dinner & washing my own shirts (all of which I do) is cussed hard for a little gold. Oh! Matilda oft is the night when laying alone on the hard ground with a blanket under me & one over me that my thoughts go back to Ohio & think of you & little Sis & wish myself with you but I am willing to stand it all to make enough to get us a home & so I can be independent of some of the darned sonabitches that felt themselves above me because I was poor. Cuss them I say & I understand they prophisy that I will never come back. Darn their stinking hides if God spares my life I will show them to be false prophits for as sure as I live we will shake hands & give a warm embrace by spring anyhow & before if you say so."

Hardship drove scores of people westward. Many migrants to the Old Northwest were New Englanders in search of the economic opportunity their worn out farms no longer provided. Most of the new settlers in the Southwest in the fifties were former residents of the Southeast, for soil exhaustion and increased competition from new western farmlands had hurt them too. Much of New England and the Southeast had become agriculturally depressed areas. A Mississippian who returned to his South Carolina birthplace after a ten-year absence found the topsoil washed away and deep gullies throughout the country; almost all the land was worn out.

This relative decline of New England and the Southeast is evident in a number of ways. Between 1840 and 1850 the population of the United States increased by 36 percent, but the average increase was 19 percent in New England and only 16 percent in the Southeastern states. Moreover, real and personal estates increased at a much slower pace in New England and the Southeast than elsewhere in the country. During the fifties wealth increased 943 percent in Iowa, 557 percent in Wisconsin, and 458 percent in Illinois, but only 33 percent in Vermont, 42 percent in Massachusetts, and 58 percent in North

Carolina. At the end of the fifties New England and the Southeast could claim only two of the ten richest states, but nine of the ten states with the lowest percentage of increase in wealth were located in these two sections. The relative decline of Charleston, South Carolina, as a port is indicative. In 1772 it ranked third among American ports. By 1800 Charleston was the fifth most populous city in the United States, and it soon became the world's greatest cotton port. But the city's importance declined rapidly as cotton production shifted westward. In 1850 Charleston ranked eleventh in population, and New Orleans exported five times as much produce. As their fellow citizens moved westward, New Englanders and Southeasterners—especially South Carolinians—saw their traditional share of the nation's wealth and political power seeping through their fingers. Even the relatively prosperous were anxious about their future.

For those who could no longer live off the land, their course was clear. They must move either to the West or to town. This uprooting of farm families had a significant influence upon American social life. First, it further undermined the pattern of family authority, which had already deteriorated. In past generations the father had been a respected patriarch. Legally his position was still one of dominance, but his actual control of his family had seriously diminished. Because extra children were a burden in an agriculturally depressed community, birth control was forced upon farm families. The father, no longer able to provide for even the children he had, lost their respect and his control over them. Young unmarried men tended to migrate westward, with or without their fathers' consent. Their departure left scores of unmarried females in the New England farm country. One county, whose population scarcely increased during half a century, had over 5,000 husbandless women in 1800, but over 17,000 in 1850. There was no place for these single women on their parents' farms. They were forced to become independent, to support themselves. So many became teachers that the term *New England schoolmarm* became a commonplace. Other girls took jobs as servants, but most farmers' daughters went to work in the textile mills. The reason: no other occupation was so profitable for women. New England school teachers earned slightly higher wages than the average mill girl, but only for part of the year. Southeasterners also worked in cotton mills, but mills were fewer in their section than in New England.

Factory work, though it gave women a chance to earn a living, was scarcely attractive by modern standards. "The abolitionists of the North have mistaken the color of American slaves," wrote a visitor to the New England cotton mills; "all the real Slaves in the United States have pale faces. There are more slaves in Lowell and Nashua alone than can be found South of the Potomac." The average working day in New England mills was between twelve and thirteen hours. In the Lowell mills the operatives worked thirteen hours a day in the summer and from daylight to dark in the winter. The routine in one factory began at 4:30 every morning when a bell awoke the workers. By five they were on the job. Two hours later they took a thirty-minute break for breakfast. At noon they had another thirty minutes for lunch. There were no other rest periods between five in the morning and seven in the evening when the factory bell signaled the end of the day's labor. For this maximum effort, the rewards were modest. Weavers in the Fall River, Massachusetts, mills received only $9.00 a month, though they worked thirteen and a quarter hours a day, twenty-six days a month. Wages for spinners and weavers in other New England mills ranged from $2.50 to $5.30 a week. Most children received from forty-two to fifty cents per week, but some young laborers were paid only thirty-three cents a week. Child workers were never paid enough to support themselves from their labor. In the case of one family a father and his seven children worked in the mill. They received $837 a year, but their living expenses equaled their total earnings. Unless the whole family worked constantly, debt to the company piled up against them.

The single factory girl was better off economically, but she had to pay a price. "The young women sleep upon an average six in a room; three beds to a room," wrote a newcomer to Lowell, where some eight thousand girls were employed in the cotton mills. "There is no privacy, no retirement here; it is almost impossible to read or write alone." Another contemporary hinted that girls eventually moved from mill work into prostitution. "The average working life of the girls that come to Lowell from Maine, New Hampshire, and Vermont is only about three years. What becomes of them then? Few of them ever marry; fewer still ever return to their native places with reputations unimpaired. 'She has worked in a factory' is almost enough to damn to infamy the most worthy and virtuous girl."

Virtuous or not, the average American woman enjoyed a degree of freedom and authority that was the envy of females elsewhere. "It is a common boast with American gentlemen that their ladies rule," wrote a visitor. "In the American home the women have, in general, all the power they wish," noted another foreigner. "Woman is the center and

the lawgiver, and the American man loves it so. He likes his wife to
have her own will at home, and loves to obey." Another observer
wrote: "The reign of the women is here complete. Unbelievable as it
may sound, even in the courts the word of a woman of the lowest
classes is given more credence than that of the most respectable man."
Still another man charged that "there are no limits to the ambitions of
the free woman in the United States. She has pleaded her case so well
that almost all careers are open to her." If some women used their freedom to preach new religions, to wear trousers, to lead humanitarian
crusades, and to advocate free love and suffrage for their sex, others ex-
ercised liberty in more conventional ways. As an American admitted,
"the ladies have all they like. They dress and go shopping and have not
a care about anything; we even live in hotels to save them the trouble of
housekeeping."

Not all women were pampered. Many supported themselves and their
families. A popular business for married women and widows was the
boarding house. "I have a good feather bed," boasted a worker from
Buffalo in 1847. "Boarding & lodgings $2 per week very good living
for that price." Competition among boarding houses was often keen, but
sometimes a certain proprietress enjoyed an advantage. "There were 8
of us in the Boarding house, mostly Young Men of various trades of em-
ployments," recalled one man. "Our Landlady was a Widow about 28
with one child. . . . Of course there was some Rivalry as to who should
be her favorite."

Many women worked hard before and after they were married—
especially western wives, who were expected to cook, wash, sew, milk,
churn, and do anything else necessary to keep the household together.
But the claim that women were worked to death at an early age while
the menfolk sat around smoking pipes is unsustained by the evidence.
Though males slightly outnumbered them, females generally lived
longer; in 1850 there were 5,311 more women than men over seventy
in the United States. "The American women have fine and gentle features, are very delicately built, and know better than any others in the
world the art of adorning themselves," wrote a traveler in the fifties.
"They are very bright in conversation, always vivacious, and passion-
ately love music, singing, and dancing. Their education is poor and they
have little understanding of how to raise children. Many, in fact, do not
wish to have any children at all, out of fear of losing their beauty, and
not infrequently resort to any remedy."

Even more serious was the charge, often repeated, that American

women were lazy and frivolous. A European insisted that the overwhelming majority of American females had "an ineradicable aversion
to any work and to household affairs. They love sweets and delicacies
to a degree that there are nowhere in the world so many dentists as
here, and all make a good living." This same man charged that American women cared nothing for love: "Let the man only have money
enough to indulge them in luxuries, then he is good enough for a husband, be he old or young, handsome or plain, religious or atheist. Let
the money vanish, and with it will go faith and love." Other visitors expressed similar views, as did many native Americans. The English traveler Harriet Martineau found in the South "perhaps the weakest women
I have anywhere seen," but she also met there "some of the strongest-
minded and most remarkable women I have ever known." One man
contended that when married American women "no longer enjoy their
passions, their love of dress, their idleness, and the other conditions
under which they live, they leave their husbands and take no notice
even of their children. Such incidents are almost a matter of course.
They make daily reading matter in the American newspapers."

In such a turbulent and ambitious society, where wives and children
could easily revolt against husbands or fathers, discipline and stability
were uncommon. "In America the family . . . does not exist," wrote
the distinguished observer Alexis de Tocqueville. "All that remains of
it are a few vestiges in the first years of childhood. . . . But as soon as
the young American approaches manhood, the ties of filial obedience
are relaxed day by day; master of his thoughts, he is soon master of his
conduct." Visitors to America in the fifties frequently complained that
American children "have their own way," are full of "self-assertion and
conceit," and "easily become spoiled to all discipline" because they
are "unaccustomed to check and to control." Twenty years earlier
James Fenimore Cooper had listed "insubordination in children, and a
general want of respect for age" as major "defects in American deportment."

There seemed no way to control young Americans—half the population was under fifteen years of age in 1850—in such an open and per-
missive society. Citizens of all ages and classes had been told countless
times by their newspapers and leaders that any man was as good as the
next and that opportunity was limitless in America. They lived in a
highly mobile society, which placed almost no restrictions on white
men. They could move where they pleased and follow almost any occupation. "Tailors, shoemakers, farmers, shop assistants become physi-

cians in thirty-two weeks," noted a visitor; "policemen, watchmen, constables all of a sudden become attorneys. Any man who feels in himself the capacity for becoming a preacher, teacher, or politician soon finds himself a sphere of activity." Success had become a way of life in America, and a move to better oneself had become a habit. People went from one state to another, from farm to city, from East to West without great difficulty or concern. Because they were in a hurry, Americans admired speed. As they gobbled their food and guzzled their drinks, they boasted that people could travel four times as fast as they had only twenty years before. Many people lived permanently in hotels, not just to please their wives, but because they were always on their way somewhere—usually up. A frequent change—of status or residence—seemed both natural and desirable. This was progress, simply part of the American way.

No one denied that Americans were obsessed with the desire to be successful. "Americans worship Mammon," wrote a traveler in 1850. "They kneel before him, setting their honor aside, day and night thinking only of amassing wealth, of building palaces." Thirteen years earlier Washington Irving coined the phrase "the Almighty Dollar" and admitted that money was the "great object of universal devotion throughout our land." Another observer reported: "Wealth is the key to respect, honor, and esteem. Almost every man is therefore constrained to become a merchant, a banker, a speculator, or a manufacturer, to secure a position that will bring a sizeable income." The search for the "fast buck" was as much a part of American life in the fifties as it is today.

A humble background was no handicap in a nation that admired ambition and claimed the amassing of wealth as a national goal. Success could be rapid and comparatively easy, for there was extraordinary opportunity for the poor to become rich or for the talented to obtain power. "Sometimes," wrote one man, "three or five years business would be so profitable to a sober and prudent merchant as to enable him to retire—sell out to his clerks . . . or engage in larger operations. I know of one house in which, in the course of twelve or fifteen years, fortunes were made by three different sets of partners." Trade not only made fortunes, it was a democratic occupation. A man could start with little and become wealthy, for there were all sorts of merchants across the country from backcountry peddlers to import-export tycoons. The country peddler might be an independent businessman or the employee of a storekeeper. The country storekeeper not only supplied a variety of goods to rural citizens; he was both their business agent and banker.

Since eastern wholesalers gave the interior merchant a year to pay for his goods, he could grant the same amount of time to his customers. Up to three-fourths of his sales were on credit, for which he received about 25 percent more. Because there were few banks in many parts of the country in the fifties, storekeepers also assumed simple banking functions. They advanced cash to farmers for taxes, doctor bills, and other emergencies.

The larger merchants, who served as the bankers and business agents of farmers and planters, were called factors. For their services, which included the supervision of the crop from the time it left the plantation until it was sold, they charged a series of fees—freight, insurance, drayage, storage, weighing, and sampling. Moreover, factors usually received a commission for supplies purchased for their clients or for money advanced against an unharvested crop.

Because they were considered a necessary adjunct to agricultural life and often enjoyed a virtual monopoly, storekeepers and factors— especially in the South—increased their economic power in the decade before the Civil War. Planters and farmers frequently were in debt to merchants; in 1861 Louisiana planters owed some forty New Orleans factors over $8 million. The factorage system supplied the planters' needs, but it was bitterly resented because it enriched the factor more than the planter and it concentrated capital in the few port cities that marketed staple crops.

All of America's ten most populous cities in 1850 were ports. The five largest—New York, Baltimore, Boston, Philadelphia, and New Orleans—were on or near the coast; the next five—Cincinnati, St. Louis, Albany, Pittsburgh, and Louisville—were river ports. For years the seaboard cities competed fiercely for the interior trade, but by 1850 New York and New Orleans had forged ahead. Every year thousands of boats brought cargoes from the Mississippi Valley to New Orleans. "Were it not for yellow fever," wrote a visitor, "New Orleans would probably be the largest and most flourishing city in the union. But the terrifying epidemic has always clogged up the flow of immigrants. They no more disembark than they hurry on to the rich farming regions of the West, where the Germans particularly have made fortunes." Unsanitary conditions as well as its seasonal and one-way trade held New Orleans back. In 1850 the city's exports were four times greater than its imports.

That same year New York City imported twice as much as it exported. Canal and river boats, trains, and ocean vessels brought goods to and from the great port of New York. "The prodigious number of cases of merchandise which I saw in New York and the commercial movement which reigned everywhere gave me the impression of an enormous fairground," wrote a foreigner in 1850. "A feverish activity seems to obsess the inhabitants. I felt myself the only idler in this nest of human ants." Canals and railroads had tied the West ever closer to the East, but the rise of New York as America's greatest port resulted more from southern trade than from canals or railroads. As early as 1822 southern produce made up over half of New York's exports. Southerners not only sent their staples, primarily cotton, to New York; they purchased most of their goods in the city—$76 million worth in 1849, $131 million worth in 1859. These figures do not include shipping fees and indirect commissions for handling southern purchases; they represent only outright sales. Part of this merchandise was consigned to large planters through factors, but much of it was bought by country merchants who personally traveled to New York to buy their yearly supply of goods.

While in New York the storekeeper invariably stayed in a "first-class" hotel—an imposing structure with well over a hundred rooms, so costly and luxurious that financial maneuvering had been necessary to build it. The management had to be professional, the servants efficient, and the accommodations, food, and drink impressive to sophisticated Europeans as well as to backwoods Americans. The American hotel offered citizens an opportunity to enjoy luxury without loss of their democratic pretensions. Some wealthy patrons paid as much as $10,000 a year for room and board. "The hotel in the United States is comfortable to a degree which astonishes and delights the European traveler," wrote a Parisian in 1846. "There are vast tables d'hote admirably served, if not well cooked (there are no good cooks outside France); elegant washrooms in each chamber, with hot and cold running water; gas lights, carpets everywhere, a large drawing room with a piano. Right in the building, on the ground floor, a barroom or tavern offers voyagers excellent American drinks with a large number of newspapers stretched out everywhere, even under one's feet."

The interior merchant usually spent more time drinking and reading newspapers in New York than he had at home. There were, after all, over 6,000 places in the city where liquor was sold in 1850; fifteen daily newspapers were available, as well as six weeklies, two monthly reviews, a quarterly, and several foreign language sheets. "Everything which might conceivably be of interest is gathered into these publications," wrote a visitor. "Many people carry on private correspondence through the medium of the press, and it is often curious and amusing to read the columns given over to personals." Scandals were so much the daily fare that one European claimed that American newspapers were "dominated by the absence of principles, by the concern with making money only. There is not a journal in the United States that is worthy of being placed beside the press of London, or the French and German periodicals. Here every kind of trash finds in the press some defender and patron, if only it will pay well enough."

Merchants saw nothing wrong with making money. That is what they were in business for, and if James Gordon Bennett's *New York Herald* could supply the public with racy stories and show a profit at the same time, so much the better. The average merchant, no matter what he professed at home, looked forward to visits in the "wicked" city. Even though eastern wholesalers supplied no party girls to entertain visiting buyers in the fifties, New York provided ample opportunity for sin. Around the Five Points section of the city visitors could see "roisterous-looking, drunken females, sitting upon the door-steps, or standing round the counter of a drinking hole." Here free Negroes and whites mingled in bars and dance halls. The section, which averaged three thousand arrests a month, had the reputation of being a national center of crime, prostitution, poverty, and drunkenness.

If the visitor preferred more polite activity he might attend the opera or dine out. He could observe the young dandies who "drove the fastest teams on Third Avenue, wore the latest fashions, sported the most unexceptionable goatees, and were the best judges of turtle soup." These "scions of Snobdom," as a contemporary called them, were rarely seen except at night, for they slept all day. Their sisters ventured out in the afternoons to department stores where they "examined the latest patterns, and turned up their pretty noses at the ordinary-looking customers. At night these young ladies were the *last* at the ball or the opera, just in time to interrupt the most exquisite part of the performance. After being fairly seated, they invariably raised their operaglasses, and began a series of ogling, tittering, bowing, turning around, and bobbing up and down, which would do credit to any tilt-tail upon the banks of a millpond."

The usual merchant, eastern or interior, followed a much more sober and conservative routine. One such successful merchant was a native New Yorker who had begun his business career as a clerk in a draper's shop some forty years before, when he was only ten, and had owned his own firm before he was twenty-five. "His energies were directed toward one single end, to make himself rich," noted an acquaintance. "And there are thousands of similar experiences in the United States." Though this merchant now had a fortune, he neither retired from business nor modified his life. He arose at sunrise every day of the year, dressed, had a cup of tea, and then departed for his office. As a wholesaler he occupied a dingy little room—badly furnished, badly ventilated, and littered with merchandise—in an immense warehouse. Nothing—rain, snow, or ice—kept him from his business. When the streets were coated with ice, he wore spiked shoes and somehow managed to get to his office. Business was more than a source of livelihood to him; it was a veritable ministry. He was as devoted as a priest to his calling. It was important to him that he arrive at the office an hour before his clerks and check the books. At nine each morning he allowed himself ten minutes for breakfast at a nearby restaurant frequented by merchants. The rest of the day he received clients in his office or toured the customshouse and exchange.

He spent little time with his wife and family—a son, seventeen, who worked for his father and twin daughters, fourteen. The merchant's wife, age thirty-five "and in the full bloom of a rather chaste and severe beauty," never left her bedroom unless she was fully dressed as if for the street. Promptly at eight, whether in January or July, mother and daughters ate breakfast, which usually consisted of fried ham and eggs washed down with large cups of coffee. After the girls went off to school, their mother put on an apron and worked along with the servants, for washing and cleaning were compulsive with her. Every day the house was scrubbed and set in order from cellar to attic. A fetish of cleanliness was common among middle-class American women. Less fastidious Europeans were amazed at "the terrific consumption of water in America, where every house has a bath, where many rooms are furnished with hot and cold running water, and where the servants wash the fronts of houses every Saturday." After the house had been cleaned to the satisfaction of the merchant's wife and everything arranged formally and a little coldly, she always retired to her room to wash and to redress. Then her shopping began—touring the stores either by carriage or on foot for from two to five hours—usually without any intention of buying anything. Even so, she would pull down bolts of cloth, look through boxes of ribbons, and try on dozens of hats. "This manner of passing time, to the despair of the salespeople, is usual among American women," noted a traveler.

Home to a quick meal and silence came merchant, wife, and children. They rarely spoke because they were tired from their various labors and because they had almost nothing to say to each other; none was interested in the dreary activities of the others. They lived their own lives together yet separately. "Such is the life of the G. family," wrote a friend, "and such is the life of almost all the families of American merchants, whatever status or fortune."

Americans flattered themselves that they were the most enlightened people on earth, but actually they admired cleverness more than learning. There were no colleges or universities in the United States to compare with the great institutions of Europe. "The shallowness of American colleges, academies, and seminaries is commonly known," admitted a scholar. "Young ladies study astronomy before they know how to spell; young men rush through a mixed-up mass of courses in two or three years without ever having mastered one of them." Learning, never loved for its own sake in America, was considered another article of commerce. Pragmatic Americans sought shortcuts to everything—to success, to wealth, to Heaven, to knowledge. The digest was already an article of faith. As one man noted, "There are shops where professional politicians make up politics, and priest factories which deal in religion. The position of a professor, or a preacher is thought of as his business. We have no time to do anything for ourselves and demand that our fellow men should earn money just as we do. We rejoice when for our comfort they manufacture in advance shoes, clothing, hats, medicine, health, morals, religion, truth, or any other commodity. For that reason, produce any absurdity whatsoever, if it is ridiculous enough to create a stir in this country it will be believed."

Americans were the healthiest people on earth, yet they constantly dosed themselves with medicines. Daily newspapers were half-filled with all kinds of quack advertisements of pills guaranteed to cure everything from cancer to syphilis. More astonishing, perfectly well people were ready to try any concoction no matter how outlandish its claims. The medicine man had already become an American institution. A less harmful fraud was that entrepreneur of public entertainment P. T. Barnum, who had by 1850 already made a fortune exhibiting freaks. One of his most profitable had been a deranged old black he claimed was George Washington's nurse. Barnum's theory was that the citizens of the United States would eventually believe anything. "They won't believe it at first," he admitted. "But I have it said, and repeated everywhere, with so much confidence and so well, that they end by believing it."

Gullibility seemed almost an American trait. As one contemporary phrased it, "a fraud will find more believers, supporters, and participants, the bigger, the sillier, and the more absurd it is." Credulous Americans followed such prophets as Andrew Jackson Davis, the "Poughkeepsie Seer"; Jemima Wilkinson, the Universal Friend; the Fox sisters, spirit rappers who convinced Horace Greeley but were later exposed as frauds; William Miller and his prediction of the end of the world; John Humphrey Noyes, the Oneida perfectionist who advocated and practiced plural marriage; the Shakers, led by Mother Ann, the "chaste" illiterate, who insisted celibacy brought perfection; and a host of others. Each new advocate or sect expected to perfect human institutions. Because Americans believed in progress and the perfectability of man, they naively hoped someone could show them a way to bring Heaven to earth. A foreigner was astonished to discover that persons he had regarded as sensible actually believed in communication with the dead. His explanation for this credibility was that Americans cared nothing for the beauty of nature, had no appreciation of art, and were too prudish to amuse themselves in extramarital affairs. "The soul must grow weary of the tinkling of dollars, of the purely material aim of their life," he wrote. "They long for excitement; the ladies grow nervous, and work themselves into trances and visions, and cheat themselves and others. Spiritual circles are formed in lieu of balls, concerts, and theaters. The gentlemen attend these representations, and are too much worn out by business to look deeply into the matter. Besides, such fancies become epidemical."

Prudishness was well established in antebellum America. The self-righteous were busy denouncing this or that. Americans, it was charged, used too much tobacco. They spat indiscriminately and filled every room with smoke. Boston, still a stronghold of Puritan morality, had actually banned smoking on the street. Other moral referees protested against popular dances, novels, and liquor. "In America," wrote a visitor, "temperance is a passion, and there is no reasoning with a passion." Most of the reformers were austere, humorless people presumptuous enough to believe that they were morally superior to their fellow citizens. A foreigner encountered one such "puritan whose modesty was comprehensive enough to stretch from the human species to the piano. One day I saw one of these instruments, the legs of which, thick as the trunk of trees, were covered with bags in the form of bathing drawers. 'They are there,' said the owner, modestly lowering her eyes, 'because it is not proper even for a piano to display naked legs.'"

Few Americans were that prudish, yet there was a dull sameness about citizens of the United States in the fifties that appalled many foreigners. Some Americans were less sober, less diligent, less wealthy than others, but most of them were remarkably alike. Americans not only dressed alike, they also thought and acted alike. They enjoyed songs they could whistle and pictures that looked like what they were supposed to represent. The arts Americans admired most were those of oratory, politics, business, and war. Science was meaningless unless it had a practical application. Philosophy was unnecessary; ambition and optimism were enough. Americans were certain theirs was the greatest country with the finest government in the world. They thought they could accomplish anything and told as half truth the tale that some forgotten American had dug the bed for the Mississippi River and had thrown the dirt out to create the Rocky Mountains. Childishly unaware of the tastelessness of their boasts, they were hurt if visitors disagreed with them.

They were in general a friendly and hospitable people, eager to be loved and admired, but they were extremely violent. Assault with a deadly weapon was common. Nor was violence confined to rural or frontier America. Men of high or low status carried pistols, bowie knives, sword canes, or dirks, and they fought with impunity. A foreigner was shocked when two Americans clashed over some petty matter. "The adversaries," he wrote, "without any regard for the crowd in which they found themselves, and at the risk of wounding innocents, reached into their pockets and each drew out a revolver. They exchanged a dozen shots in the open street and the fight did not end until one of them fell with a shattered shoulder. No one was astonished at this impromptu duel; it was hardly questioned."

A broad cultural unity softened and shaded the diversity of late antebellum society. Of course, within this national culture, Americans displayed a range of varied and often contradictory traits. They were materialistic yet generous, practical yet undisciplined, equalitarian yet snobbish, prudish yet profligate, friendly yet violent. Their turbulent, pragmatic society promoted mobility, both horizontal and vertical, and opportunity. But it also encouraged greed and brutality along with self-confidence and ambition. Most Americans, like the Ohioan who sought gold in California, wanted to "be independent of . . . the darned sonabitches that felt themselves above me because I was poor." In their desire to catch up or to get ahead they had learned to ignore or to justify their own unlovely characteristics but to recognize and to denounce those same characteristics in their fellow countrymen. In a sense Civil

War soldiers were correct about each other; Rebs and Yanks often had all the unadmired traits their opponents claimed. What few soldiers on either side were willing to admit was that their enemies were "just like our own boys."

CHAPTER II

Were the Whigs a Class Party in Alabama?

"The Whig party in the South," writes Arthur C. Cole, its most comprehensive examiner, "was from its origin, and continued to be throughout its history, the party of the planter and slave-holder." Led by aristocrats, its "members formed a broadcloth and silk stocking party embracing a large part of the wealth, intelligence, and blue blood of the South." [1]

This concept of the Whigs as a class party has not only been incorporated into textbooks [2] but has been endorsed almost without exception by serious students of the period. As eminent a scholar as U. B. Phillips, for example, believed that the "southern people tended generally to be Democrats unless there were special considerations to the contrary" such as "the social class consciousness of the squires. . . . The squires almost with one accord joined the Whigs throughout the south," except in the Carolinas.[3] Following Cole and Phillips, students of the Whig party in various southern states have generally reached similar conclusions.[4] Indeed, it has become almost a stereotype to characterize southern Whigs as owners of "stately mansions, surrounded with almost every comfort of the day and with many luxuries"; as "men of culture and of broad interests"—"educated in the polished manners of their class" ("often they had received a college education in the North")—

who earnestly believed "that their less fortunate neighbors were not fit to associate with them socially or politically." [5]

"Very early," writes Theodore H. Jack about Alabama, "the ultra democratic attitude of the Jackson men began to be distasteful to the developing aristocratic sentiment on the plantations." In those sections where "cotton was king and the large plantation was the predominant economic institution, it was natural for the Whig party to develop its greatest strength." Thus, in Alabama the Whig party "rapidly became the 'broadcloth' party, the party of the wealthier and more cultivated people." [6] Such distinguished scholars as Thomas P. Abernethy and Albert B. Moore have also stressed the strength of the Whigs in the Alabama Black Belt. [7] Abernethy points out, however, that the Whigs cannot be explained simply as the party of the planters. "The solidly Democratic vote in northern Alabama," he writes, "in spite of the large number of slaves in the Tennessee Valley, indicates that the rivalry between the two sections of the State had much to do with political alignments." [8] Moore also admits that "from the outset there was a considerable planter contingent in the Democratic party." [9]

How nearly correct, then, are the generalizations? Were the Alabama Whigs almost exclusively large planters and slaveholders; the Democrats small farmers and nonslaveholders? Do the county returns for the six presidential elections (1836 through 1856) in which there was a Whig nominee show that the Whigs were a class party? Do the background, education, occupations, and religious affiliations of the men elected to Congress and to the Alabama legislature suggest that the Whigs were "the party of the wealthier and more cultivated people"?

It cannot be denied that many Whig voters lived in the Alabama Black Belt; nor is it denied that the Democrats received more votes than the Whigs in most of the counties where there were few slaves. What has not been sufficiently emphasized, however, is that the Whigs did not receive votes just in the Black Belt or that areas of small farms were not the only Democratic strongholds. For twenty years the Whig party was a major political organization in Alabama with supporters in every county. Although never able to carry the state, Whig presidential nominees received 42 percent of the votes cast in the six presidential elections between 1836 and 1856. [10] Some of the largest majorities given Whigs were polled in counties where there were few slaves, and some of the largest majorities given Democrats were polled in counties where there were many slaves. [11] Covington and Madison counties were conspicuous examples. Ranking very low in slaveholding, Covington returned Whig majorities in every presidential election except one. Madison, with over half its population slave, gave the Democratic candidates large majorities in every election.

TABLE 2–1

Whig Vote by Counties

Slave population of counties	Whig vote 0–45%			Whig vote 45–50%			Whig vote 50–55%			Whig vote 55–65%			Whig vote 65–100%		
	over 50 %	30-50 %	0-30 %	over 50 %	30-50 %	0-30 %	over 50 %	30-50 %	0-30 %	over 50 %	30-50 %	0-30 %	over 50 %	30-50 %	0-30 %
1836	3	6	12	0	5	1	1	3	2	4	2	2	6	0	2
1840	2	5	13	1	4	1	2	0	1	8	6	2	1	1	2
1844	3	7	15	2	3	0	7	2	3	2	4	0	0	0	0
1848	1	2	12	1	1	0	2	3	2	5	3	3	2	1	1
1852	8	9	20	4	3	1	3	2	1	0	0	0	0	0	0
1856	8	8	17	1	4	2	5	0	0	1	1	1	0	0	1
TOTAL	25	37	89	9	20	5	20	10	9	20	16	8	9	2	6

Whig strength was not based solely upon planters. An analysis of the presidential elections from 1836 through 1856 shows only slight correlation between slaveholding and the Whig vote.[12] In only three of the sixteen counties where over half of the population was slave did Whig candidates receive a majority in every election. In three of these same sixteen counties Democratic candidates also received a majority in every election. The other ten leading slaveholding counties were inconsistent in their loyalties, and frequently the contests were close—a shift of 5 percent in the vote would have brought defeat in nearly half of the Whig and in 36 percent of the Democratic victories.

TABLE 2–2

Correlation Between Whig Vote and Slave Population

1836	.534
1840	.583
1844	.671
1848	.523
1852	.630
1856	.492

Between 1836 and 1856, thirty-eight different individuals represented Alabama in the United States Congress—twenty-six Democrats,
eleven Whigs, and one Know-Nothing.[13] During the same years, 990
men from fifty-two counties were elected to the state legislature.[14] Party
affiliations for 414 (41.7 percent) could be determined—244 were
Democrats, 167 were Whigs, two were both Democrats and Whigs during their tenure, and one was a Know-Nothing.[15]

Persons of varied background and personality sat in both Congress
and the state legislature: college professor and carpenter; preacher and
drunkard; [16] Catholic and Jew; a member of the Sons of Temperance
and a glutton; [17] men from very wealthy families and men whose fathers
were poor. The congressmen included such well-known figures as Vice
President William R. King; blimplike Dixon H. Lewis; fire-eating William L. Yancey; the able speaker and writer John Gayle; prematurely
gray-haired Francis S. Lyons; and the brilliant and erratic Jeremiah
Clemens, who confessed that "he was obliged to drink to bring his genius down to a level with Mr. Y[ancey]'s." [18] Capable and principled
men could be found in both parties, as could demagogues and political
chameleons. Of the latter types no better examples can be suggested
than Democrat W. R. W. Cobb, "friend of the poor against the rich,"
who "sang homely songs which he had composed for his stump
speeches" (one began: "Uncle Sam is rich enough to give us all a farm")
and resorted to such tricks as "the rattling of tinware and crockery to
keep the attention of his audiences" while winking and "punctuating his
phrases by chewing with great gusto a piece of onion and the coarsest
'pone' bread"; [19] and the "master stump speaker" Henry W. Hilliard,
successively a Whig, a Know-Nothing, a Democrat, a Bell man in 1860,
a Radical Republican, a Greeley man in 1872, and finally an unsuccessful Republican candidate for Congress in 1876.[20] Two Whig legislators
were notorious jokers. Exceedingly fond of playing pranks on his
friends, Robert Dougherty of Macon County allegedly rode an alligator
over a mile in the Alabama River.[21] Richard H. Ricks of Franklin was
also "noted for his eccentricities and his waggery." Wearing "his hair
and beard long, and a blouse coat, which drew much attention upon
him," Ricks was "so addicted to sport that, on joint ballot of the two
Houses, he was apt to vote for 'John Smith,' his favorite candidate." [22]

If the representatives of the people of Alabama varied in personality,
they were remarkably alike in place of birth. The overwhelming majority of both congressmen and legislators were born in the South.[23] Over
half of the Whigs as well as the Democrats were born in either the Car-

olinas or Georgia; more Democrats were born in South Carolina than in any other state, more Whigs in Georgia.

Biographical data were not found on the social origins of all the Democratic and Whig congressmen and legislators, but the information that was obtained makes it clear that a number of both Democrats and Whigs had the advantage of being born into wealthy families. It is also clear that often Whigs as well as Democrats were of humble origin. If the Democrats sometimes sent "common men" to Congress and to the state legislature, so did the Whigs—"poor boy" candidates were not restricted to one party. For example, the Democrats could boast of such congressmen as Edmund S. Dargan, who was so poor that he had to walk from North Carolina to Autauga County, Alabama, and who, despite his limited education, taught school while studying law; [24] or of Benjamin Fitzpatrick, who "never attended school more than six months" but was offered the choice of running for vice president on the Douglas ticket.[25] The Whigs could claim congressmen like William R. Smith, who began life as an orphan, "without means and without influential friends," and rose from tailor's apprentice to college president; [26] or George W. Crabb, who migrated from Tennessee with little more apparent equipment for success than a common-school education but returned to Alabama from the "Indian war in Florida . . . the idol of his men" and assured of political "preferment." [27]

In the state legislature sat such simple Whigs as Luke R. Simmons, a "plain farmer," [28] and poorly educated James Cain, one of the "class of men," according to William Garrett, "who have been aptly styled 'the bone and sinew of the country.' " [29] There, too, sat Benjamin H. Baker, who "grew up with grave disadvantages"; [30] George N. Stewart, son of a common sailor in the United States Navy; [31] and Henry W. Cox, who, as his biographer described his quest for legal training, "succeeded over many difficulties in getting to the bar." [32] Of "humble parentage" also was William H. Fowler, who worked "at different times with a tailor, a printer, and a druggist." [33] Such men certainly do not confirm the theory that the Whig party was made up of "blue bloods." Probably most of the congressmen and legislators—Whig and Democratic—came about as close to being "aristocrats" as did legislator Thomas McCarroll Prince, a Whig merchant of Mobile. While visiting in Europe, one story goes, he registered at a hotel as "Thomas McCarroll Prince of Mobile." Large crowds gathered, and he was treated as visiting royalty until it was discovered "that the absence of a punctuation mark, and not 'blue blood' " had made him one of the nobility.[34]

TABLE 2–3

Distribution by Place of Birth and Educational Background

	Place of birth by percentage			Educational background by percentage		
	Born in the South	Born in the North	Born else-where	Limited or only common schooling	More than common schooling but not college graduates	College graduates
Congressmen						
Whigs	90.9	9.1	—	36.4	27.2	36.4
Democrats	100.0	—	—	38.5	23.0	38.5
Legislators						
Whigs	92.3	7.7	—	30.8	25.3	43.9
Democrats	96.1	3.3	0.6	20.3	25.0	54.7
Party unknown	100.0	—	—	32.0	40.0	28.0

A sizable number of both Democrats and Whigs were college graduates, but, surprisingly enough, the Democrats appear to have had more formal education than the Whigs. Over half (51.5 percent) of the Democratic congressmen and legislators whose educational background could be determined were college graduates, while only 43.1 percent of the Whigs could claim degrees. Moreover, a higher percentage of Democrats (10.4) than Whigs (5.9) received degrees from northern colleges.[35] Indeed, the only congressmen who attended colleges outside the South were Democrats—Eli S. Shorter received both academic and law degrees from Yale, and William L. Yancey attended Williams College but left before graduating.[36] Democrat Robert B. Lindsay, a graduate of St. Andrew's University, Scotland,[37] was the only legislator to attend a foreign university.

As would be expected in a group of successful politicians, over half of the congressmen and legislators were lawyers.[38] All eleven Whig and twenty-four of the twenty-six Democratic congressmen were lawyers. (No evidence could be found that wealthy Democrat William M. Payne had any other occupation than that of a "large scale" planter,[39] or that Democrat W. R. W. Cobb was more than a former "peddler of clocks" who became a rich merchant.[40]) Nearly all of the congressmen, however, had concomitant occupations. Besides being lawyers, two Whigs and five Democrats were also planters. Democrat David Hubbard combined his legal practice with merchandising, planting, and manufacturing.[41] Democrat James F. Dowdell was also a Methodist preacher; and Whig Joab Lawler was "a receiver of public money" and a Baptist preacher.[42] Democrats William L. Yancey and James E. Belser and Whig William R. Smith were editors as well as lawyers; [43] Whig Henry W. Hilliard was a professor of English literature at the University of Alabama; and litterateur Jere Clemens, a Democrat, wrote four novels.[44]

Planting was listed as an occupation of ninety-nine (47.6 percent) Democratic and forty-nine (34.5 percent) Whig congressmen and legislators. Nineteen Whigs and thirty-eight Democrats were described by their biographers as either a "planter of large means," or an "extensive planter," or a "planter of considerable wealth." Whig legislator Robert M. Patton, for example, is said to have owned over three hundred slaves, while Democratic legislator John W. Portis is reported to have owned "not less than 100,000 acres." [45]

A slightly higher percentage of Whigs than Democrats were professional men, but about the same percentage of Whigs as Democrats were in business. Sixteen Democrats and thirteen Whigs were merchants; seven Democrats and four Whigs were bankers; three Democrats and four Whigs were connected with railroads; and two Democrats and two Whigs were manufacturers. Eleven Democrats and five Whigs were listed only as businessmen, or their business was described too vaguely for specific classification. Such, for example, was Democrat Eldridge Mallard, who was said to be "the keeper of a very popular house of entertainment." [46] Ten Democrats and eight Whigs were listed merely as farmers.

Earlier in life a number of congressmen and legislators had pursued occupations not listed in Table 2–4. Before obtaining more suitable positions, eleven Whigs and eleven Democrats had taught school—often while they were studying law. Six Whigs and five Democrats had been store clerks; two Whigs had been printing apprentices; one Whig and two Democrats had worked on farms; one Whig had been an apprentice to a tailor; two Democrats had been mail riders; one had been a plantation overseer, another an apprentice to a cottin gin maker, one a carpenter, and one a saddler.

Many congressmen and legislators were charged with being godless men, like Whig legislator Hardin Perkins, who "seemed to manifest no concern whatever for his spiritual condition, or for the responsibilities of a future life." "Most of our public men," lamented Garrett, "instead

TABLE 2–4

Distribution by Occupation

| | Congressmen | | Legislators | | Party unknown % |
	Whigs %	Democrats %	Whigs %	Democrats %	
Planter	18.2	23.1	35.9	51.1	36.4
Large	18.2	15.4	13.0	18.7	12.1
Farmer	—	—	6.1	5.5	—
Lawyer	100.0	92.3	55.0	54.4	51.5
Professional	36.4	11.4	23.7	14.7	15.2
Physician	—	—	12.2	6.6	6.1
Minister	9.1	3.8	3.8	3.8	9.1
Teacher	9.1	—	—	0.5	—
Author	9.1	—	0.8	—	—
Editor	9.1	7.6	6.9	3.8	—
Business	—	11.5	22.9	22.0	18.3
Merchant	—	7.7	9.9	7.7	6.1
Banker	—	—	3.1	3.8	6.1
Railroad	—	—	3.1	1.6	—
Hotel	—	—	0.8	1.2	—
Insurance	—	—	0.8	—	—
Manufacturer	—	3.8	1.4	1.2	—
Real Estate	—	—	—.	0.5	—
Other	—	—	3.8	6.0	6.1
Total number of men	11	26	131	182	33

of being selected for high moral virtue, seem to repudiate all qualifications of this nature." [47] Whatever the reason, church membership could be ascertained for only 14 percent of the congressmen and legislators.[48] Most of the Whigs as well as the Democrats were Methodists or Baptists; there were few Episcopalians in either party.

Both the presidential election returns and the background, education, occupations, and religious affiliations of the Alabama congressmen and legislators suggest that some of the general statements about the Whig party need qualification. To say that the Whigs were the party of the large planter and slaveholder seems to be too much of an oversimplification. The correlation between the Whig vote and slaveholding in Alabama is slight. Some of the largest Whig majorities were received in counties where there were few slaves. Moreover, if the Whigs had relied exclusively upon planter support, it would have been impossible for them to have polled 42 percent of the vote. Less than a third of the people of Alabama owned slaves.

Certainly it cannot be proved by the men who sat in Congress and in

TABLE 2–5

Distribution by Religious Affiliation

| | Congressmen | | Legislators | | |
	Whigs	Democrats	Whigs	Democrats	Unknown
Methodist	2	2	16	34	6
Baptist	1	4	10	21	2
Presbyterian	2	0	9	17	0
Episcopalian	1	1	3	7	0
Catholic	1	0	0	0	0
Jew	0	1	0	0	0
Congregationalist	0	0	1	0	0
Unitarian	0	0	0	1	0
Lutheran	0	0	0	1	0

the Alabama legislature that great social differences existed between the two parties. On the contrary, the successful candidates for whom biographical information was found appear to have been more alike than different. Generally they were born in the same part of the South; their education was similar, as were their occupations and religious affiliations. Both parties elected large planters as well as plain farmers— "self-made" men as well as men born into wealthy families.

In the state as a whole it may have indeed been true that more large planters were Whigs than Democrats. But if the men they sent to Congress and to the state legislature are any indication, the Whigs were no more exclusively the "silk stocking" party in Alabama than the Democracy was exclusively the party of the "common man."

NOTES

1. Arthur C. Cole, *The Whig Party in the South* (Washington, 1913), pp. 69, 71–72.

2. See Harry J. Carman and Harold C. Syrett, *A History of the American People* (New York, 1952), 1:385; John D. Hicks, *The Federal Union: A History of the United States to 1865* (Boston, 1948), pp. 446–47; Samuel E. Morison and Henry S. Commager, *The Growth of the American Republic*, 4th ed. (New York, 1950), 1:555; Merle Curti *et al.*, *An American History* (New York, 1950), 1:464; and Robert S. Cotterill, *The Old South* (Glendale, Calif., 1936), p. 161.

3. U. B. Phillips, "The Southern Whigs, 1834–1854," in *Essays in American History Dedicated to Frederick Jackson Turner*, ed. Guy Stanton Ford (New York, 1910), p. 215.

4. See Theodore H. Jack, *Sectionalism and Party Politics in Alabama, 1819–1842* (Menasha, Wis., 1919), p. 31; Henry H. Simms, *The Rise of the Whigs in Virginia, 1824–1840* (Richmond, 1929), pp. 164–66; James E. Winston, "The Mississippi Whigs and the Tariff, 1834–1844," *Mississippi Valley Historical Review* 22 (1935):506; and to a lesser extent Paul Murray, *The Whig Party in Georgia, 1825–1853* (Chapel Hill, N.C., 1948), pp. 2–3. Murray finds many similarities between Whigs and Democrats in Georgia; and in Tennessee, according to Thomas B. Alexander, a "comparison of Whig with Democratic counties on the basis of geography, soil, slaveholding, urbanization, and concentration of capital or business and professional men reveals only imperfect correlations between the political map and the geographic or economic map. . . . No simple dichotomy explains the political geography of Tennessee." "Thomas A. R. Nelson as an Example of Whig Conservatism in Tennessee," *Tennessee Historical Quarterly* 15 (1956):17.

5. Cole, *Whig Party*, p. 70. Writing a quarter of a century after Cole and Phillips, Charles S. Sydnor suggested that "one should not forget that ambitious politicians were calculating their chances of advancement and were throwing their influence to the party that held out the better prospects. The chief activity of Southern politicians in the 1830's and 1840's consisted in struggles for local place and power rather than in contests over any principles that differentiated the national parties." Sydnor nevertheless concluded that "the Whigs were strongest in the planting counties [except in North Carolina], and it is sometimes said that they owned three fourths of the slaves in the South." *The Development of Southern Sectionalism, 1819–1848* (Baton Rouge, 1948), pp. 318–19.

A more recent study by Charles G. Sellers, Jr., treated the Whigs as a class party, but contended that instead of being planter dominated "the Whig party in the South was controlled by urban commercial and banking interests, supported by a majority of planters, who were economically dependent on banking and commercial facilities." "Who Were the Southern Whigs?" *American Historical Review* 59 (1954):335–46.

6. Jack, *Sectionalism and Party Politics,* p. 31.

7. Thomas P. Abernethy, *The Formative Period in Alabama, 1815–1828* (Montgomery, 1922), p. 146, and Albert B. Moore, *History of Alabama* (Tuscaloosa, 1951), pp. 160–61. According to Moore, "The two parties . . . rested upon social and economic foundations. . . . The Whig party was the 'broadcloth' party; it drew its strength from the men of slaves and means who lived in the Black Belt and in the western counties of the Tennessee Valley and the business interests affiliated with them. The Democratic party," on the other hand, "was supported principally by farmers and the small business classes of the other parts of the State. Generally speaking, the Whig party was a south Alabama party and the Democratic party dominated north Alabama."

8. Abernethy, *Formative Period in Alabama*, p. 146.

9. Moore, *History of Alabama*, p. 161.

10. Clanton W. Williams, ed., "Presidential Election Returns and Related Data for Ante-Bellum Alabama," *Alabama Review* 1 (1948):279–93 and 2 (1949):64–71.

11. See Table 2–1, which is based upon data found in Williams, "Presidential Election Returns."

12. See Table 2–2, which is also based upon Williams's material. The returns show only slight correlation between Whig vote and (1) per capita

wealth; (2) percentage of families owning slaves; and (3) average acreage per family. The formula used in determining correlation was Spearman's rank correlation coefficient.

13. Allen Johnson, Dumas Malone, and Harris E. Starr, eds., *Dictionary of American Biography* (New York, 1928–1944), hereafter cited as *DAB;* Thomas M. Owen, *History of Alabama and Dictionary of Alabama Biography* (Chicago, 1921); William Garrett, *Reminiscences of Public Men in Alabama* (Atlanta, 1872); Willis Brewer, *Alabama: Her History, Resources, War Record, and Public Men* (Montgomery, 1872); and *Biographical Directory of the American Congress* . . . (Washington, 1950) were used in gathering biographical data on these men. William R. Smith was a Union Democrat, a Union Whig, and a Know-Nothing during his tenure in Congress. *Biographical Directory of Congress*, p. 1837; *DAB*, 27:367.

14. Twenty-five congressmen, either before or after their terms in Washington, sat in the state legislature, but—in order to avoid duplication —they are not included in the 990 (neither are the men who were elected to the legislature first as Whigs or Democrats and later as Know-Nothings). Party affiliations could be determined for 48.3 percent (seventy-seven Democrats and eighty-four Whigs) of the men who represented the sixteen counties where over half the population was slave; for 46.9 percent (ninety-five Democrats and sixty-three Whigs) of the men who represented the fifteen counties where slaves comprised from 30 to 50 percent of the population; and for 28.8 percent (seventy-two Democrats and twenty Whigs) of the men who represented the twenty-one counties where less than 30 percent of the population was slave.

15. The principal sources used in gathering material on these men were *Journal of the House of Representatives of the State of Alabama,* 1835–1856; *Journal of the Senate* . . . *of Alabama,* 1835–1856; Garrett, *Reminiscences;* Owen, *History of Alabama;* and Brewer, *Alabama.* Some information was also obtained from various county histories.

16. President Polk recorded that his friend Felix G. McConnell committed suicide because "of the effects of intemperance." Allan Nevins, ed., *Polk: The Diary of a President, 1845–1849* (New York, 1952), pp. 145–47. It was also suggested that Jeremiah Clemens "colored his water a little too deeply." Lewy Dorman, *Party Politics in Alabama from 1850 through 1860* (Wetumpka, Ala., 1935), pp. 41–42, 132 n.; Brewer, *Alabama,* p. 363. According to Garrett, Whig legislator Henry C. Lea became a drunkard. And not only was Democratic legislator Hugh M. Rodgers charged with being a drunkard but also with being a thief. Garrett, *Reminiscences,* pp. 162, 280–81.

17. Franklin W. Bowdon's "only enemy was his own appetite, which impaired his usefulness, and cut him off in the zenith of life." Brewer, *Alabama,* p. 540.

18. *Ibid.,* p. 363.

19. Dorman, *Party Politics in Alabama,* pp. 58–59.

20. *DAB*, 9:54–55.

21. Garrett, *Reminiscences,* p. 354.

22. *Ibid.,* p. 505.

23. See Table 2–3. Place of birth was determined for all of the Whig and Democratic congressmen and for 281 (28.3 percent) legislators—153 Democrats, 104 Whigs, and 24 men whose party was not determined.

24. *DAB*, 5:74.

25. *Ibid.*, 6:439.

26. Brewer, *Alabama*, pp. 561–62; *DAB*, 17:367.

27. Although only a lieutenant colonel in one of the Alabama regiments in the Indian War, Crabb was after the peace "immediately elected a Major-General." *Biographical Directory of Congress*, p. 1027; Garrett, *Reminiscences*, p. 53. Democratic legislator John H. Garrett of Cherokee County, who "was fond of talking of duels and the code of honor which prevailed among the chivalry" in his native South Carolina, also owed much of his political success to his popularity with the militia. "He had quite a taste for military life, and was elected a Major General of Alabama Militia." Garrett, *Reminiscences*, pp. 179–80.

28. Garrett, *Reminiscences*, pp. 196–97.

29. *Ibid.*, p. 239. Cain's simplicity was reported to have been a factor in his victory over Democrat Eldridge Mallard. Mallard's "family were fond of stylish display, hardly in keeping with the times, and this fact was used by his political opponent, James Cain, in defeating him in 1841 and 1842." James M. Dombhart, *History of Walker County, Its Towns and Its People* (Thornton, Ark., 1937), pp. 275–76.

30. Brewer, *Alabama*, p. 514.

31. Owen, *History of Alabama*, 4:1622.

32. *Ibid.*, 3:407.

33. Brewer, *Alabama*, p. 269.

34. *Ibid.*, p. 172; Garrett, *Reminiscences*, p. 193.

35. See Table 2–3. Educational background was determined for all of the Whig and Democratic congressmen and for 244 (24.6 percent) legislators —128 Democrats, 91 Whigs, and 25 men whose party was not determined.

Sixty-five Democrats and thirty-eight Whigs were graduated from southern colleges: nineteen Democrats and seven Whigs from the University of Alabama (also, Democrat C. C. Clay, Jr., received a law degree from the University of Virginia; Democrat Joseph P. Safford received a law degree from Yale; and Democrat Lewis M. Stone received a law degree from Harvard), thirteen Democrats and three Whigs from the University of Georgia (Democrat J. L. M. Curry also received a law degree from Harvard), ten Democrats and eight Whigs from the University of South Carolina (or South Carolina College), five Democrats and three Whigs from the University of Virginia, five Democrats and six Whigs from the University of North Carolina, two Democrats and two Whigs from the University of Tennessee, four Democrats and one Whig from La Grange College, two Democrats and four Whigs from Cumberland, two Democrats from Transylvania, one Democrat from Randolph-Macon, one Democrat from Greenville College, one Whig from Emory, one Whig from Louisville Medical College, one Whig from Charleston Medical College, and one Whig from St. Joseph College, Kentucky.

Fourteen Democrats and six Whigs received degrees from northern colleges: two Democrats and four Whigs from Princeton, four Democrats and one Whig from Yale, two Democrats from Harvard, two Democrats from the Philadelphia Medical College, one Democrat from the University of Pennsylvania, one Democrat from Amherst, one Democrat from the United States Military Academy, and one Democrat and one Whig from Middlebury College, Vermont.

36. Owen, *History of Alabama*, 4:1551; *DAB*, 20:592.

37. Brewer, *Alabama*, p. 190.

38. See Table 2–4. Occupations were determined for all of the Whig and Democratic congressmen and for 346 (34.9 percent) legislators—182 Democrats, 131 Whigs, and 33 men whose party was not ascertained. A considerable number of men, however, had more than one vocation; it was not unusual to find as many as three occupations listed for one man. Each occupation is noted in Table 2–4.

39. Garrett, *Reminiscences*, p. 100; Owen, *History of Alabama*, 4:1331.

40. Brewer, *Alabama*, p. 286; Garrett, *Reminiscences*, p. 395; Owen, *History of Alabama*, 3:357–58.

41. Hubbard also was "the leading promoter of Alabama's first railroad." *DAB*, 9:322.

42. Owen, *History of Alabama*, 3:502; 4:1015–16.

43. Brewer, *Alabama*, p. 450; *DAB*, 20:592–93; 17:367.

44. *DAB*, 9:54; 4:191.

45. Owen, *History of Alabama*, 4:1328; Garrett, *Reminiscences*, pp. 366–67.

46. Dombhart, *History of Walker County*, p. 275.

47. Garrett, *Reminiscences*, p. 192.

48. See Table 2–5. Religious affiliations were determined for 15 (40.5 percent) congressmen and 128 (12.9 percent) legislators.

CHAPTER III

Sex, Women, and the "Old Army" Officers

Friends and enemies of the United States Military Academy agreed that West Point—where the overwhelming majority of the officers of the "Old Army" [1] began their military careers between the age of fifteen and twenty—left its mark upon these young men. Their experience at the academy, it might be argued, was somewhat analogous to the "frontier experience" described by Frederick Jackson Turner. At West Point, cadets were stripped of their previous habits and ways and reshaped by an environment that stressed discipline and conformity. Instructors insisted that they could and did homogenize the "most heterogeneous [material] imaginable—youth of good education, poor education, no education at all; from the plow, the office, the machine shop, luxury, destitution, competence; with brilliant, mediocre, or little ability; with high moral development, or with tendencies colored by demoralizing environment; with strict and with lax views of the obligations of truth. From these are . . . weeded out the impossible, and the rest are . . . molded [into] men. . . ." Academy authorities boasted that "no other institution in the world has so strongly impressed its stamp upon the whole body of its alumni." [2]

Above all, it was asserted, the West Point experience created officers and gentlemen of high moral character. "The Military Academy stands primarily for *character*," stated the institution's centennial history; "the paramount feature of West Point's work is its character developing and forming power." Antebellum observers, one historian noted, "seldom failed to be impressed with the character of the officers who were their hosts." A visitor praised the officer corps for "its moral character, its spirit of discipline, and its sentiment of honor and patriotism." Another traveler described the young West Point graduate he met on the upper Mississippi River as "a gentleman, . . . high minded, honorable, strictly honest and correct in all his deportment." [3]

To test this generalization, I have examined the attitudes and actions of West Point graduates regarding sex, women, and marriage. These topics were selected for investigation because sexual behavior was considered one of the strongest indicators of character in the nineteenth century. If the West Point experience actually produced a uniform value structure, this homogeneity should be apparent in the sex life of "Old Army" officers.

The relatively isolated location of West Point as well as the academy's restrictive routine limited contact between antebellum cadets and females and doubtless encouraged what an instructor called the "clean habits of life." "The moral discipline of the institution is perfect," announced the Board of Visitors in 1828; "the avenues to vice are closed, and the temptations to dissipation . . . have been vigilantly guarded against." "Our recreations are very few," complained a cadet in 1830. "They consist chiefly in walking over a plain about 800 yards in diameter & in the enjoyment of each other's society (which, to me at least, is rather more of a bore than anything else) when it is not study hours or drill. By far the most profitable & pleasant of our time is . . . spent in the mess hall. There are a very few ladies on the Point & those, who are here, are pretty old & ugly which is not at all congenial with my taste. . . ." Girls attended such occasions as the annual fall dance, but usually females were so scarce at West Point that cadets practiced dancing with each other. "It is rather dry business dancing without ladies," admitted one young man. [4]

The scarcity of girls at the academy probably caused cadets to act with more than usual adolescent awkwardness when in the company of females. "I forgot to describe my meeting with Miss Margaret Robinson," wrote Cadet Edmund Kirby Smith in 1844. "A party of us had taken a stroll through the woods Saturday afternoon to breathe the fresh air, gather chestnuts & on our return in passing a party of ladies & officers I heard someone exclaim—why really there's Edmund Smith. In consternation at being caught in such a plight for I was rather deshabile & with a mouth full of chestnuts I shook her warmly by the hand, but in my first attempt to express my pleasure at the meeting out flew the chestnuts bountifully distributed on all sides; had it not been for her open countenance beaming with delight I should have felt rather awkward—as it was I had a hearty laugh over it on my return to quarters." [5]

Another cadet complained: "There is so little variety in the dismal routine of a cadet's life. We live isolated as it were in this insulated spot. There is little or no intercourse existing between the Cadets & the citizens living on the point. The small number of citizens & the ill breeding of some of the cadets (many of whom are perfect boors) render it probable that the nonintercourse will continue. We are never allowed to leave the point during the academic term. . . ." [6]

The wives of army officers who lived at or visited West Point unquestionably taught the cadets much of what they knew about females. "Mrs. [Winfield] Scott and her daughters have been creating quite an excitement here," noted a cadet in 1844. "If I was the Old General I should be dreadfully jealous—Mrs. Scott holds her levee to forty or fifty Cadets. . . . Gives them parties, sends them daily fruit, cakes &c.—and never seems at ease till she gets a crowd of Cadets (her heart's corps as she calls them) around her. She is very much liked and would make quite a popular superintendent." Other army wives also entertained cadets, though usually less elaborately than Mrs. Scott. "I spent a pleasant afternoon with . . . [the wife of General Edmund Pendleton Gaines] and another lady, whose name I have forgotten," reported Cadet Alexander McRae, who was not attracted to all females. "Mrs. G asked me to take her daughter (a child of about 14 or 15) to the ball, and dance with her; which I, as politely as possible, declined." [7]

In 1833 a foreign visitor charged that the contact between cadets and women at West Point was not always innocent. "As no watch is kept over the cadets at night," claimed an Englishman, "some leave their rooms and repair to haunts of dissipation among the hills, known only to themselves, where they meet women of loose character, eat pork and molasses, drink, and chew tobacco. . . ." [8]

Some cadets undoubtedly engaged in heterosexual intercourse while at West Point, but opportunities for coitus were probably infrequent. "We are kept tremendously strict, I assure you," announced one cadet. Another lad reported that life at the military academy consisted of "temperance, cleanliness, and regular diet." Yet in 1846 a cadet reportedly sneaked two prostitutes into his room where he kept them overnight. They were discovered the next morning, and he was forced to resign from the academy. [9]

Surely talk and teasing about sexual experiences, real and imagined, abounded among cadets. At least one such incident led to violence. When a cadet from South Carolina suggested that Emory Upton had been intimate with Negro girls at Oberlin College, which he had attended before coming to West Point, Upton challenged his accuser to a duel. They fought with swords in the dark; Upton was slightly wounded.[10]

A few homosexual relationships probably developed. Though I have discovered no overt acts mentioned in letters, it seems unlikely that none occurred among young men living in such close contact over a prolonged period of time. Latent homosexuality, if nothing more, seems indicated in the letters of Cadet Stephen Dodson Ramseur to his friend David Schenck. Some of the phrases Ramseur used are: "remember, my dear Dave, that in my breast beats a heart that will ever cling to you"; "I know you, Dave, and I love you"; "whenever I write to you my blood rapidly approaches the boiling point"; and "I love you as ever." On January 24, 1858, Ramseur confessed: "I wish that I could change my pen & paper for a seat by your side. I could say many things that I can not write; and then to look upon your dear face, to feel the warm grasp of your hand and to hear kind words of Hope & encouragement that you always bestow upon me. Would not all this make my heart overflow and would I not then be able to express how dearly I love you." On March 27, 1858, Ramseur wrote: "Would that I could tell you the depth and intensity of the affection I feel for you." "But it is impossible for me to portray the depth of the affection I bear you. *You know it is tender* and deep." And on January 5, 1859, Ramseur admitted: "my Dear Old Dave! God Bless you! I wish I could *sleep with you tonight*. We would sleep a heap wouldn't we? How I long to hear of your adventures you! Patience! There's a good time coming!" Ramseur's youthful difficulty in establishing his male sexual identity, perhaps exacerbated by the scarcity of females at Davidson College and at West Point, apparently eased as time passed. Before his death at Cedar Creek in 1864, Ramseur married and fathered a child.[11]

Masturbation and nocturnal (perhaps even spontaneous) emissions probably were the most common sexual outlets for cadets. One young man recalled "the most beautiful creature" he ever beheld. "I have dreamed of her several times," he confessed. Another cadet revealed in a letter to a relative just how strong his fantasies of females were. "I do think there are some of the prettiest girls in Virginia that have flourished since the days of Helen," he wrote. "Angelic creatures! At this moment me thinks I see you standing in all the array of loveliness . . .

your alabaster skin—the auburn locks describing curves of unimagined beauty as they hang in graceful negligence over foreheads too pure for earthly mould. Oh! Oh! Oh how I do wish you all had but one mouth and that I could kiss it. Happy—thrice happy—would I be. I must hold in though. I am like gun powder whenever the subject is broached—off like lightning." [12]

Yet if one cadet considered his stay at West Point sexually frustrating, another cadet apparently thought otherwise. "I frequently refer to the four years spent at the Military Academy as the happiest period of my life," stated John S. Hatheway in 1852.[13]

After their graduation from West Point officers usually enjoyed more frequent and freer contact with women. "I have [already] been to one party in the city," announced Lieutenant Lafayette McLaws just after his arrival in Baton Rouge. "The ladies are not handsome, of their other qualifications I cannot say anything for my acquaintance does not as yet extend beyond a mere party introduction." In 1859 from California, Lieutenant Edward Dillon wrote: "Benecia contains I presume as large a number of respectable women as any place in Cal, and it was with some regret that I left it. Besides a number of resident ladies, it boasts two female academies, where you may find the sex, of all colors, nations, and degrees, from the pure Castillian to the christianized Chinawoman." [14]

Officers were socially acceptable in nearly any society; consequently, wherever they were stationed, they got to know the local females. "I am perfectly delighted with Louisville & the only drawback to my pleasure is the anticipation of having to return to the frontier to fried bacon and Indians," admitted Lieutenant Richard S. Ewell in 1845. "There are a number of *beautiful* women in this place and as unsophisticated a personage as myself would most certainly fall a victim were it not that one heals the wounds left by another." General Philip H. Sheridan recalled that in 1854, when he was a young officer stationed on the southern border, the Mexican commandant nearby often held dances to which the Americans were invited. "We generally danced in a long hall on a hard dirt floor," noted Sheridan. "The girls sat on one side of the hall, chaperoned by their mothers or some old duennas, and the men on the other. When the music struck up each man asked the lady whom his eyes had already selected to dance with him, and it was not etiquette for her to refuse—no engagements being allowed before the music began. When the dance, which was generally a long waltz, was over, he seated his partner, and then went to a little counter at the end of the room and bought his dulcinea a plate of the candies and sweetmeats provided. Sometimes she accepted them, but most generally pointed to her duenna or chaperon behind, who held up her apron and caught the refreshments as they were slid into it from the plate. The greatest decorum was maintained at these dances, primitively as they were conducted; and in a region so completely cut off from the world, their influence was undoubtedly beneficial to a considerable degree in softening the rough edges. . . ." [15]

Such limited, but sexually stimulating, contact with women doubtless hurried some young officers toward marriage. In 1859 Lieutenant Edward Dillon informed his sister that a fellow officer "will marry when he next goes home, since he seems to be scrupulous of late in courting every woman he meets: somebody will surely take him up." And Dillon added: "I want you and mother to prepare some young woman, for a favourable reception of myself, and if I don't add the finishing stroke to the work when I get leave, it will be because of utter inability." Another officer explained to his nephew, a West Point cadet, just how to win a girl: "my little horse is beyond compare. I am going to take him away with me, break him & offer him to my sweetheart. I flatter myself she'll never resist the united attractions of myself & Tigertail. . . ." To most young officers marriage apparently seemed desirable. In 1840 West Point cadets debated "whether it would be beneficial to the service to prohibit officers of the army under the rank of captain from being married." The negative side won the debate. [16]

Officers married various types of women for various reasons. Certain men took a calculating, self-interested approach. "How often do unforseen accidents occur to change our most maturely considered plans," observed Lieutenant Robert Anderson, who had just been assigned to instruct cadets in artillery at West Point. "This winter I had hoped to have seen you—for 1837 I had planned to visit Europe—in 1838 I was to return and forthwith look around for a wife. But here comes a new change over my affairs, should I receive a permanent situation here. I may feel it a duty to my country to consider at once the propriety of taking a wife. I shall make no exertions to change my situation until I consider it a duty," Anderson promised his mother. "Much do I owe to you, my dear Mother, and to my dear Father, for your care and prudent management of me. I expect that you did not whip me as often as I deserved. . . . Never mind I'll have my boys whipped enough to make up for it. If I can find a wife who will educate her children so as to make them as contented as I am (barring a few touches of the rheumatism)

I'll marry her directly, even if she has not more than twenty thousand Dollars for her fortune." [17]

Marriage into a wealthy family provided some men the means they needed to leave the army. Captain Braxton Bragg admitted in 1848: "I cannot live out of the army, until I get a rich wife. . . ." He got one the next year, but he still could not leave the army because, as an officer noted: "her estate is so arranged as to be unavailable to either of them at present." In 1856, soon after his wife received her inheritance, Bragg resigned from the army and with her money purchased a large sugar-cane plantation and 105 slaves. Not all officers who married rich women resigned, of course, but those who did apparently were not denounced by their former comrades. An officer informed his sister in 1859: "Two officers of my Regiment have married and resigned within the last year, and it is likely that one or two more will go and do like-wise. I believe you know both [Archibald I.] Harrison & [William H. F.] Lee, both nice gentlemen, whose resignations we all regret, while we must admit, that in marrying rich women, and settling down in a decent country, they have acted most sensibly." [18]

The supply of rich girls was never sufficient to meet the demand; most officers married females of modest or no fortune they had known back home or had met at army posts. "I called this afternoon on Capt. [Nathaniel C.] McRae who is now in command at the barracks at New-port opposite this place," a lieutenant wrote from Cincinnati. "His daughter, Miss Virginia, is the belle among the young officers stationed here." From Jefferson Barracks, Missouri, in 1844 Lieutenant Richard S. Ewell stated: "This is the best country for single ladies I ever saw in my life. They are hardly allowed to come of age before they are en-gaged to be married however ugly they may be. Except the Misses Gar-lands I have not seen a pretty girl or [an] interesting one since I have been here." [19] Ewell's standards may have been higher than those of other officers, who often married officers' daughters—one suspects— simply because they were there.

Some ambitious men no doubt hoped to win favor by marrying a high-ranking officer's daughter, but many young officers unquestionably were attracted to girls who understood army life. "Every afternoon we have . . . drill," wrote the West Point superintendent's daughter; "it is my favorite military pastime to sit on our piazza and watch it. You would laugh to see the interest I take in it, many of the maneuvores [sic], in fact I may say all, are familiar to me, for I have read the 'Tac-tics,' and sometimes my enthusiastic delight, at some well executed command, causes me to clap my hands, regardless of transgressing the limits of etiquette. But my fondness for the drill is a secret between ourselves, for I would not have civilians know what a thorough army girl I am." It was argued that the daughters of officers were more likely to accompany their husbands to remote outposts, perhaps because they knew what temptations single officers encountered on the frontier. A traveler lamented that officers were too frequently "exiled" on the frontier, "far removed from cultivated female society, and in daily contact with the refuse of the human race." Lydia Lane, daughter of a major, emphasized the hardship she and other wives of officers experienced living in outposts. She recalled too how one wife, Mrs. Abner Doubleday, "was more afraid of a mouse than anything in the world. I remember she had a frame fixed around her bed and covered with netting to keep them out. She did not seem to dread snakes at all, nothing but an awful mouse!" [20]

Some officers, for various reasons, were in no hurry to marry. Many were simply too poor. A large number of the West Point cadets, though from middle-class families, could expect little or no financial aid from home. Many, probably a majority, of the cadets were at the military academy because it was free, because their families could not afford to educate them elsewhere. In 1831 Cadet Benjamin S. Ewell refused to ask for summer leave because the expenses of the trip home "would require a much larger sum than the present condition of Mother's finances would admit of her sending." He also refused to borrow money from his sister. "I am very much obliged to you for your generous offer," he informed her, "but I could not think of depriving you of the pittance you have earned. . . ." It was quite common for junior officers to be in debt for some time following their graduation from the military academy. In 1839 Cadet William T. Sherman asked his mother for "$5 to satisfy some little debts." He promised to repay her as soon as he received his commission as a lieutenant. Then his income—"upwards of $700 yearly independent of quarters and fuel"—would "be amply sufficient" for a single man stationed at one of "the Western posts. To be sure," admitted Sherman, "the outfit upon graduation will be quite heavy but it is generally so arranged as to be paid for gradually at different periods of the year." In 1835 Lieutenant Robert Anderson asked his mother: "Will you promise, if I can marry well, that you will come and spend some of the summer months with your new daughter? Remember that [my brothers] John, Charles, and William only got married by accident before I did. I have always been well disposed in that way, and have been prevented by untoward circumstances, such as having no house to live in, not having pay enough to support a wife &c. . . ." [21]

A few officers simply considered marriage unsuitable to army life. "A beautiful life this military life of ours isn't it?" asked Major John S. Hatheway. "Such variety, such unexpected incidents, here today, gone yesterday. Still to a good for nothing old bachelor (like myself) who has no one but himself and soldiers to care for it is not without its attractions, far from it, but it is no place for a family, the army. I have come to that conclusion from long experience and mature deliberation, and I *think* I may safely say, so long as your brother John is an officer of the U.S. Army so long you may write him down 'Old Bachelor.' " [22]

Some officers remained single because they were too occupied at the moment with other activities. Upon being assigned to duty as an instructor at West Point, Lieutenant Edmund Kirby Smith confided to his diary: "in truth I have avoided society and pass the greater portion of my time in my own room. . . . I feel a distaste for the gaities and enjoyments of society and much prefer the quiet and seclusion of my own room. Moreover I came to West Point solely for the purpose of study and improvement, and care not for flitting away my time in idle and ceremoneous calls of society." [23] To a nephew who accused him of being more interested in women than in war, Lieutenant Joseph E. Johnston replied: "no, no, Pres: women are pleasant & attractive creatures, beyond denial. When one has nothing else to think of, or to excite him—but those who believe such a story know me little. There are not—never were—women enough in the world to allure me from the chance of one hostile shot." [24]

The reactions of officers to Indian women were as varied as to white women. "Many of the Officers have Cherokee Mistresses, a scrape I intend to keep out of both on account of my purse and taste," announced a lieutenant. "Occasionally a good looking half breed may be seen but generally they are a dirty set and all have a smoky odor about them which is particularly disagreeable to me at the distance of ten yards for I was never closer." [25]

A number of men, of course, got much closer to the "dusky damsels" than the fastidious lieutenant. In 1847 an Oregon settler wrote: "I am decidedly opposed to military posts among Indians. *A dragoon camp is the gate of hell*—the wickedest place I ever saw." And a soldier admitted: "As a general rule, the Indians resent any special attention to the young females of their race by the white man. Only by long residence among them, and a line of conduct on the part of the white man that wins their confidence, is this race prejudice overcome. It is well understood among them that a large majority of soldiers—at least ninety-nine out of a hundred—who seek the society of their girls do so merely to spend agreeably the passing hour, and that their special attention cannot be relied on as indicating any desire for marital relations." One officer who married an Indian was so ostracized by his fellow officers that he secured a transfer and abandoned his wife and child. She followed, however, and her devotion impressed him so much that he resigned his commission and settled with her and the child in Galena, Illinois.[26]

Wherever they were stationed, officers who wanted temporary relationships with women could usually find them. "I have not yet procured you a bedfellow for the coming winter," the Chief Justice of Utah Territory apologized to an officer in 1858. "I have spoken to one woman and she says if her husband is agreed to it she would like to go but not until she is freed from her present *interesting* condition. She says she has a sister who is the 2nd wife of an old *Cap* and she has one child and wants to leave him and she will send and inquire if she will cook and wash for you. I think she will do—I told her sister to let me know. I think also that if she does not succeed in that *quarter* I will in some other—hold *on a little*." From Louisville in 1845 Lieutenant Richard S. Ewell wrote: "somebody rapped at my door just then & lo and behold a waiter came in with a bouquet of the finest flowers with a card on which was written in a *female* hand 'From a friend, a Cincinnati bouquet.' These ladies do certainly plague one out of his life. . . . The Bouquet . . . came I presume from a widow whom I have, or rather who has been sparking me & who at present is on a visit to Cin'ti. She is rich and is engaged to be married but like most widows is fond of a flirtation. Do you remember [Franklin] Saunders who graduated at West Point in 37 & belonged to your section? He was regularly victimized by this same widow. . . ." Later Ewell wrote: "I am obliged to you for your offer to select a finer specimen of the genus woman than can be found in New Mex., but as you have not seen these latter I doubt your capability of judging. Yet awhile these are good enough for me." [27]

Officers usually were more demanding when they sought wives. One man revealed his views in discussing his sister and her boyfriend. "Elizabeth does wrong in asking him to ride about with her," he wrote. "It is not at all delicate and Mother ought to put a stop to it. Reports very injurious to Elizabeth's reputation might be the consequence." "In this 'world that we live in' too much care cannot be taken to prevent malicious reports being spread—and a female ought to be particularly cautious," he concluded. Most officers probably agreed that a virtuous reputation for a woman was a valuable commodity in the marriage market. "A Christian woman is the most Heavenly of earthly creatures," announced Lieutenant William D. Pender. "Darling," he wrote his wife, "I love you more than I ever knew, and how much superior you are to any of the ladies around you. You have goodness, Oh! how good; intelligence, youth & beauty; what more could I ask? If I were not satisfied I would indeed, be difficult to please. Please, be assured my own precious wife that I ask for nothing more in my wife." Another officer insisted: "There is something enobling and elevating in the society of refined women which is seen and felt by all who come in contact with them. No garrison is complete without ladies, and there should be a number at every military post." [28]

Yet another officer charged that most army wives were selfish schemers who spent more than their husbands made, drank excessively, and flirted outrageously. "There is a freedom of manners among ladies of the Army that does not obtain in the best civilian society," stated Lieutenant Duane M. Greene. "Married ladies may accept costly presents and receive little attentions and visits from agreeable bachelors without provoking the jealousy of their husbands or offending the general sense of propriety." The "gay and lighthearted" wives of officers took "advantage of every opportunity for enjoyment"; they regarded "all occasions and circumstances as favorable for 'sport.' " The wife of one post commander boldly walked hand in hand across the parade ground at noon with a bachelor, remembered Greene; nor was it unusual for wives to "bestow their smiles and approving glances upon the debauches who show the least regard for the proprieties of refined society," or for a woman to get her husband promoted "by the adroit manipulation of her admirers." [29]

The validity of Greene's charges is difficult to determine. Army life —characterized by long and frequent separations of husbands and wives and by the forced familiarity of garrison life, especially on the frontier —unquestionably promoted a certain "freedom of manners." But it is impossible to establish whether the wives of "Old Army" officers were more adulterous than the wives of antebellum American civilians. The sexual attitudes and actions of army wives, like those of army officers, apparently varied widely.

Even the soundest marriages probably suffered when assignments kept officers apart from their wives and children for a long time. From Mexico City in 1847 Captain Benjamin Huger wrote a friend: "Personally I should not mind spending a year or two here more or less, but there is the family at home. Boys will grow up—& my presence with them is of great importance. So I am in earnest in asking to be relieved in the spring." [30]

After nearly two years on the west coast away from his family, Captain Ulysses S. Grant wrote his wife: "You do not know how forsaken I feel here." To dull his loneliness, he drank; "misery loves company," he noted, "and there are a number in just the same fix with myself, and . . . some who have been separated much longer from their families than I have." A few months later, in 1854, the separation became too much for Grant to endure; he resigned his commission.[31]

In 1836 an officer's wife wrote her husband: "You bid me be happy. Dearest, I *cannot* be happy when I am separated from you; for although I may be cheerful, I always feel that there is something wanting—some part of myself missing, dearer than my right arm." The following year she admitted: "You have been gone two weeks, my beloved, and what long, long weeks they have been to me. You bade me forget you dearest, while we are separated, but I can not. I dream of you—I think of you always. I frequently take my *siesta* after dinner but I have been thinking of giving it up. I don't like it so much as I did when I had *company*. I dream of you and feel so lonely when I wake and find that you are not there." [32]

"Oh! darling you know not what a pleasure looking at your likeness gives me," one lieutenant, away on patrol, informed his wife: "It is almost like looking at your self. If I could see that self, but we must make the best of it. We will love each other, enjoy the company of each other so much the more when we meet. How I will pet you, hold you in my lap, in fact do every thing that will please you." [33]

Colonel Robert E. Lee told newly wed Mrs. Winfield Scott Hancock: "I understand that you contemplate deserting your post, which is by your husband's side, and that you are not going to California with him. If you will pardon me, I should like to give you a little advice. You must not think of doing this. As one considerably older than Hancock, and having had greater experience, I consider it fatal to the future happiness of young married people . . . to live apart, either for a short or long time." [34]

One officer complained after his arrival at Jefferson Barracks, Missouri, in 1844: "There is no garrison here but a few grass widows belonging to the 2d Regt. & very poor company . . . they make—always grumbling about their Husbands. I never saw a place so well calculated . . . to cure an officer of a matrimonial disposition." Two months later the situation was just as unpleasant. "Several families of the 4th were left here, when the Regiment went to La., expecting the Regt. to return soon," complained a sociable officer, "but their absent Husbands & lovers occupy the thought & conversation so much when one visits them that it is quite a bore to call." [35]

An absence often caused husbands and wives to worry about what their spouses might be doing. To his wife, who had admitted attending a dance while he was away, an officer wrote: "Honey I am glad you do not dance the fancy dances with any one but me, for I should feel jealous of having any one but myself putting his arm around your waist. I do not think the less of other ladies for doing those things, but prefer your not doing so. One thing certain Capt. Smith must never do it again. That I am determined upon." Even General John E. Wool complained to his wife: "I have not received a line from you. . . . If I had not heard from you indirectly I would have concluded you were sick. . . . Miss Foote said she had received a letter from some friend . . . who informed her that she had seen you a short time before at a party . . . when you looked uncommonly well as *young* and as *beautiful* as any one in the room, all which has induced me to believe that you have not been sick but probably very busy. . . ." At another time the general informed his wife: "Don't be jealous because the old folks are . . . kind to me during my stay in this country, I mean the old Ladies, who think *I look remarkably young considering how old I am.* As for the Young Girls you know I don't look at them however much they may look at me. I always turn my back upon their pretty faces. That is just as you would wish and you know I always do as you wish." [36]

Some officers clearly had reason to be jealous. From New Mexico an officer wrote: "I believe . . . a man would do better to marry in this country, provided he never was so imprudent as to return home at unreasonable hrs. or when not expected. A Maj. [Oliver L.] Shepherd, Infy. passed the other day with his wife, a Mexican about 15 yrs old whom he married 6 or 8 months since. They stopped here during the heat of the day & the prospects ahead for him made me feel melancholy. He is a fool & coarse brute & neglects this girl very much. There were scoldings & disputations when they got into the carriage & temper in the greatest abundance. She, raised among those whose virtue was very easy, young & neglected by her husband, who is cross & not agreeable . . . has, as I can see, hardly one chance in fifty of keeping within bounds. The first sproutings looked almost ready to burst forth—I have no doubt when he finds the horns full grown he will make a devil of a fuss just as if they were not entirely owing to his stupid & brutal course." [37]

In 1860 a friend wrote handsome Lieutenant James B. McPherson, who was stationed in San Francisco: "It is not necessary for me of course, to give you any advice as to your intercourse with women, your experience has doubtless perfected your education. I will merely say to you, never take a *respectable married* woman to an assignation house, & run the risk of detection; rather wait your opportunity at home, & make haste with the operation, after the fashion of the Ram, quick, but *often."* [38]

The brazen conduct of some men shocked their fellow officers. During the Mexican War Lieutenant John Pope and another officer were "accused of kidnapping two Mexican women, one 14 yrs old . . . for carnal purposes. One thing is certain," noted an officer, "the women live with them now, and ride thru the city with them in defiance of decency in an open carriage furnished by the Q[uarter] M[aster] Dept." [39]

Other officers were equally outraged by the adulterous acts of certain army wives. "Men can not fully understand the goodness of a good woman," an officer admitted to his wife. "They are so much our superiors. . . . And oh! darling a bad woman; did you see that Mrs. [John M.] Brannan, wife of Capt. B. who was supposed to have been residing in New York nearly one year ago was seen in Florence [?] with Lt. [Powell T.] Wyman. She ought to be burnt, & he quartered, for after every thing else to have abused the confidence of a brother officer. We of all others ought to protect each others wives, having to place confidence in each other. It seems to me, if I were in poor Brannan's place, I should go crazy, after first committing murder." [40]

Officers tended to caricature women as either devils or angels. Public contact with a loose woman, one whose flirtations and indiscretions might jeopardize the reputation of her husband or companion, was socially and professionally dangerous, though private intercourse with such a woman often did not produce guilt or tarnish self-respect. A wife, on the other hand, might be placed on a pedestal and idealized. Neither stereotype allowed women the humanity in vice or virtue that men allowed themselves.

A stereotyped view of the opposite sex was not confined to officers, or even to men. The cultural patterns that often encouraged men to treat women as sex objects also encouraged women to see men as lustful and sometimes foolish animals. The attitude toward men expressed by Eliza Johnston, wife of Colonel Albert Sidney Johnston, probably represented the popular biases of her time and sex. From the Texas frontier, she wrote in her diary on March 30, 1856: "I made a discovery through my cook the other day hearing her say a poor woman was very sick in camp with a young baby 5 weeks old and both neglected. I told her to go and see if I could have anything done for her & asked where her husband was she said she was Lieutenant [Charles W.] Fields mistress & the baby was his. he had taken a woman from her good decent husband in Missouri and brought her here to Texas. oh! you immoral men what should be your fate for all the sorrow you cause in this world. I never can talk to the man with pleasure or patience again & yet he is considered a gentleman and a fine officer. I do not know why but I have had a dislike to that man ever since I first knew him in Austin." A day later Mrs. Johnston noted: "Mr. Field keeps his mistress now openly in the camp. I get all this news from Mrs. Capt. [James] Oak[e]s who I veryly believe would cause trouble in Heaven, 'memo' I must beware of her. . . . I listen to all, but say nothing. Mrs. Capt. [Innis N.] Palmer had her first babe about 2 weeks since a bride of just a year, and being still in bed she is receiving all the young gentlemen at the post and the strangers of the court martial. what strange things people do. The night of the birth of her babe she was walking the room in great pain when Lieut. [Cornelius] Van Camp knocked at the door. Capt Palmer foolish man opened the door and asked him to walk in & take a seat, which he did, and the poor woman sat down in an arm chair and dared not even groan. there he sat and talked until at last he remarked her countenance when he said Mrs Palmer you look sick. shortly after, he left. what a goose the husband is." [41]

Some officers were shocked by certain sex habits, especially those of foreigners.[42] "People rarely marry in this region, particularly among the lower class," reported an officer from Baja California. "They 'take on' as a soldier would say. They don't know what *chastity* is. I have seen mothers selling their daughters for two, three, four and six dollars. I am told that in the Ranchos in the interior it is no uncommon thing for a father to have connection with his daughter. The country is cursed with Mexican blood. Yet I am told that it is virtuous, when compared with some parts of Mexico." [43]

One of the most intolerant officers to observe and to comment on the sexual morals of foreigners was Captain Edmund Kirby Smith, who visited Europe in 1858. In France and Germany, where he saw women working "in the most public places" and "engaged in the legitimate occupations of men," he was disgusted. "Women are thus taken from their household duties and out of their legitimate sphere & forced into positions & occupations, whence they soon lose their modesty & where their morality soon forsakes them," he charged.

On July 9 he noted in his diary: "I have seen in one hour more beautiful women in . . . Vienna than in all the rest of Europe combined, and with it find morality at a lower par than elsewhere; twenty-five out of thirty of the children born here are said to be illegitimate, and intrigue seems to be the order of the day. As a check upon the immorality of the Viennese, the Emperor of Austria was advised to licence houses where women of doubtful character could live together under the surveillance of the Police—he refused, saying 'that in that case he would have to build one grand roof over Vienna & licence the whole city.' " Smith reported special hospitals where unmarried pregnant women went "in the most secret manner" to have their children.

Smith believed "that whilst the public taste was improved the morals must be deteriorated" by the Liechtenstein Art Gallery, which was filled with "lewd & lascivious subjects . . . in all the rich coloring and nudity of nature . . . with the scenes & acts so vividly represented that nothing is left to the imagination. . . . Why the most broken down old blaze could not walk through some of these European galleries, without feeling the blood course through his veins in rapturous excitement," charged Smith, "and yet the halls swarm with women of every age & clime and sphere of society—the middle age matron and the young girl just budding into womanhood may be seen side by side commenting on and criticizing the rape of . . . Europa, or the more scriptural subject of Susannah and the Elders."

Of all the places in Europe Smith visited, he was most critical of Italy. "The Italian characteristics now first show themselves, rags, garlic & misery—bare legged Lazzeroni and jolly Pappas," he sneered on July 30. After visiting the excavations of Pompeii, he wrote : "I noticed that the houses were generally marked with some sign indicating the occupation of their inmates; the houses of ill-fame were decorated with a huge *indescribable arrangement,* sculptured in stone over the street door, and frequent recurrence of these buildings with sign rampant was quite significant of the tastes of the Pompeians." "The pictures (mural or fresco) in many of the houses were good," admitted Smith, "but the large number of licentious and obscene subjects indicated a depraved state of morals and habits. The luxurious and licentious mode of life of the Romans was the cause of their downfall, and its consequence are exhibited in the miserable race which now represent that once great and powerful people. In no other part of the enlightened world has human nature so retrograded; the mass of men are under five feet, and the large proportion of dwarfs and hideous specimens of deformity . . . is as distressing as it is remarkable." [44]

It is impossible to know, of course, just how many officers of the "Old Army" accepted Smith's code of sexual morality. Some—maybe most—did, but certainly there were exceptions. Smith saw nothing humorous in sex; to him it was a sober and often an immoral subject. This was not the case with a number of officers, who considered sex a suitable topic for jokes. "Major [Granville O.] Haller started to York [Pennsylvania] this morning to be married to-morrow to a Miss Cox," an officer informed another. "He has taken a warm time for it and though the nights are now at the shortest I think he will find them long enough." Candidly and with apparent amusement Ulysses S. Grant wrote his fiancée in 1845: "I was . . . returning [to barracks from New Orleans] between 1 and 2 o'clock at night when I discovered a man and a woman that I thought I knew, footing it to the city carrying a large bundle of clothes. I galloped down to the Barracks to asc[er]tain if the persons that I suspected were absent or not and found that they were. I was ordered immediately back to apprehend them, which by the assistance of some of the City Watchmen I was able to do. I had the man put in the watch house and brought the *lady* back behind me on my horse to her husband, who she had left asleep and ignorant of her absence. Quite an adventure wasn't it?" To a friend, an officer wrote: "[Lieutenant Henry W.] Slocum has an heir in the person of a daughter. He seemed to be not much elated but took it as if he were used to such things. [Lieutenant Truman] Seymour's wife still resembles the barren fig-tree, producing no fruit. It does not proceed from want of moisture about the roots, for Seymour's *root* is kept pretty constantly in motion so his friends say." [45]

When Congressman Daniel E. Sickles killed Philip Barton Key, son of "The Star-Spangled Banner's" author, for seducing Mrs. Sickles, officers differed in their reactions.[46] "I have sent you several copies of the N.Y. Herald, containing the account of the trial of Sickles," wrote one young man. "No doubt the trial is full of interest to you as it is to all. He was acquitted as every one supposed he would be." Another man informed a lieutenant stationed in San Francisco: "I presume the bachelors of your city were very much affected as the young men, or rather single men, of New York which was, that no *unmarried* man was known to have an *erection* for at least *ten days after* the death of poor Barton Key!" [47]

The diverse sexual attitudes and actions revealed in the writing of "Old Army" officers refutes the claim that they were homogenized by the West Point experience. They disagreed on when and on whom to marry, and even on whether or not to marry. Some officers pampered and sheltered their wives; others neglected them. Women were treated as sex objects by certain officers at certain times, but these or other officers often regarded females as companions, as aids in professional or social advancement, or as sources of income. At least some officers copulated with the wives of fellow officers. Certain officers kept mistresses. Frequently officers denounced each other's actions. Those with robust or indiscriminate tastes were censured by those with more subdued sexual drives, who in turn were laughed at by the bawdy and the uninhibited. The range was wide: from an Edmund Kirby Smith, who was disgusted by the "lewd & lascivious" paintings in the Liechtenstein Gallery, to a John Pope, who allegedly kidnapped a fourteen-year-old Mexican girl "for carnal purposes," to a William D. Pender, who uninhibitedly informed his wife: "Speaking of health, I have a cure for the *piles* and if you suffer in the least please try it. Let Marshall get you a piece of tarred rope, such as used about ships—light it, then blow out the flames and smoke your piles. If the first smoking does not cure you try again in a day or so, and if you find it does any good repeat till it ceases to trouble you. Try this, for I know it to be good." [48]

Some officers, of course, avoided any discussion of sex in their letters or diaries; others made only vague or disguised references to the subject. Rarely did those who refused to write openly about sex reveal as clearly through the use of symbolism their conscious or unconscious sexual wishes as did former "Old Army" officer P. G. T. Beauregard. In 1862, after he had become a Confederate general, Beauregard wrote to Miss Augusta J. Evans: "Permit me to send you by one of my aids . . . the pen with which I have written all my orders & reports of battles from the fall of Sumter to 'Shiloh' inclusive. It is now like myself, a little the worst for the wear & tear of over 15 months' active service in the cause of our country—but will still do its duty faithfully, if handled with care.

"I beg you to believe that I do not send it to you, on acct. of the importance I attach to it, but the ladies here seem to prize so highly my *pencil,* that I have been presumptuous enough to think, that one who writes so ably & beautifully as yourself, would probably appreciate still more my *pen,* however unattractive in appearance it may be." [49]

NOTES

1. Civil War officers on both sides referred to the antebellum United States Army as the Old Army to distinguish it from the army—Union or Confederate—in which they served after 1860.

2. John A. Logan, *The Volunteer Soldier of America* (Chicago, 1887), p. 406 ff; *The Centennial of the United States Military Academy at West Point, New York, 1802–1902* (Washington, 1904), 1:474, 472.

3. *Centennial of the United States Military Academy,* 1:470, 471; Sidney Forman, *West Point: A History of the United States Military Academy* (New York, 1950), p. 150 ff; Stephen E. Ambrose, *Duty, Honor, Country: A History of West Point* (Baltimore, 1966), p. 147 ff; Russell F. Weigley, *History of the United States Army* (New York, 1967), pp. 168–69; Francis Paul Prucha, *The Sword of the Republic: The United States Army on the Frontier, 1783–1846* (New York, 1969), pp. 331–32.

4. *Centennial of the United States Military Academy,* 1:471; Ambrose, *Duty, Honor, Country,* p. 150; Benjamin S. Ewell to Rebecca L. Ewell, April 10, 1830, Benjamin Stoddert Ewell Papers, College of William and Mary, Williamsburg, Va.; Hazard Stevens, *The Life of Isaac Ingalls Stevens* (Boston, 1900), 1:36–38; Isaac I. Stevens to Aaron Cumming, Jr., August 30, 1835, Isaac Ingalls Stevens Papers, University of Washington, Seattle.

5. Edmund Kirby Smith to his mother, February [1844], Edmund Kirby Smith Papers, Southern Historical Collection, University of North Carolina, Chapel Hill.

6. Benjamin S. Ewell to Paul H. Ewell, April 1, 1830, B. S. Ewell Papers.

7. Edmund Kirby Smith to his mother, September 24, 1844, Smith Papers; Mrs. Robert E. Lee to E. P. Alexander, January 1854, Edward Porter Alexander Papers, Library of Congress, Washington; Alexander McRae to his father [1848?], John McRae Papers, Southern Historical Collection, University of North Carolina.

8. "Notes on the Army of the United States," *Military and Naval Magazine of the United States* 1 (1833):104.

9. Stevens, *Life of Isaac Ingalls Stevens,* 1:30. Elizabeth Ellis to Charles Ellis, July 16, 1832, Ellis-Allan Papers, Library of Congress; Ambrose, *Duty, Honor, Country,* pp. 159–60.

10. Morris Schaff, *The Spirit of Old West Point* (Boston, 1907), pp. 142–48.

11. Stephen Dodson Ramseur to David Schenck, January 28, February 4, 1858, March 1, 1859, September 15, January 24, March 27, 1858, January 5, 1859, Stephen Dodson Ramseur Papers, Southern Historical Collection, University of North Carolina; Ezra J. Warner, *Generals in Gray: Lives of the Confederate Commanders* (Baton Rouge, 1959), pp. 251–52.

12. S. D. Ramseur to David Schenck, November 8, 1857, Ramseur Papers; Benjamin S. Ewell to Rebecca L. Ewell, November 22, 1835, B. S. Ewell Papers.

13. John S. Hatheway to his sister, April 15, 1852, Hatheway Family Papers, Cornell University, Ithaca, N.Y.

14. Lafayette McLaws to his father, November 20, 1844, Lafayette McLaws Papers, Southern Historical Collection, University of North Carolina; Edward Dillon to "Dear Jennie," November 20, 1859, Dillon-Polk Papers, Southern Historical Collection, University of North Carolina.

15. Richard S. Ewell to Benjamin S. Ewell, February 28, 1845, Richard Stoddert Ewell Papers, Library of Congress; Philip H. Sheridan, *Personal Memoirs* (New York, 1888), 1:32–33.

16. Edward Dillon to "Dear Jennie," November 20, 1859, Dillon-Polk Papers; Joseph E. Johnston to J. Preston Johnston, November 18 [1839], Joseph E. Johnston Papers, College of William and Mary; *Centennial of the USMA*, 2:99.

17. Robert Anderson to his mother, November 21, 1835, Robert Anderson Papers, Library of Congress.

18. Braxton Bragg to Marcellus C. M. Hammond, August 15, 1848, James H. Hammond Papers, Library of Congress; H. B. Judd to W. T. Sherman, July 4, 1850, William T. Sherman Papers, Library of Congress; Grady McWhiney, *Braxton Bragg and Confederate Defeat*, vol. 1, *Field Command* (New York, 1969), p. 141; Edward Dillon to "Dear Jennie," November 20, 1859, Dillon-Polk Papers.

19. Alexander McRae to his father, October 15 [1857?], McRae Papers; Richard S. Ewell to Benjamin S. Ewell, August 3, 1844, R. S. Ewell Papers.

20. Sue P. Delafield to James B. McPherson, September 18, 1859, James Birdseye McPherson Papers, Library of Congress; Charles J. Latrobe, *The Rambler in North America* (London, 1835), 2:205; Lydia Spencer Lane, *I Married a Soldier, or, Old Days in the Old Army* (Philadelphia, 1893), pp. 20, 48. See also Sheridan, *Personal Memoirs*, 1:20.

21. Benjamin S. Ewell to Rebecca L. Ewell, March 4, 1831, B. S. Ewell Papers; W. T. Sherman to his mother, September 30, 1839, Sherman Papers; Robert Anderson to his mother, November 21, 1835, Anderson Papers.

22. John S. Hatheway to his sister, May 1, 1851, Hatheway Family Papers.

23. Edmund Kirby Smith Diary and Scrapbook, December 5, 1849, Smith Papers.

24. Joseph E. Johnston to J. Preston Johnston, April 4, 1843, Johnston Papers.

25. Richard S. Ewell to Benjamin S. Ewell, February 2, 1841, R. S. Ewell Papers.

26. Andrew Rodgers to his uncle, October 16, 1847, Rodgers Family Papers, Newberry Library, Chicago; John B. Beall, *In Barrack and Field* (Nashville, 1906), p. 266; Elizabeth Ellet, *Summer Rambles in the West* (New York, 1853), pp. 49–50.

27. Delena R. Eckels to Lieutenant [Clarence E.?] Bennett, August 12, 1858, Thomas L. Kane Papers, Yale University, New Haven, Conn., quoted in Stanley P. Hirshson, *The Lion of the Lord: A Biography of Brigham Young* (New York, 1969), pp. 249–50; Richard S. Ewell to Benja-

min S. Ewell, February 28, 1845, December 23, 1852, R. S. Ewell Papers.

28. Benjamin S. Ewell to Rebecca L. Ewell, November 22, 1835, B. S. Ewell Papers; William D. Pender to his wife, August 2, May 17, 1860, William Dorsey Pender Papers, Southern Historical Collection, University of North Carolina; R. W. Johnson, *A Soldier's Reminiscences in Peace and War* (Philadelphia, 1886), p. 27.

29. Duane Merritt Greene, *Ladies and Officers of the United States Army, or, American Aristocracy: A Sketch of the Social Life and Character of the Army* (Chicago, 1880), pp. 84, 87, 43, 65, 75, 77.

30. Benjamin Huger to George Talcott, October 27, 1847, Mexican War Letters, Pruyn Collection, Cornell University.

31. Lloyd Lewis, *Captain Sam Grant* (Boston, 1950), pp. 325, 328–29.

32. Julia Howe to her husband, November 30 [1836], June 13, 1837, C. S. Howe Papers, Southern Historical Collection, University of North Carolina.

33. William D. Pender to his wife, May 15, 1860, Pender Papers.

34. Mrs. Winfield Scott Hancock, *Reminiscences of Winfield Scott Hancock* (New York, 1887), pp. 46–47.

35. Richard S. Ewell to Benjamin S. Ewell, August 3, October 17, 1844, R. S. Ewell Papers.

36. William D. Pender to his wife, August 2, 1860, Pender Papers; John E. Wool to his wife, April 15, February 2, 1838, John E. Wool Papers, New York State Library, Albany.

37. Richard S. Ewell to Benjamin S. Ewell, July 21, 1852, R. S. Ewell Papers.

38. "Harry" to James B. McPherson, October 20, 1860, McPherson Papers.

39. Braxton Bragg to Samuel G. French, October 13, 1847, Samuel G. French Papers, United States Military Academy, West Point, N.Y.

40. William D. Pender to his wife, June 19, 1860, Pender Papers.

41. Charles P. Roland and Richard C. Robbins, eds., "The Diary of Eliza (Mrs. Albert Sidney) Johnston: The Second Cavalry Comes to Texas," *Southwestern Historical Quarterly* 60 (1957):493–95.

42. In the material examined on the Old Army, blacks were not mentioned in a sexual context, but in 1866 at Fort Philip Kearny a special order warned that "the notorious 'Colored Susan' " was a woman of "bad repute," and in 1876 an officer's wife accused her Negro maid of spreading "a *bad disease*" among the soldiers. See Robert A. Murray, *Military Posts in the Powder River Country of Wyoming, 1865–1894* (Lincoln, 1968), p. 57, and Abe Laufe, ed., *An Army Doctor's Wife on the Frontier: Letters from Alaska and the Far West, 1874–1878* (Pittsburgh, 1962), pp. 181–82.

43. H. S. Benton to "Dear Joe," September 27, 1847, Sherman Papers.

44. Edmund Kirby Smith Diary and Scrapbook, June 14, July 9, 10, 30, September 2, 1858, Smith Papers.

45. Richard S. Ewell to Benjamin S. Ewell, June 20, 1849, R. S. Ewell Papers; U. S. Grant to Julia Dent, July 17, 1845, in *The Papers of Ulysses S. Grant*, ed. John Y. Simon, 4 vols. to date (Carbondale, Ill., 1967–), 1:52; William P. Craighill to James B. McPherson, April 4, 1855, McPherson Papers.

46. For an account of the diversity of civilian opinion on the case, see Allan Nevins and Milton Halsey Thomas, eds., *The Diary of George Templeton Strong* (New York, 1952), 2:440, 447–49, 456–57.

47. Stephen Dodson Ramseur to David Schenck, April 29, 1859, Ramseur Papers; "Harry" to James B. McPherson, October 20, 1860, McPherson Papers.

48. William D. Pender to his wife, August 23 [1860], Pender Papers.

49. P. G. T. Beauregard to Augusta J. Evans, July 24, 1862 (copy), P. G. T. Beauregard Papers, Library of Congress.

CHAPTER IV

Ulysses S. Grant's Pre–Civil War Military Education

It is often claimed that Ulysses S. Grant became a successful general for an astonishing reason—because he failed to learn the formal military lessons taught to all pre–Civil War professional soldiers. "In his studies he was lazy and careless," noted a contemporary. "Instead of studying a lesson, he would merely read it over once or twice. . . ." Grant's poor scholarship, so the argument runs, left him ignorant of the military theories and practices that more bookish officers memorized. "It is true," writes T. Harry Williams, "that Grant was not versed in doctrine, but his comparative ignorance was an advantage. Other generals were enslaved by their devotion to traditional methods." Grant, on the other hand, never allowed military orthodoxy to supersede common sense. In this way, argues Bruce Catton, "Grant was . . . definitely unprofessional. His attitude . . . was much more the attitude of the civilian than of the trained soldier. . . ." Unburdened by the sterile dogma that handicapped so many of his contemporaries, Grant was thus free to act pragmatically and successfully.[1]

Was Grant as uncommitted to orthodox military doctrines as this thesis suggests? What were his pre–Civil War military experiences? What lessons did he learn and from whom? What did he read on the art of war? Who were his heroes?

Grant spent fifteen years in the army before the Civil War. His military career began as a cadet at West Point in 1839. After four years of study, he was graduated from the military academy and commissioned a brevet second lieutenant in the Fourth Infantry in 1843. For the next three years he was stationed at various posts in Missouri, Louisiana, and Texas. During the Mexican War, Grant served with both Generals Zachary Taylor and Winfield Scott and received brevet promotions for gallant conduct in the battles of Molino del Rey and Chapultepec. Even so, it took Grant ten years to reach the rank of captain. In 1854, after a lonely assignment on the Pacific Coast, he resigned his commission to be with his family.[2]

Grant claimed to have had mixed feelings about a military career. In his *Memoirs,* written some forty years after he was a cadet at West Point, Grant recalled: "A military life had no charms for me, and I had not the faintest idea of staying in the army even if I should be graduated, which I did not expect." But in a letter to a cousin, written soon after Grant arrived at West Point, he announced: "On the whole I like the place very much. so much that I would not go away on any account. The fact is if a man graduates here he [is] safe fer life, let him go where he will. There is much to dislike but more to like. I mean to study hard and stay if it be possible. . . ."[3]

Despite his promise to study hard, Grant compiled a mediocre record at the military academy. He ranked twenty-first among the thirty-nine students in his graduating class. His marks in military subjects during his final year were even less impressive; he ranked twenty-fifth in artillery tactics and twenty-eighth in infantry tactics. "I did not take hold of my studies," Grant later confessed; "in fact I rarely ever read over a lesson the second time during my entire cadetship." Furthermore, he admitted that he had considered the encampments, at which many practical military lessons were taught, "very wearisome and uninteresting."[4]

It is often asserted that the two men who influenced the military thinking of Civil War commanders the most were Henri Jomini and Dennis Hart Mahan. Every graduate of the United States Military Academy before 1861, it is claimed, had been exposed to the ideas of Jomini, an interpreter of Napoleonic warfare, who was considered the foremost authority on tactics and strategy. One officer remarked that "many a Civil War general went into battle with a sword in one hand and Jomini's *Summary of the Art of War* in the other." And in the words of Professor T. Harry Williams: "the American who did more than any other to popularize Jomini was Dennis Hart Mahan, who . . .

[taught] at West Point . . . [for over thirty years] and who influenced a whole generation of soldiers. He interpreted Jomini both in the classroom and in his writings." "Probably no one man had a more direct and formative impact [than Mahan] on the thinking of the war's commanders." [5]

Yet neither Jomini nor Mahan seems to have had much influence upon Grant's military thinking. The evidence here admittedly is mostly negative. Grant claimed that he had never read any of Jomini's works. There is no reason to doubt this. Jomini's works were all written in French, a language of which Grant had little knowledge. He admitted that, as a student of French, "my standing was very low." Not until 1859, long after Grant had left West Point, was Jomini's *Summary of the Art of War* used as a textbook in tactics at the military academy, and then only in translation. There may have been books by Jomini in the West Point library when Grant was a cadet, but there is no evidence that he looked at any. Most of the books Grant read at the academy were, he guiltily confessed, novels. [6]

It is true that Grant was exposed to Mahan's views in class, but there is no real evidence that he either fully understood them or was affected by them. Unlike his friend William T. Sherman—who announced in 1862: "Should any officer high or low . . . be ignorant of his tactics, regulations, or . . . of the principles of the Art of War (Mahan and Jomini), it would be a lasting disgrace"—Grant never mentioned his old professor in letters or reminiscences. Mahan recalled years later that Cadet Grant had quiet manners and a boyish face, and that he was not an outstanding student. [7]

There are several reasons why Grant learned little about the art of war at West Point. None of his instructors, including Mahan, excited him. His earliest hero was not a professor, but General Winfield Scott. "During my first year's encampment," recalled Grant, "General Scott visited West Point, and reviewed the cadets. With his commanding figure, his colossal size and showy uniform, I thought him the finest specimen of manhood my eyes had ever beheld, and the most to be envied. I could never resemble him in appearance, but I believe I did have a presentiment for a moment that some day I should occupy his place on review. . . ."

Grant may have been a lackadaisical student because he was shy and could not bear to be laughed at. He was far more concerned about his appearance than about his knowledge of warfare. "If I were to come home now with my uniform on," he wrote in 1839, "you would laugh at my appearance. . . . My pants sit as tight to my skin as the bark to a tree and if I do not walk *military,* that is if I bend over quickly or run, they are very apt to crack with a report as loud as a pistol." "If you were to see me at a distance, the first question you would ask would be, 'is that a Fish or an animal'?" "When I come home in two years (if I live) . . . I shall astonish you *natives.* . . . I hope you wont take me for a Babboon." Any desire Grant may have had to be conspicuous—to copy even in a modest way his first hero's ornate dress—vanished soon after he left West Point. "I was impatient to get on my uniform and see how it looked, and probably wanted my old school-mates, particularly the girls, to see me in it," Grant remembered. But the "conceit was knocked out of me by two little circumstances . . . which gave me a distaste for military uniform that I never recovered from." The first incident occurred while Grant was riding down a street in his uniform, "imagining that every one was looking" at him; "a little urchin, bareheaded, barefooted, with dirty and ragged pants," said to Grant: "Soldier! will you work? No, sir-ee; I'll sell my shirt first!!" Grant was even more embarrassed when he returned home to find a "rather dissipated" stableman parading about in a pair of sky-blue pantaloons that were just the color of Grant's own uniform trousers. "The joke was a huge one in the mind of many . . . people, and was much enjoyed by them," admitted Grant, "but I did not appreciate it so highly." [8]

Still another reason why Grant, as well as other cadets, learned little about the art of war at West Point was because too little time was devoted to the subject. Mahan mixed lessons on strategy and tactics into his engineering course for fourth-year students. "But few lectures [on the art of war] were given by Professor Mahan," recalled a former cadet, "and these were restricted almost entirely to short descriptions of campaigns and battles, with criticisms upon the tactical positions involved." An officer told a commission that was investigating instruction at the academy in 1860: "I do not think enough importance is attached to the study or standing in the several branches of tactics. These are not taught sufficiently." Most of the officers questioned by the commission agreed that cadets received inadequate instruction in strategy and tactics. "At present," complained a major, "even the infantry tactics is taught by officers of other corps, . . . taken almost hap-hazard, and who . . . have neither the antecedents nor position necessary to inculcate in the cadets a proper appreciation of its merits." A lieutenant who taught a section on "the theory of strategy and grand tactics" at West Point stated that the time allotted to his course "permits little more than the learning of principles." Another instructor announced: "The time given to strategy is . . . entirely too little. The subject is one of the very gravest importance, and in no other branch of the military art is 'a little learning' so dangerous a thing." Yet the superintendent of the academy warned that "it would not be well to have the [academic] standard . . . for graduating made too high. The demands of our service," he said, "do not require it." [9]

It was easy enough for young cadets, studying in an environment where academic standards were not exceptionally high and most learning was done by rote, to misinterpret, oversimplify, or simply forget much of what Mahan taught. Grant and most other cadets apparently learned just enough to satisfy their examiners, but once they had passed the course—like so many students before and after them—they quickly forgot what they had been taught. That was not difficult. Mahan's views were neither unequivocal nor always precisely stated. [10]

Nor was much done at West Point or at army posts to stimulate men to further study. Regulations sometimes discouraged cadets from using the library, and some did not check out a single volume during their four years at the academy. "One of the important objects of education is to give habits of judicious reading," noted General Joseph E. Johnston in 1860. "The present academic course [at West Point] is not calculated to do so. The abstruse sciences, to which the time of the cadet is mainly devoted, can, in after life, interest none whose pursuits do not require their frequent application, and therefore officers of the Army generally do not retain their school habits." An instructor at the academy testified: "I have never known . . . of a single instance of an officer studying theoretically his profession (when away from West Point) after graduating." Lieutenant John M. Schofield of the First Artillery wrote: "It would be well if artillery officers could study after graduating, but my experience has been that they have no time. Without such subsequent study the elementary instruction is in a great measure lost." And another officer pointed out that the army offered "no incentive to exertion and study beyond the personal satisfaction each officer must feel who has a consciousness of having done his duty. The careless and ignorant officer is promoted, in his turn, with as much certainty as the accomplished and conscientious one." [11]

There is nothing in either his letters or reminiscences to suggest that Grant spent any time studying his profession after he left West Point. Perhaps that is why he could write: "Soldiering is a very pleasant occupation generally. . . . " Years later he recalled that except for one instance: "I . . . never looked at a copy of tactics from the time of my graduation [from West Point]." That exception occurred when he received his first Civil War command. "I got a copy of [Hardee's] tactics and studied one lesson," Grant admitted. "I perceived at once, however, that Hardee's tactics—a mere translation from the French with Hardee's name attached—was nothing more than common sense. . . . I found no trouble in giving commands that would take my regiment where I wanted it to go. . . . I do not believe that the officers of the regiment ever discovered that I had never studied the tactics that I used."

His writings indicate that Grant knew something of Napoleon Bonaparte's campaigns, but references to the Corsican are brief and suggest no more than what Grant might have remembered from his studies at West Point. For example, in 1845 Grant teasingly told his fiancée that her brother would have time "to prove himself a second Napoleon as you always said he would." Later, in describing the American flanking movement at Cerro Gordo, Grant suggested that the "undertaking [was] almost equal to Bonapartes Crossing the Alps." And finally, in his *Memoirs,* Grant wrote: "I never admired the character of the first Napoleon; but I recognize his great genius." [12]

Most of what Grant knew about war in 1861 he had learned not from lectures or from books, but from his own combat experience in Mexico. In his first action, at Palo Alto and Resaca de la Palma, he discovered something significant about himself. Combat was not as upsetting as he had supposed it would be; under fire he had been steady and calm. "Although the balls were whizing thick and fast about me," he wrote Julia Dent, whom he later married, "I did not feel a sensation of fear until nearly the close of the firing [when] a ball struck close by me killing one man instantly, it nocked Capt. Page's under Jaw entirely off and broke in the roof of his mouth, and nocked Lt. Wallen and one Sergeant down besides. . . ." To a friend, Grant explained: "You want to know what my feelings were on the field of battle! I do not know that I felt any peculiar sensation. War seems much less horrible to persons engaged in it than to those who read of the battles." [13]

These and subsequent battles strongly influenced Grant in other ways. He learned the value of regular troops and rigid discipline. Anyone who believes that Grant had an unprofessional approach to war should look carefully at the general's own words. "The victories in Mexico were, in every instance, over vastly superior numbers," Grant recalled. "There were two reasons for this. Both General Scott and General Taylor had such armies as are not often got together," continued Grant. "At the battles of Palo Alto and Resaca-de-la-Palma, General Taylor had a small army, but it was composed exclusively of regular troops, under the best of drill and discipline. Every officer, from the highest to the lowest, was educated in his profession, not at West Point necessarily, but in the camp, in garrison, and many of them in Indian wars. The rank and file were probably inferior, as material out of which to make an army, to the volunteers that participated in all the later battles of the war; but they were brave men, and then drill and discipline brought out all there was in them. A better army, man for man, probably never faced an enemy than the one commanded by General Taylor in the earliest two engagements of the Mexican war. The volunteers who followed were of better material, but without drill or discipline at the start. They were associated with so many disciplined men and professionally educated officers, that when they went into engagements it was with a confidence they would not have felt otherwise. They became soldiers themselves almost at once." [14]

The campaigns of Taylor and Scott were the highlights of Grant's pre–Civil War military education. From them Grant learned strategies and tactics he would use in the Civil War. For example, his Vicksburg campaign was similar to Scott's bold march to Mexico City. Grant's account in his *Memoirs* of Scott's campaign could have been, with only a few changes, a fair description of his own brilliant moves that culminated in the capture of Vicksburg. "He invaded a populous country, penetrating . . . into the interior," wrote Grant; "he was without a base; the enemy was always intrenched, always on the defensive; yet he won every battle. . . ." [15]

Grant also saw Taylor's and Scott's forces attack and drive the Mexicans from both open fields and fortified positions. He reported with some amazement to Julia after the battle at Resaca de la Palma: "Grape shot and musket balls were let fly from both sides making dreadful havoc. Our men [con]tinued to advance . . . in sp[ite] of [their] shots, to the very mouths of the cannon an[d] killed and took prisoner the Mexicans . . . , taking cannon ammunition and all. . . ." After the Americans had successfully stormed Monterrey, Grant wrote: "The city is built almost entirely of stone and with very thick walls. We found all their streets baricaded and the whole place well defended with artillery, and taking together the strength of the place and the means the Mexicans had of defending it it is almost incredible that the American army now are in possession here." [16]

Gradually Grant accepted these attacks, which at first he had considered incredible, as standard tactics. Why not? They always succeeded. The American forces were invincible. Not only had they won every battle; when they attacked they inflicted heavier casualties than they suffered. By the spring of 1847 Grant could write of the American attack at Cerro Gordo, which he witnessed: "As our men finally swept over and into the [Mexican] works, my heart was sad at the fate that held me from sharing in that brave and brilliant assault." [17]

Grant never forgot those assault tactics that had been so successful in Mexico. He used them in the Civil War, often to his own detriment. They did not work so well for him as they had for Scott and Taylor. The reason was simple: the standard infantry weapon of the Mexican War, the smoothbore musket, had been replaced by a superior rifled musket. The single-shot, rifled muzzleloader could be fired two or three times a minute; it could stop an attack at up to four hundred yards; and it could kill at a distance of one thousand yards. This weapon became the great killer of the Civil War. Because of the rifle's increased range and accuracy, Civil War infantry assaults were bloody, sometimes suicidal, affairs. For the first time in over a century defenders gained the advantage in warfare. "Put a man [with a rifle] in a hole," noted Colonel Theodore Lyman, "and he will beat off three times his number, even if he is not a very good soldier." A few entrenched men armed with rifles could hold a position against great odds. "Before we left [the] North Anna [in May 1864]," wrote a Federal soldier, "I discovered that our infantry were tired of charging earthworks; a good man behind an earthwork was equal to three good men outside it."

But Grant simply would not accept the fact that the rifle had revolutionized tactics. He continued to order assaults against strongly defended positions; he seemed captivated by tactics that in Mexico had brought victories but in the Civil War usually brought only costly repulses. Finally, after losing 7,000 men in a frontal attack at Cold Harbor in June 1864, Grant admitted: "I regret this assault more than any one I have ever ordered. I regarded it as a stern necessity, and believed that it would bring compensating results; but, as it proved, no advantages have been gained sufficient to justify the heavy losses suffered." [18]

Some lessons are difficult to unlearn, especially those taught to young people by respected instructors. Taylor and Scott were not merely Grant's commanders; they were his heroes. It is understandable that their tactics and strategies had a lasting influence upon him. "I never thought at the time to doubt the infallibility of these two generals," he

confessed. Nevertheless, there are two questionable letters that show—
if indeed they were written by Grant—that he did suggest in 1847 that
Scott might have picked a better route into Mexico City. Still, Grant insisted that "the opinion of a lieutenant, where it differs from that of his
commanding General, *must* be founded on *ignorance*." [19]

Though he admired and learned from both Taylor and Scott, Grant
left no doubt which man influenced him the most. "Both were pleasant
to serve under—Taylor was pleasant to serve with," wrote Grant, who
announced after the Mexican War's opening battles: "history will count
the victory just achieved [by General Taylor] one of the greatest on record." And he later informed his fiancée that he had so much confidence in Taylor's military skill that "I do not feel my Dear Julia the
slightest apprehention as to our success in ev[e]ry large battle that we
may have with the enemy no matter how superior they may be to us in
numbers." [20]

What Grant later recalled in his *Memoirs* about Taylor is especially
significant because it reveals not only what Grant admired in his old
general but also how many of Taylor's characteristics and military practices he adopted. Taylor, he noted, "was opposed to anything like plun-
dering by the troops." So was Grant. "Taylor was not an officer to trouble the administration much with his demands, but was inclined to do
the best he could with the means given him." So was Grant. "Taylor
never made any great show or parade, either of uniform or retinue."
Neither did Grant. Taylor "moved about the field in which he was operating to see through his own eyes the situation." So did Grant. "Taylor
was not a conversationalist." Neither was Grant. But on paper Taylor
"could put his meaning so plainly that there could be no mistaking it.
He knew how to express what he wanted to say in the fewest well-cho-
sen words. . . ." So did Grant. And finally Grant said of Taylor what
so many writers have said of Grant: "No soldier could face either danger or responsibility more calmly than he. These are qualities," Grant
noted, "more rarely found than genius or physical courage." [21]

The similarities between Taylor and Grant are too great to be accounted for by coincidence. At the outset of the Mexican War Grant
doubtless admired Taylor partly because Grant, even as a young soldier,
was already much like the old general. But it also seems clear that Taylor, to a greater extent than has been realized, became Grant's military
model. No other man so profoundly influenced Grant's pre–Civil War
military education. "The art of war is simple enough," Grant once remarked. "Find out where your enemy is. Get at him as soon as you can.

Strike at him as hard as you can, and keep moving on." [22] Zachary Taylor himself could not have given a better definition of how to fight.

It is ironic that a Southerner and a slaveholder had such a strong influence upon the Civil War's most successful Union general.

NOTES

1. Horace Porter, *Campaigning with Grant,* ed. Wayne C. Temple (Bloomington, Ind., 1961), p. 342; T. Harry Williams, *McClellan, Sherman and Grant* (New Brunswick, N.J., 1962), p. 104; Bruce Catton, "The Generalship of Ulysses S. Grant," in *Grant, Lee, Lincoln and the Radicals,* ed. Grady McWhiney (Evanston, Ill., 1964), p. 11.

2. The best account of Grant's pre–Civil War career is Lloyd Lewis, *Captain Sam Grant* (Boston, 1950); for the exact dates of Grant's military assignments see Francis B. Heitman, *Historical Register and Dictionary of the United States Army* (Washington, 1903), 1:470.

3. U. S. Grant, *Personal Memoirs* (New York, 1885), 1:38; Grant to R. McKinstry Griffith, September 22, 1839, in *The Papers of Ulysses S. Grant,* ed. John Y. Simon, 4 vols. to date (Carbondale, Ill. 1967–), 1:6.

4. Lewis, *Captain Sam Grant,* p. 95; *Personal Memoirs,* 1:38.

5. David Donald, *Lincoln Reconsidered* (New York, 1956), pp. 82–102; T. Harry Williams, "The Military Leadership of North and South," in *Why the North Won the Civil War,* ed. David Donald (Baton Rouge, 1960), pp. 23–47. See also Catton, "Generalship of Grant," pp. 3–30, and T. Harry Williams, *Americans at War: The Development of the American Military System* (New York, 1962).

6. Williams, "The Military Leadership of North and South," p. 43; Grant, *Personal Memoirs,* 1:39; Samuel E. Tillman, "The Academic History of the Military Academy, 1802–1902," in *The Centennial of the United States Military Academy at West Point, New York* (Washington, 1904), 1:278–79; Edward S. Holden and W. L. Ostrander, "A Tentative List of Text-books Used in the United States Military Academy at West Point from 1802 to 1902," *ibid.,* 458, 464.

7. U.S. War Department, *War of the Rebellion: A Compilation of the Official Records of the Union and Confederate Armies* (Washington, 1880–1901), Series 1, 17, pt. 2:119; D. H. Mahan, "The Cadet Life of Grant and Sherman," *Army and Navy Journal* (March 31, 1866):507.

8. Grant, *Personal Memoirs,* 1:41–44; Grant to R. McKinstry Griffith, September 22, 1839, in *Papers of Grant,* 1:6-7.

9. *Report of the* [1860] *Commission to Examine into the Organization, System of Discipline, and Course of Instruction of the United States Military Academy at West Point* (Washington, 1881), pp. 74, 156, 76, 164, 133.

10. Dennis Hart Mahan, *A Treatise on Field Fortification* (New York, 1862); Mahan to "Dear Sir," April 5, 1834, David B. Harris Papers, Duke University; Mahan, *Advanced-Guard, Out-Post, and Detachment Service of Troops, with the Essential Principles of Strategy, and Grand Tactics for the Use of Officers of the Militia and Volunteers* (New York, 1864).

11. *Report of the* [1860] *Commission,* pp. 82, 100, 170, 77, 114, 79. Library policy apparently discouraged book borrowing at West Point. Several people complained in 1860 that cadets were allowed to "take out but a single volume, and that from Saturday noon till Monday morning."

12. Grant, *Personal Memoirs,* 1:252–53; Grant to Julia Dent, June, July 6, 1845; Grant to John W. Love, May 3, 1847, in *Papers of Grant,* 1:46, 47, 136; Grant, *Personal Memoirs,* 2:547.

13. Grant to Julia Dent, May 11, 1846; Grant to John W. Love, June 26, 1846, in *Papers of Grant,* 1:85, 97.

14. Grant, *Personal Memoirs,* 1:167–68.

15. *Ibid.,* p. 166.

16. Grant to Julia Dent, May 11, October 3, 1846, in *Papers of Grant,* 1:85–86, 112.

17. Grant to unknown addressee, April 24, 1847, *ibid.,* p. 134.

18. Arcadi Gluckman, *United States Muskets, Rifles and Carbines* (Harrisburg, 1959), pp. 229–44; Francis A. Lord, "Strong Right Arm of the Infantry: The '61 Springfield Rifle Musket," *Civil War Times Illustrated* 1 (1962):43; Jac Weller, "Imported Confederate Shoulder Weapons," *Civil War History* 5 (1959):170–71, 180, 158; George R. Agassiz, ed., *Meade's Headquarters, 1863–1865: Letters of Colonel Theodore Lyman* (Boston, 1922), p. 224; Frank Wilkeson, *The Soldier in Battle, or Life in the Ranks of the Army of the Potomac* (New York, 1896), p. 99; Porter, *Campaigning with Grant,* p. 179.

19. Grant, *Personal Memoirs,* 1:167; Grant to unknown addressee, August 22, September 12, 1847, in *Papers of Grant,* 1:144–45.

20. Grant to Julia Dent, May 11, June 5, 1846, in *Papers of Grant,* pp. 87, 90.

21. Grant, *Personal Memoirs,* 1:85, 99–100, 138, 139.

22. Quoted in Williams, "The Military Leadership North and South," p. 51.

CHAPTER V

The Confederacy's First Shot

Thirty years ago Charles W. Ramsdell charged that Abraham Lincoln, "having decided that there was no other way than war for the salvation of his administration, his party, and the Union, maneuvered the Confederates into firing the first shot in order that they, rather than he, should take the blame of beginning bloodshed." [1]

The ensuing uproar, especially among Lincoln scholars, was predictable. Many distinguished historians joined the debate; some supported the Ramsdell thesis, but most attacked it. In works published in the early 1940s James G. Randall and David M. Potter claimed Lincoln sought peace rather than war. A few years later Kenneth M. Stampp concluded: "one cannot indict Lincoln for [sending relief to Fort Sumter] . . . unless one challenges the universal standards of 'practical' statesmen and the whole concept of 'national interest.' This was a thing worth fighting for! If Lincoln was no pacifist, neither were his contemporaries, North and South. Southern leaders must share with him the responsibility for a resort to force." [2]

Recent scholarship also contends that Jefferson Davis was as responsible as Lincoln, if not more so, for the outbreak of hostilities. "The firing on Sumter was an act of rash emotionalism," stated Allan Nevins in 1959. "The astute Alexander H. Stephens, counseling delay, showed more statesmanship than Jefferson Davis." And in 1963 Richard N. Current suggested that "the Ramsdell thesis, turned inside out, could be applied to Davis with as much justice as it had been applied to Lincoln.

One could argue that political and not military necessity led Davis to order the firing of the first shot. The very life of the Confederacy, the growth upon which that life depended, was at stake. So were the pride, the prestige, and the position of Davis." "Biographers of Davis and historians of the Confederacy have evaded or obscured their hero's role in the Sumter affair," charged Current. "They have digressed to levy accusations or innuendos at Lincoln. If they have any concern for historical objectivity, however, they should face frankly the question of Davis's responsibility for the coming of the war." "After all," Current concluded, "Lincoln did not order the guns to fire. Davis did." [3]

Those who consider the Confederates aggressors have a strong case, and, as Current claimed, southern historians and Davis biographers have evaded or obscured what the Confederate president and his associates actually did to bring on war. But so have northern historians; they have been too engrossed in defending Lincoln against Ramsdell's charges to give much attention to Davis and the Confederates. Too few scholars have mined beyond the most obvious printed sources on the Confederate side or looked beyond Sumter. The Lincoln-Sumter story, explained in elaborate detail by numerous historians,[4] is too well known to be recounted here. It probably has been overtold already. What has been neglected—what historians have missed—is how events at Fort Sumter were determined by what happened and by what failed to happen at Fort Pickens.

In March 1861, the only significant forts within the Confederacy still occupied by Federal forces were Sumter, in Charleston harbor, and Pickens, near Pensacola, Florida. After a badly planned and bloodless attempt by Alabama and Florida militia to capture Fort Pickens in early January, President James Buchanan and the Confederate government agreed to a truce. Stephen R. Mallory, a former United States senator from Florida, announced that Southerners had no intention of attacking Fort Pickens, "but, on the contrary, we desire to keep the peace, and if the present status be preserved we will guarantee that no attack will be made upon it." Nine former senators—including Jefferson Davis and Judah P. Benjamin—joined Mallory in opposition to any Confederate attempt to take the fort. "We think no assault should be made," they wrote on January 18. "The possession of the fort is not worth one drop of blood to us." [5]

President Buchanan also opposed any action that might appear aggressive. At his direction, the secretaries of war and the navy wrote the commander of the naval squadron off Pensacola on January 29: "In consequence of the assurances received from Mr. Mallory . . . that Fort Pickens would not be assaulted, you are instructed not to land the company on board the *Brooklyn* unless said fort shall be attacked." The day before this letter was written, the president asked Congress "to abstain from passing any law calculated to produce a collision of arms." Thereafter, through February, the Navy Department instructed the commanders of ships near Fort Pickens to "act strictly on the defensive." [6]

Buchanan's successor was less cautious. In the preliminary draft of his first inaugural address, Lincoln wrote: "All the power at my disposal will be used to reclaim the public property and places which have fallen; to hold, occupy and possess these, and all other property and places belonging to the government, . . . but beyond what may be necessary for these, there will be no invasion of any State." Secretary of State William H. Seward begged the president to substitute for this strong statement a promise to use his power "with discretion in every case and . . . with a view and a hope of a peaceful solution of the national troubles and the restoration of fraternal sympathies and affections." Lincoln's friend Orville H. Browning also suggested that the phrase "to reclaim the public property and places which have fallen" was too strong. "On principle the passage is right as it now stands," Browning agreed. "But cannot that be accomplished as well, or even better without announcing the purpose in your inaugural?" Lincoln did modify his address, but he left no doubt that he intended to hold Sumter and Pickens. [7]

It is certain that by early March both Lincoln and Davis had decided to violate the truce, but neither knew what the other intended. On March 10 General Braxton Bragg took command of southern forces near Pensacola with instructions from the Confederate War Department to report his "wants in respect to artillery and the munitions of war, having in view the . . . reduction of Fort Pickens." Two days later a Union ship started south with an order to Captain Israel Vogdes aboard the U. S. S. *Brooklyn.* "At the first favorable moment," read the order, "you will land with your company, re-enforce Fort Pickens, and hold the same till further orders." [8]

But the senior American naval officer off Pensacola, Captain Henry A. Adams, refused to obey the order. "I have declined to land the men . . . as it would be in direct violation of the orders from the Navy Department under which I am acting," he wrote Secretary of the Navy Gideon Welles on April 1. To reinforce Pickens, argued Adams, "would most certainly be viewed as a hostile act, and would be resisted to the utmost. No one acquainted with the feelings of the military assembled under Genl Bragg can doubt that it would be considered not only a declaration, but an act of war. It would be a serious thing to bring on by any precipitation a collision which may be entirely against the wishes of the administration. At present both sides are faithfully observing the agreement entered into by the U.S. Government with Mr. Mallory. . . ." Adams reminded Welles: "This agreement binds us not to reinforce Fort Pickens unless it shall be attacked or threatened. It binds them not to attack it unless we should attempt to reinforce it. I saw Genl Bragg on the 30th ulto., who reassured me the conditions on their part should not be violated." [9]

Bragg had been less than honest with Adams. Only insufficient means, not regard for the truce, prevented the Confederates from attacking Fort Pickens. By the end of March Bragg commanded a force of 1,116 men, and 5,000 additional troops were on the way to Pensacola, but he was not yet ready to fight. He believed that the erection of a new battery at Pickens was "a virtual violation of the [truce] agreement; and the threat of President Lincoln in his inaugural is sufficient justification of the means we are adopting." But Bragg "deemed it prudent not to bring the agreement to an abrupt termination." The Union fleet off Pensacola was too strong, and he was still unprepared. "According to my notions," he admitted to his wife, "things here are in a most deplorable condition. . . . Our troops are raw volunteers, without officers, and without discipline, each man with an idea that he can whip the world, and believing that nothing is necessary but go . . . take Fort Pickens and all the Navy." It would not be that easy. The fort was on Santa Rosa Island, a mile and a half across Pensacola Bay from the mainland. Bragg had neither the firepower nor the ships necessary to isolate the Federal garrison. He believed that unless "the U.S. troops attack us no fighting can occur here for a long time, as we are totally unprepared. . . . Fort Pickens cannot be taken without a regular siege, and we have no means to carry that on. . . ." [10]

Yet the Confederate War Department insisted that Bragg submit a plan to take Pickens, and he suggested three possibilities—a regular siege, a flank attack upon the fort from Santa Rosa Island, or a direct assault. If the operation was to be undertaken immediately, he favored an infantry assault on the fort after its walls had been broken by heavy guns and mortars. The other alternatives would require many more guns and men than he had or could reasonably expect to have for some time. Bragg explained to Adjutant General Samuel Cooper on March 27: "I

entertain little doubt of being able to batter [the fort's walls] . . .
down with 10 inch guns . . . when an assaulting party from this side
aided by a false attack on the Island might carry the work with the Bayonet. It will be difficult at this distance to determine when the breach is
fully effected, . . . and should the enemy resist us by landing heavy re-
enforcements it would be a desperate struggle. A knowledge, however,
that success or entire destruction was inevitable would nerve our men to
the work." [11]

While Confederate authorities discussed what action, if any, Bragg
should take, the Federals prepared to reinforce Pickens. On April 6,
after Lincoln learned that his earlier reinforcement instructions had not
been obeyed, Gideon Welles informed Captain Henry A. Adams: "The
[Navy] Department regrets that you did not comply with the . . . orders.
. . . You will immediately, on the first favorable opportunity after re-
ceipt of this order, afford every facility to Capt. Vogdes . . . to enable
him to land the troops under his command [at Fort Pickens]. . . ." [12]

When Bragg received reports that additional troops might soon land
at Pickens, he was uncertain what he should do. On April 5, he wired
Secretary Walker: "Should the agreement not to re-enforce be violated,
may I attack?" Walker replied that same day with three questions: "Can
you prevent re-enforcements being landed at other points on Santa Rosa
Island other than the docks? Do you mean by 'attack' the opening of
your guns upon the fort or upon the ships? If the former, would your
operations be confined to battering the fort?" [13]

"I can control the dock," Bragg answered the next day, "but re-
enforcements can be landed on the outside of Santa Rosa Island in spite
of me. The ships, except the Wyandotte, are beyond my range. She can
be driven off or destroyed. Any attack by us now must be secretly made
by escalade. My batteries are not ready for breaching, and we are entirely deficient in ammunition. No landing should be made on Santa
Rosa Island with our present means." [14]

It was still unclear to Bragg just what the War Department expected
of him. In a letter to Adjutant General Cooper on April 5, Bragg asked
how far he should "be governed by the articles of agreement now existing here?" He could not prevent the landing of reinforcements, but he
might make it hazardous. Moreover, he might take Pickens by escalade
before it could be reinforced. He would get ready for an escalade,
"should it be deemed advisable at any time." Nevertheless, as "long as
diplomatic intercourse is going on," he informed Cooper, "I shall not feel
authorized to bring on a collision, as now advised." Yet the next day

Bragg seemed less certain. To Secretary Walker, he announced: "I do not hesitate to believe we are entirely absolved from all obligations under the [truce] agreement," and he wanted to know if he was "free to act when a favourable occasion might offer?" [15]

On April 6, the day he asked Walker for instructions, Bragg received from Jefferson Davis a remarkably candid letter, which historians of the first shot controversy have overlooked. It was written, in the President's words, "freely and hurriedly" by "your old comrade in arms, who hopes much, and expects much for you, and from you."

Unofficial

MONTGOMERY, ALA.
April 3, 1861.

MY DEAR GENL,

The Secty of War communicated to you last night by telegraph our latest information and the suppositions derived from it. It is, there is much reason to believe, with a view to exhibit forms and relieve the effect of the necessary abandonment of Sumter that is proposed to reinforce Pickens, but it is also possible that it may be intended to attempt the reinforcement of both. They will it is said avoid collision with you by landing their forces upon the Island and after the garrison is sufficient will bring in supplies defying your batteries.

You will not have failed to notice that the tone of the Northern press indicates a desire to prove a *military* necessity for the abandonment of both Sumter & Pickens.

It is already asserted that your batteries will not permit the landing of supplies, and soon this may be charged among the short comings of Mr. Buchannan [sic]. Per contra there is manifested a desire to show what can be done at Pensacola as proof of what would have been done at Charleston. In the latter view they may seek to throw both men and supplies into Pickens by landing on Santa Rosa beyond the range of your guns. It is scarcely to be doubted that for political reasons the U.S. govt. will avoid making an attack so long as the hope of retaining the border states remains. There would be to us an advantage in so placing them that an attack by them would be a necessity, but when we are ready to relieve our territory and jurisdiction of the presence of a foreign garrison that advantage is overbalanced by other considerations. The case of Pensacola then is reduced [to] the more palpable elements of a military problem and your measures may without disturbing views be directed to the capture of Fort Pickens and the defense of the harbor. You will soon have I hope a force sufficient to occupy all the points necessary for that end. As many additional troops as may be required can be promptly furnished.

Instruction, organization and discipline must proceed with active operations; you will appreciate the circumstances which rendered such objectionable combination an unavoidable condition. Your batteries on the main shore are I am informed nearly complete and their converging fire may I hope compensate somewhat for their too distant location from the work to be battered.

To secure the time necessary for you to effect a breach will it not be necessary to embarrass the use of the guns of Pickens which bear upon your works? Can this be done by a mortar battery placed on the Island so as to take those guns in reverse? In the same connection: could you establish gun batteries on the Island so as to drive off the shipping and prevent a junction of the land and naval forces? A mortar battery could I suppose be established in a night, secure from fire & from sortie when you have a sufficient force to justify a partition of your army. If that first step the establishment of a mortar battery was permitted you could establish gun batteries also, and then carry forward your approaches until you were attacked. Then all your batteries being opened, shells falling in the Fort from front and from rear must prove rapidly destructive to the garrison, and open to you several modes of success. 1st. By surrender. Second. By abandonment if you had not been able to command the shipping. Third. By breach of front wall or explosion of glacis mines exposing the work to capture by assault. Fourth. By evacuation on the plea that the means at the disposal of their government had not been sufficient to prevent the investment of the Fort and its reduction by famine.

I have written to you freely and hurriedly because I wished to exchange views with you and felt assured that you would understand that there was no purpose to dictate; and under an entire confidence that your judgment would control your conduct, and could only be influenced by a suggestion, in so far as it might excite a train of thought out of the channel which the constant contemplation of a particular view is apt to wear. Though you are addressed upon official matters yet I wish to regard this not as a letter of the President but of your old comrade in arms, who hopes much, and expects much for you, and from you.

Very respectfully & truly yrs,
JEFFN DAVIS [16]

This letter indicates that Davis was willing to start the war. He would have liked to do precisely what Ramsdell claimed Lincoln did— maneuver the enemy into firing the first shot—but the Confederate president considered such a scheme, in his own words, "overbalanced by other considerations." Davis counseled action—"your measures may without disturbing views be directed to the capture of Fort Pickens"— and the tone of his letter implied that he expected Bragg to take the fort should he fire the first shot.

Bragg could make no such promise. In his reply to the President's letter on April 7, he stated: "Subsequent information has strengthened the opinion against the attack by way of Santa Rosa Island. . . . Regular approaches by any but veteran troops are very difficult under the most favorable circumstances, but when attended, as in this case, by a combination of the most unfavorable circumstances, they become almost impossible." "The placing of a mortar battery on the Island as you suggest would have a good effect," Bragg admitted, "but the same thing can be accomplished from this side without dividing our force." Bragg believed a Confederate landing on the island would result in the immediate reinforcement of Pickens. He could suggest only one possible and somewhat hazardous way to capture the fort before reinforcements landed. "The plan which just at this time might succeed," Bragg wrote, "is that of an escalade by ladders. My troops are eager, and will risk anything to avoid a long investment on this sand beach. Ignorant in a great degree of the danger they would go at it with a will, and with ordinary good luck would carry the point. Our greatest deficiency is the want of means to reach the Island properly and secretly." [17]

Davis doubtless considered an escalade too risky. If it failed, the Confederates would be branded as aggressors and have nothing tangible to show for it. Though Bragg prepared for an escalade, permission to assault Pickens never came. On April 8, Walker ordered Bragg to prevent the reinforcement of the fort at "every hazard." Bragg might have considered this permission to attack had Walker written nothing else but in a subsequent message the secretary of war warned: "The expression 'at all hazard' in my dispatch of this morning was not intended to require you to land upon the Island. The presumption is that reinforcement will be attempted at the Docks, and this I hope you can and will prevent, though it should lead to assault on your works. The belief here is that they will not only attempt to reinforce the Fort but also to retake the Navy Yard." [18]

Bragg, who had been less than enthusiastic in his recommendation that the Confederates attack Pickens, began to doubt his ability to check a determined Union assault on the Pensacola defenses. " [We] will do our best," he promised Walker on April 9, "but supplies are short for a continued resistance. [We also] want transportation to move guns, shot and troops." [19]

While Bragg strengthened his defenses, Confederate officials in Montgomery shifted their attention to Fort Sumter. Throughout March and early April they had ordered the Confederate commander at Charleston, General P. G. T. Beauregard, to prevent the reinforcement of Sumter but otherwise to remain on the defensive.[20] But on April 10—after it became clear that Pickens was an unlikely place to start the conflict and Lincoln had informed the Confederates that supplies were on the way to Sumter—Walker ordered Beauregard to demand the fort's "evacuation, and if this is refused proceed, in such manner as you may determine, to reduce it." [21]

The rest of the story is familiar enough. The Federal commander, of course, refused to evacuate Sumter, and at 4:30 a.m. on April 12, Beauregard's guns opened fire. The next day Walker wired Bragg: "Sumter is ours." [22]

At that point Bragg was too busy with his own problems to rejoice. On the night of April 12 the first wave of Federal reinforcements reached Fort Pickens. One of Bragg's reconnaissance vessels discovered the landing on the seaward side of the island, but was detained by the Federals until their troops were safely ashore. Bragg reported that when the reinforcements landed he "was making every effort for an escalade, had my party all detailed, and was waiting notice of the readiness of the Engineers. . . . Of course," he asserted, "such a movement now is impossible. . . ." Five days later four more companies of Union troops reached Pickens without opposition. [23]

The first shot had been fired because neither Lincoln nor Davis tried very hard to avoid a collision. Lincoln had no desire to shoot first, but he was determined to hold the forts, and he readily broke the informal truce Buchanan had established. Davis, too, had little regard for the truce agreement. He supported it only when it seemed advantageous. He encouraged Bragg to capture Fort Pickens, but when Bragg insisted that the only possible way to take Pickens was by a reckless assault which might become an embarrassing failure, Davis shifted his attention to Sumter and directed Beauregard to open fire. Thus war came at Fort Sumter only because the Confederates were neither subtle enough nor strong enough to begin it at Fort Pickens.

NOTES

1. Charles W. Ramsdell, "Lincoln and Fort Sumter," *Journal of Southern History* 3 (1937):259–88.

2. James G. Randall, "When War Came in 1861," *Abraham Lincoln Quarterly* 1 (1940):3–42; idem, *Lincoln the President*, 2 vols., *Springfield to Bull Run* (New York, 1945), 1:311–50; idem, *Lincoln the Liberal Statesman* (New York, 1945), pp. 88–117; David M. Potter, *Lincoln and His Party in the Secession Crisis* (New Haven, 1942), pp. 315–75; Kenneth M. Stampp, "Lincoln and the Strategy of Defense in the Crisis of 1861," *Journal of Southern History* 11 (1945): 297–323; idem, *And the War Came: The North and the Secession Crisis, 1860–1861* (Baton Rouge, 1950), pp. 263–86.

3. Allan Nevins, *The War for the Union: The Improvised War, 1861–1862* (New York, 1959), pp. 12–74; Richard N. Current, "The Confederates and the First Shot," *Civil War History* 7 (1961):357–69; idem, *Lincoln and the First Shot* (Philadelphia, 1963), *passim*, but especially p. 201.

4. In addition to the works already cited, see John S. Tilley, *Lincoln Takes Command* (Chapel Hill, 1941); Kenneth P. Williams, *Lincoln Finds a General: A Military Study of the Civil War,* 5 vols. (New York, 1949–1959), 1:16–59; W. A. Swanberg, *First Blood: The Story of Fort Sumter* (New York, 1957); David R. Barbee, "The Line of Blood—Lincoln and the Coming of the War," *Tennessee Historical Quarterly* 16 (1957):3–54; Ludwell H. Johnson, "Fort Sumter and Confederate Diplomacy," *Journal of Southern History* 26 (1960):441–77; Bruce Catton, *The Coming Fury* (New York, 1961), pp. 271–313; and Ari Hoogenboom, "Gustavus Fox and the Relief of Fort Sumter," *Civil War History* 9 (1963):383–98.

5. U.S. War Dept., *The War of the Rebellion: A Compilation of the Official Records of the Union and Confederate Armies* (Washington, 1880–1901), Series 1, 1:354, 444–45. Hereafter cited as *OR,* with all references to Series 1.

6. *OR,* 1:355–56; James D. Richardson, ed., *A Compilation of the Messages and Papers of the Presidents, 1789–1910,* 10 vols. (New York, 1911), 5:662; Isaac Toucey to Capts. James Glynn and Henry A. Adams, and Cmdr. Charles H. Poor, January 21, 1861 (copy), Gustavus V. Fox Papers, New York Historical Society, New York; Toucey to Capts. James Glynn and William S. Walker, and Lt. Adam J. Slemmer, January 29, 1861 (copy), *ibid.;* Toucey to Walker, Adams, and Poor, February 16, 1861 (copy), *ibid.* I am grateful to Professor Ari Hoogenboom for copies of these letters from the Fox Papers.

7. Roy P. Basler, ed., *The Collected Works of Abraham Lincoln,* 9 vols. (New Brunswick, 1953), 4:254, 266. Randall, *Lincoln the President,* 1:332, believed Lincoln would have evacuated Fort Sumter if Buchanan had allowed the reinforcement of Fort Pickens.

8. Braxton Bragg to Maj. George Deas, March 10, 1861 (copy), William P. Palmer Collection of Braxton Bragg Papers, Western Reserve Historical Society, Cleveland; *OR,* 1:449; *Official Records of the Union and Confederate Navies in the War of the Rebellion* (Washington, 1894–1927), Series 1, 4:90.

9. Henry A. Adams to Gideon Welles, April 1, 1861, Fox Papers.

10. Bragg to Adj. Gen. Samuel Cooper, March 13, 1861 (copy), Palmer Collection; Bragg to Mrs. Bragg, March 11, 1861, William K. Bixby Collection of Braxton Bragg Papers, Missouri Historical Society, St. Louis; *OR,* 1:454–55.

11. Bragg to Cooper, March 27, 1861 (copy), Palmer Collection.

12. Gideon Welles to Henry A. Adams, April 6, 1861, Fox Papers.

13. *OR,* 1:455–56.

14. *Ibid.,* p. 456.

15. Bragg to Cooper, April 5, 1861 (copy), Palmer Collection; *OR,* 1:456–57. The same day he told Walker that the Federals had broken the truce, Bragg wrote Richard Taylor: "Our truce remains in force. 'They are not to reinforce. We are not to attack.' It is being carried out by both parties so far." Bragg to Taylor, April 6, 1861, Urquhart Collection of Richard Taylor Papers, Tulane University, New Orleans.

16. Davis to Bragg, April 3, 1861, Palmer Collection. This letter is cited in only one of the many works on the first shot controversy—Bruce Catton's *The Coming Fury,* p. 492.

17. Bragg to Davis, April 7, 1861 (copy), Palmer Collection.

18. Walker to Bragg, 8 a.m. and 4 p.m., April 8, 1861, *ibid.*

19. *OR,* 1:458; Bragg to Walker, April 9, 1861 (copy), Palmer Collection.

20. On April 2, for example, Walker wrote Beauregard: "You are specially instructed . . . to keep yourself in a state of the amplest preparation and most perfect readiness to repell invasion, acting in all respects—save only in commencing an assault or attack, except to repell an invading or re-inforcing force—precisely as if you were in the presence of any enemy contemplating to surprise you." *OR,* 1:272, 285, 289, 291.

21. *Ibid.,* p. 297.

22. *Ibid.,* p. 305; Walker to Bragg, April 13, 1861, Leroy Pope Walker Collection, Chicago Historical Society, Chicago.

23. Henry A. Adams to Gideon Welles, April 14, 18, 1861, Fox Papers; Harvey Brown to Adams, April 17, 1861, *ibid.; OR,* 1:460–61; Bragg to Cooper, April 13, 15, 1861 (copies), Palmer Collection; Bragg to Henry A. Adams, April 14, 1861 (copy), *ibid.*

CHAPTER VI

Jefferson Davis
and His Generals

Jefferson Davis was, in the words of a contemporary, "the heart and brains" of the Confederate government. He spent fifteen or more hours a day at his duties—receiving visitors, writing letters, consulting his advisers, revising or initiating projects to win the war. Thomas DeLeon claimed that Davis "managed the War Department, in all its various details, in addition to other manifold labors; finding time not only to give it a general supervision, but to go into all the minutiae of the working of its bureaux, the choice of all its officers, or agents, and the very disbursement of its appropriations." Davis appointed and removed generals, advised them on strategy and tactics, and often decided when and where they should fight. He was the man most responsible for the way the Confederacy fought the Civil War.

Davis seems to have had no doubts about his ability to direct a war. He had spent a dozen years in the army, including four years as a cadet at the United States Military Academy (1824–28), five years as a second lieutenant in the First Infantry (1828–33), two years as a first lieutenant in the First Dragoons (1833–35), and one year as colonel of the First Mississippi Volunteer Rifles during the Mexican War (1846–47). He had participated in the Black Hawk War (1832) and in two Mexican War battles. At Monterrey and Buena Vista, where he had been wounded in the foot, Davis had fought courageously. In addition to his years in the army, he had served as President Franklin Pierce's secretary of war (1853–57), and he had been chairman of the Senate's Military Affairs Committee. All of these activities had given him confidence in his military ability. "By early education, by years of service in the army, by other years spent in administering the U.S. War Dept.," Davis boasted, "I had learned the usages of war." [1]

Davis believed that he was a talented soldier. He had said before the Confederacy was formed that he would rather be commander in chief of its army than its president. Of course he knew that under the United States Constitution the commander in chief of the army was the president; and he could have guessed that it would be so under the constitution the Confederates would adopt. Davis was not a devious man, but neither was he overly modest. He told his wife during the Civil War: "If I could take one wing [of the army] and Lee the other, I think we could between us wrest a victory from those people." [2]

Contemporaries also had faith in Davis's military ability. When the Mississippi legislature appropriated $150,000 to purchase arms in 1859, Governor John J. Pettis asked Davis's advice on how to spend the money. In 1861 an enthusiastic newspaperman compared "Gen. Davis" favorably with General George Washington, and Louis T. Wigfall, who later became one of the president's strongest critics, said: "Davis has the wisdom and sagacity of the statesman . . . the courage and discretion of the soldier. . . . I know of no man so competent to inaugurate a Government at such a time." Just after Davis became president, William L. Yancey declared: "The man and the hour have met." He praised Davis as a "soldier, distinguished upon the field of battle, wise in council, terrible in the charge." A few months later a clerk in the Confederate War Department noted the almost universal belief that Davis "possessed military genius of a high order." [3]

The new Confederate president appeared to be just what the South needed. If war came, the organizers of the Confederacy reasoned, it would be well to have a politician heading the government who had more military experience than any other presidential prospect. It was believed that Davis had the knowledge and the experience to direct military operations, that he understood strategy and tactics, and that because he knew who was who among American professional soldiers he would appoint the ablest men to high rank. [4]

The widespread belief among Southerners at the war's outset that Davis was the right man to lead them soon changed. In June 1861 Mrs. Davis informed her mother: "When Jeff goes to the encampments [of soldiers] they go on like wild Indians, scream, catch hold of him, call out 'I am from Tennessee, I'm from Kentucky, I'm from Mississippi,

God bless your soul.' The other day a volunteer stepped up to the carriage & said 'God bless you, Madam, & keep you well,' with a deep bow. They seize little Jeff & kiss him. It seems as if Jeff's stock has suddenly risen." Yet early in 1862 Howell Cobb told his wife that one "might almost use the term *odious*" in describing the attitude of Confederate congressmen toward Davis. Only patriotism prevented them from rebelling against the president, wrote Cobb; "I—(who have never received a kindness at his hands)—have to interpose between him and his former pets to save him from bitter attacks on the floor of Congress." "Davis is preverse and obstinate," insisted Cobb, "and unless we can beat some liberal and just notions into his head, we shall have much trouble in the future. . . ." A few months later an editor considered Davis "cold, haughty, peevish, narrow-minded, pigheaded, malignant" —"the cause of our undoing. While he lives, there is no hope for us." And in November 1862 a major in the commissary department said that he "used to think Jefferson Davis a *mule,* but a good *mule.*" Now he considered him "a jackass." [5]

Such criticism of Davis would hardly have surprised Winfield Scott. The old general, with whom Davis had feuded when he was secretary of war, had said in 1861: "I am amazed that any man of judgment should hope for the success of any cause in which Jefferson Davis is a leader. There is a contamination in his touch. . . . He is not a cheap Judas. I do not think he would have sold the Saviour for thirty shillings; but for the successorship of Pontius Pilate he would have betrayed Christ and the apostles and the whole Christian Church!" [6]

If Scott's words seem unduly biased and exaggerated, it is worth noting that Davis's own chief of ordnance, General Josiah Gorgas, wrote in his diary: "The President seems to respect the opinions of no one; and has, I fear, little appreciation of services rendered, unless the party enjoys his good opinion. He seems to be an indifferent judge of men, and is guided more by prejudice than by sound, discriminating judgment." And Senator C. C. Clay, a Davis supporter, admitted that the president "will not ask or receive counsel and indeed seems predisposed to go exactly the way his friends advise him not to go." [7]

On the other hand, a number of prominent men continued to support the president. In August 1864 the editor of *De Bow's Review* said that Davis was as "brave as Ajax and as wise as Ulysses," and in 1865 Congressman Warren Akin wrote: "I had a long conversation with the President yesterday. He has been greatly wronged. . . . The President is not the stern, puffed up man he is represented to be. He was as polite, attentive and communicative to me as I could wish. He listened patiently to all I said and when he differed with me he would give his reasons for it. He was very cordial. . . . And many gentlemen tell me the same thing as to his manner with them. His enemies have done him great injustice. He is a patriot and a good man, I think." [8]

Different people simply saw different qualities in Davis. To those who admired him he appeared able, modest, polite, loyal, agreeable, and self-sacrificing—an accomplished and a dedicated patriot. To his enemies he seemed ruthless, cold, stubborn, petty, and prejudiced—an incompetent executive with poor judgment.[9]

On one point friends and enemies of the president agreed: his health was poor. This sick man, who suffered constantly from insomnia, dyspepsia, and neuralgia, was often incapacitated by such diseases as malaria. "Jeff has been for nearly eight weeks confined to the house," admitted Mrs. Davis in 1858. The next year Davis wrote his friend Franklin Pierce: "I . . . have been seriously ill, though now free of disease, my strength has not been restored and there is therefore constant apprehension of a relapse." Just before the war a reporter described Davis as having "the face of a corpse, the form of a skeleton." "You are surprised to see him walking," wrote Murat Halstead in 1860. "Look at the haggard, sunken, weary eye—the thin white wrinkled lips clasped close upon the teeth in anguish. That is the mouth of a brave but impatient sufferer. See the ghastly white, hollow, bitterly puckered cheek, the high, sharp cheek bone, the pale brow full of fine wrinkles, the grizzly hair, prematurely gray; and see the thin, bloodless, bony, nervous hands!" Almost everyone who saw Davis during the Civil War commented upon his sickly appearance. He seemed, to the English reporter William H. Russell, to have "a very haggard, care-worn, and pain-drawn look." In 1861 a future congressman wrote: "The president looks thin & feeble." That same year a war clerk observed: "The President is sick. . . . I did not know until to-day that he is blind of an eye." Two years later an English officer remarked that Davis looked "older than I expected. He is only fifty-six, but his face is emaciated and much wrinkled. He is nearly six feet high, but is extremely thin and stoops. . . . I was . . . told he had lost the sight of his left eye from a recent illness." [10]

Not only was the president sickly; so were many of his military advisers. Their gatherings sometimes resembled a hospital ward more than an assembly of war directors. Davis's first secretary of war, Leroy Pope Walker, was described in 1860 as "a tall . . . man, with long pale

face . . . whose health is feeble." A member of the War Department
noted in May 1861: "Mr. Walker . . . is fast working himself down.
He has not yet learned how to avoid unnecessary labor. . . . He stands
somewhat on ceremony with his brother officials, and accords and ex-
acts the etiquette natural to a sensitive gentleman who has never been
broken on the wheel of office. I predict for him a short career." By
June, Walker's health had failed; he remained secretary of war until
September 1861, but most of the time he was too ill to come to his office. George W. Randolph, secretary of war for eight months in 1862,
had pulmonary tuberculosis, and James A. Seddon, who had the longest
tenure of any secretary of war, was often incapacitated by neuralgia and
other illnesses. Albert T. Bledsoe, the assistant secretary of war, advised Davis that Seddon was too feeble to head the War Department.
"The labor of the office would kill him in one month," insisted Bledsoe.
"Mr. Seddon has no physique to sustain him," observed war clerk John
B. Jones, who also stated that Seddon lacked both "energy and knowledge of war." "He is . . . frail in health," noted Jones. "He will not remain long in office if he attempts to perform all the duties." Six months
later Jones remarked: "Secretary Seddon is gaunt and emaciated. . . .
He looks like a dead man galvanized into muscular animation. His eyes
are sunken, and his features have the hue of a man who has been in his
grave a full month." After two more months of hard work Seddon looked
to Jones like a "corpse which had been buried two months. The circles
round his eyes are absolutely black." Another contemporary remembered
Seddon as "an old man broken with the storms of state." [11]

Some of the soldiers Davis named to the War Department looked and
acted more dead than alive. Three of the most prominent were Colonel
Lucius B. Northrop, the Confederacy's highly criticized commissary
general; Adjutant and Inspector General Samuel Cooper; and General
Braxton Bragg. Colonel Northrop, whom Mrs. Mary Chesnut called an
"eccentric creature" because he wore folded newspapers across his chest
instead of underwear, had been on permanent sick leave from the
United States Army for twenty-two years before Davis appointed him
commissary general. "The reason for his appointment to . . . the most
responsible bureau of the War Department was a mystery," admitted a
contemporary. General Cooper, often described as too old and too feeble to take the field, had not been in the field for nearly thirty years.
During the war he was often ill and out of his office. "Genl. Cooper still
sick & can't be seen," wrote an officer in 1862. General Bragg, whom
Davis brought to Richmond in 1864 to help him conduct military oper-

ations, was at the time the most discredited general in the Confederacy
and one of the sickliest. Bragg had enough illnesses to keep a squad of
doctors busy—dyspepsia, rheumatism, chronic boils, a liver ailment,
extreme nervousness, and severe migraine headaches. Some of his
illness—and perhaps his often erratic and irascible behavior—may
have been caused by the medicine he took. Before the war Bragg admitted that he was suffering from his "old Florida complaint of the *liver*.
. . . Every summer I have these attacks," he explained to a friend,
"and I can now only keep about by almost living on Mercury (Blue
Mass & Calomel). No constitution can stand it." [12]

A remarkable number of the South's highest ranking field officers had
physical handicaps or health problems. Bragg was sick during much of
the time he commanded Confederate forces in the West. General John
Bell Hood, who lost a leg at Chickamauga and the use of an arm at
Gettysburg, had to be strapped into his saddle when he commanded the
Army of Tennessee. In 1862 General P. G. T. Beauregard had to retire
from army command because of illness. General Joseph E. Johnston,
who had been wounded several times in action against Indians and
Mexicans before the Civil War, was again hit twice at Fair Oaks—first
by a bullet in the shoulder and a few moments later by a shell fragment,
which unhorsed him. For nearly six months during the critical summer
and fall of 1862 he was incapacitated, and even after he returned to
duty he often was, in his own words, "too feeble to command an army."
In April 1863, when President Davis ordered him to take command of
the South's second most important army, Johnston was "seriously sick."
He explained: "I . . . am not now able to serve in the field." Later,
when he was ordered to assume command of forces in Mississippi,
Johnston replied: "I shall go immediately, although unfit for field-
service." [13]

There is a tendency to think of Robert E. Lee as a superman who
was never ill, but he was bedridden for some days in the spring of 1863
with "inflammation of the heart-sac" and a serious throat infection.
This condition plus occasional attacks of rheumatism "enfeebled" and
forced him "to take more rest." In August 1863, after the Gettysburg
campaign, Lee asked Davis to relieve him from command of the Army
of Northern Virginia: "I do this with the most earnestness because no
one is more aware than myself of my inability for the duties of my position. I cannot even accomplish what I myself desire. How can I fulfil
the expectations of others? In addition I sensibly feel the growing failure of my bodily strength. I have not yet recovered from the attack I
experienced the past spring. I am becoming more and more incapable

of exertion, and am thus prevented from making the personal examina-
tions and giving the personal supervision to the operations in the field
which I feel to be necessary. I am so dull that in making use of the eyes
of others I am frequently misled. Everything, therefore, points to the
advantages to be derived from a new commander, and I the more anx-
iously urge the matter upon Your Excellency from my belief that a
younger and abler man than myself can readily be attained." Though
Davis refused to replace Lee, the general's health continued to decline.
In October 1863 an attack of "sciatica," "rheumatism," or "lumbago"
made it impossible for Lee to ride for about a week, and during the
critical campaign against Grant in May and June 1864 Lee was debili-
tated for ten days by sickness.[14]

Even Lee's trusted lieutenant, Thomas J. ("Stonewall") Jackson, had
or imagined he had a wide range of ailments—dyspepsia, liver distur-
bances, nervousness, eye strain, rheumatism, chilblains, cold feet, malaria, bilious attacks, neuralgia, fevers, and chronic inflammation of the
throat, nose, and ears as well as "a slight distortion of the spine." By
sitting "straight up, . . . without touching the back of his chair," Jackson believed that he "could keep his internal organs from being con-
stricted." He also treated himself with buttermilk, freshly cooked corn-
bread, much fruit—especially lemons—and cold water. "I have been
quite unwell," he announced in 1850, "and had it not have been for my
judicious application of water, I can not say what would have been the
consequences." Active campaigning seemed to improve his health.[15]

The poor health of so many of Davis's subordinates does not necessarily suggest that the Confederate president had a psychological affinity
for sick people, though one might speculate that this was the case. Sickness is after all an aspect of weakness, and there is abundant evidence
that Davis liked to surround himself with weak subordinates. "He was
not only President and secretary of five departments—which naturally
caused some errors," stated a contemporary, "but that spice of the dic-
tator in him made him quite willing to shoulder the responsibilities of
all the positions. . . ." He had six different secretaries of war in four
years.[16]

If empathy bound Davis to some of his infirm subordinates, there is
no evidence that these men received or retained their high offices solely
because the president considered them fellow sufferers; indeed, he insisted that his military appointments were based on merit alone. "Due
care was taken to prevent the appointment of incompetent or unworthy
persons to be officers of the army," Davis stated after the war. And several historians have supported his claim. The president "gave just as

few high commissions to politicians as possible," writes a recent biographer. To a critic, Davis wrote: "It would be easy to justify the appointments which have been made of Brig. Genls. by stating the reasons in each case, but suffice it to say that I have endeavored to avoid bad selections by relying on military rather than political recommendations." [17]

Yet political considerations influenced Davis more than he admitted. Nearly 30 percent of the generals he named in 1861 were political appointees. For example, Humphrey Marshall of Kentucky, despite his military training and experience, was clearly a political general. Less than a year after his graduation from the United States Military Academy, Marshall had resigned from the army. Later he served as a volunteer in the Mexican War, where, according to one report, his "regiment did some fine running & no fighting." Elected to Congress seven times as a Whig, Marshall had tried to keep Kentucky neutral in 1861. After he had failed, Davis appointed him a Confederate brigadier general. Marshall spent much of his time writing long letters of complaint to Davis. These finally goaded the president into a reply that revealed why he had appointed Marshall. "When you were offered a position of rank and responsibility in our army," Davis stated, "it was my hope that you would prove beneficial to our cause. . . . [I believed] in your assured conviction of your ability to recruit an army of Kentuckians, who would rally to your standard." But Marshall proved to be neither an able recruiter nor an able general. In 1863 he resigned his army commission and entered the Confederate Congress. [18]

Other political generals included John C. Breckinridge of Kentucky, who had been a member of Congress, vice-president of the United States, and a candidate for president in 1860; Robert Toombs of Georgia, who resigned as Confederate secretary of state to enter the army; Louis T. Wigfall of Texas, who had been expelled from the United States Senate; James Chesnut, Jr., a former senator from South Carolina and a member of the Provisional Confederate Congress, who became a member of Davis's military staff; Milledge L. Bonham, a South Carolina congressman; Lawrence O. Branch, a member of a politically prominent North Carolina family; Howell Cobb of Georgia, former Speaker of the United States House of Representatives; John B. Floyd, at one time governor of Virginia and recently President Buchanan's secretary of war; Leroy Pope Walker of Alabama, who was for a short time Davis's secretary of war; and two former Virginia governors, William ("Extra Billy") Smith and Henry A. Wise. [19]

Pressure to appoint political generals was strong. Davis had the thankless task of organizing an effective army while at the same time including in it officers of diverse political opinion from all states and regions of the South. In a letter of July 13, 1861, Governor Isham G. Harris of Tennessee thanked the president for appointing three Tennesseeans to the rank of brigadier general, "but," the governor noted, "they are all Democrats." He wanted Davis to name some "other generals" from Tennessee, including a few Whigs. "It is a political necessity," Harris explained, "that the Whig element be fully recognized." Davis agreed; in fact, he had appointed two additional generals from Tennessee just a few days before receiving Harris's letter. One of these men was Felix Zollicoffer, an influential Whig, who had supported John Bell for the presidency in 1860 and had been a member of the aborted Washington Peace Conference. In 1862 two Alabama politicians protested that the president had appointed only five generals from their state. They recommended to him four politicians who "seem to us entitled to respectful consideration in competition with other civilians, from other States, which have already their full proportion, or more, of General officers." [20]

A few of Davis's political generals were assets, but many of them proved to be worthless soldiers and sources of embarrassment to the president. John B. Floyd, for example, was removed from command after he shirked his responsibility at Fort Donelson. After much criticism of his conduct at the battle of Elkhorn Tavern, General Albert Pike, a prominent Arkansas Whig, resigned from the army. General William H. Carroll, a Tennesseean whose father had been six times governor of the state, was removed from command "for drunkenness, incompetency, and neglect of duty." General Roger A. Pryor, a former Virginia congressman, was left without military duties in 1863. Robert Toombs and Louis T. Wigfall soon resigned from the army and spent much of the war criticizing Davis. In the summer of 1863 Wigfall announced: "Davis's mind is becoming unsettled. No sane man would act as he is acting. I fear that his bad health and bad temper are undermining his reason, and that the foundation is already sapped." Henry A. Wise had been appointed a general because he was popular in the western counties of Virginia. After he had helped raise a number of regiments, Davis ignored him. "This war has produced no more emphatic a failure than Wise," remarked a member of the administration. Outraged by this ignominy, Wise denounced the president and his family as "little, low, vulgar people." [21]

Davis liked to tell certain people that none of his appointees was a political general, but he also liked to say to others—especially to demanding politicians—that he had appointed a fair number of representatives from each state and party. Thus two conflicting impressions grew —that the president appointed either too many or almost no politicians to high military positions. A general complained that professional soldiers "have seen themselves overlooked by their government, while their juniors in years of service and I think their inferiors . . . were put over them in rank. . . ." Civilians, on the other hand, often objected to what one man called the president's "irrepressible *West Pointism.*" Davis tried to defend himself against both charges. "I know that among some of our people," he wrote in 1863, "an impression prevailed that I was unduly partial to those officers who had received an education at the Military Academy and was willing to concede something to that impression though I did not recognize its justice." [22]

Davis knew that, whatever his personal desires, all of his generals could not be West Point graduates. First, there simply were not that many West Pointers available. A common misconception is that in 1861 most of America's experienced soldiers were Southerners who resigned their commissions in the United States Army to join the Confederacy. Actually, Northerners comprised nearly 60 percent of the regular army officers at the outbreak of the Civil War. Of the army's 1,080 officers, only 286 entered the Confederate service; 184 of these were graduates of the United States Military Academy. Over 600 West Point graduates remained in the Federal army. Of the approximately 900 West Point graduates then in civil life, fewer than 225 joined the Confederate army. Second, too many West Point graduates were young and inexperienced soldiers. Of the 286 men who resigned from the United States Army to enter Confederate service only 24 were majors or above in the Old Army; most of the others were junior officers, some quite recent graduates of West Point. Though the president welcomed these young men, he appointed few of them to high rank early in the war.[23]

The 88 men appointed generals by Davis in 1861 fell into three categories: first, 40 regular United States Army officers who resigned their commissions in 1861 to join the Confederacy (all but 2 of them, David E. Twiggs and William W. Loring, were West Point graduates); [24] second, 23 West Pointers who had resigned from the regular army some years prior to 1861; and third, 25 men who had neither attended the United States Military Academy nor served in the regular army. All these men had in common at least one thing—they were either civil or military leaders. The 40 regulars who became Confederate generals in

1861 had been captains or above in the United States Army at the war's outset.[25]

Military training alone did not ensure high rank. Fewer than half of the West Point graduates who offered their services to the Confederacy ever became generals. Between 1861 and 1865 Jefferson Davis appointed 425 men to the rank of brigadier general or higher. Almost two-thirds of these men had had some military experience prior to the Civil War, but much of that experience had consisted of militia service, attendance at military schools, or expeditions against Indians. No fewer than 153 Confederate generals were lawyers or politicians when the Civil War began; 55 were businessmen, and 42 were farmers or planters. Only 34 percent of the Confederate generals were graduates of the United States Military Academy, and only 29 percent were professional soldiers when the war began.[26]

Some men, it was charged, received or were denied high rank simply because the president liked or disliked them. William L. Yancey claimed that Davis's appointments "are often conferred as rewards to friends and are refused as punishments inflicted upon enemies." And Senator James L. Orr said that the "President's attachment for Genl. Bragg could be likened to nothing else than the blind & gloating love of a mother for a deformed & misshapen offspring." [27]

Despite Davis's disclaimer to a critic—"nor will I consent to be influenced in the exercise of the appointing power which I hold as a trust for the public good, by personal favor or personal resentment"—there is evidence to support the charge that the president did reward his friends. In 1861 he commissioned at least five generals who had little military experience but were his close friends. Three of these men had been with him at West Point: Thomas F. Drayton, Hugh W. Mercer, and Leonidas Polk. All had left the United States Army while they were still lieutenants. Drayton became a planter and a railroad builder in South Carolina; Mercer became cashier of a bank in Savannah; and Polk became the Episcopal missionary bishop of the Southwest. At the time Davis appointed these men Confederate generals, they had been out of military service for twenty-five or more years. Polk, who had spent a grand total of five months as an officer after his graduation from West Point in 1827, was made a major general by Davis on June 25, 1861.[28]

Richard Griffith, while a lieutenant in the First Mississippi Rifles during the Mexican War, had "formed a warm and lasting friendship with his commanding officer, Jefferson Davis." This brief military association must have been enough to convince Davis that Griffith had leadership ability. He was appointed brigadier general in the Confederate service before he had been in a Civil War battle.[29]

Richard Taylor, son of General Zachary Taylor, was the brother of Davis's first wife. Taylor had no military experience prior to the Civil War except that gained from a childhood spent at various army posts and a brief stint as his father's secretary during the Mexican War, but Davis quickly promoted him to general. "This promotion," Taylor recalled, "seriously embarrassed me. Of the four colonels whose regiments constituted the brigade, I was the junior in commission, and the three others had been present and 'won their spurs' at the recent battle [of First Manassas], so far the only important one of the war. Besides, my known friendship for President Davis . . . would justify the opinion that my promotion was due to favouritism." [30]

At times Davis also used his appointing power to punish his enemies. He apparently struck the name of Arthur M. Manigault off the list of colonels recommended for promotion to brigadier because a personal letter of Manigault's that was critical of Davis had been published. "I admit having written the letter & must abide the consequences," explained Manigault. "It is a matter of . . . great surprise to me . . . , its publication in any newspaper, . . . as to the best of my recollection, I placed it in the post office at Knoxville myself." [31]

Contrary to the claims of Davis and certain historians, it is clear that qualities other than military ability and experience influenced the appointment of some generals, but what about the Confederacy's highest ranking officers? Did political considerations, friendship with the president, or other factors affect their selection and promotion?

Only six men—Samuel Cooper, Albert Sidney Johnston, Robert E. Lee, Joseph E. Johnston, Pierre Gustave Toutant Beauregard, and Braxton Bragg—ever became full generals in the regular Confederate army.[32] The Confederacy's senior general both in age and in rank was Samuel Cooper. When the president appointed him the highest ranking general in the Confederacy, Cooper was sixty-four years old. No one could deny that he had years of military experience. At the time he joined the Confederacy, Cooper could boast of forty-eight years of continuous service in the United States Army; since 1838 he had been in Washington, D.C., at a desk job. He became the adjutant and inspector general of the Confederacy, the position he had held in the Old Army since 1852.[33]

In time of peace, Cooper might have been a satisfactory figurehead for the adjutant general's office. But he was incapable of handling the complex and demanding task of organizing and administering the Confederacy's armies. The chief of the Confederate Bureau of War, Robert G. H. Kean, claimed that Cooper was totally incompetent: "It is so manifest that nothing but the irrepressible *West Pointism* of the President, and that other peculiarity of preferring accommodating, civil-spoken persons of small capacity about him, can account for his retention." Kean charged that Cooper had no idea of the condition of any army. "There has never been a time when the A. I. General could give even a tolerably close *guess* of the whole force on the rolls of the army, still less of the *effective* force. He is most of the time *out* of his office. There is not one paper a week which bears evidence of his personal examination. He never decides anything, rarely ever *reports* upon a question, and when he does the report is very thin." [34]

Why did Davis appoint and retain such a person? Was it because, as Kean claimed, the president favored professional soldiers and graduates of the United States Military Academy and liked "civil-spoken persons of small capacity about him"? Perhaps so. Davis, when he was President Pierce's secretary of war, had worked closely and gotten along well with Cooper. "Having known him most favorably and intimately as Adjutant-General of the United States Army," recalled Davis, "the value of his services in the organization of a new army was considered so great that I invited him to take the position of Adjutant-General of the Confederate Army, which he accepted without a question either as to relative rank or anything else." [35] Davis liked people who agreed with him. If they did not, they usually left his administration.

Perhaps another reason why Davis appointed Cooper adjutant and inspector general was that there was simply nothing else to do with the man. Contemporaries agreed that he was unsuited for field service. What could the president do other than give Cooper the same job that he had held for the past nine years? To have done otherwise would have insulted Cooper—a native of New Jersey who had sacrificed a secure position to join the Confederacy—and created political problems for the Davis administration, for Cooper was married to the sister of Senator James M. Mason of Virginia.[36]

If the appointment of Cooper appears to have been motivated by personal and political considerations, that of the second highest ranking Confederate general, Albert Sidney Johnston, was based upon personal friendship and admiration. Davis and Sidney Johnston had been friends since the 1820s. They had attended West Point together, where Johnston had treated Davis like a younger brother; they had served together on the Illinois frontier as young lieutenants in the Black Hawk War; and they had been under fire together at Monterrey in the Mexican War.[37]

Johnston was fifty-eight years old when the Civil War began; twenty-seven of those years had been spent in active military service or training. After four years at West Point (1822–1826), Johnston served eight years as a lieutenant in the Sixth Infantry. He resigned from the army in 1834, but two years later he enlisted as a private in the Army of the Texas Republic. He quickly rose to the rank of senior brigadier general. He next served two years (1838–40) as Texas's secretary of war. After Texas became a part of the United States and the Mexican War began, Johnston assumed command of the First Texas Volunteer Infantry with the rank of colonel. A month later, when the unit's enlistment ended, most of the men went home, and Johnston was left without a command. But he remained in Mexico, and General Zachary Taylor appointed him inspector general on the staff of General William O. Butler, commander of a division of volunteers. Johnston helped steady the volunteers after Butler was wounded at Monterrey. When Taylor became president, he appointed Johnston a major in the army's Paymaster Department. Relief from this position, which Johnston disliked, came after six years when he was promoted to the rank of full colonel and given command of the Second United States Cavalry. Political influence, including the support of Jefferson Davis, who was then secretary of war, helped Johnston get his new command. His next opportunity came in 1857 when he was selected to lead an army to Utah to prevent a Mormon uprising. His successful occupation of Utah won him promotion to brevet brigadier general. When the Civil War began, Johnston was in California commanding the Department of the Pacific. He immediately resigned his commission and started overland with a small party. He arrived in Richmond in September 1861 and called at the Confederate White House only to be told that the president was too ill to see visitors. Davis, who from his sickbed heard sounds on the floor below, supposedly called out: "That is Sidney Johnston's step. Bring him up." Davis got out of bed and "for several days at various intervals," he recalled, "we conversed with the freedom and confidence belonging to the close friendship which had existed between us for many years. Consequent upon a remark made by me, he asked to what duty I would assign him, and, when answered, to serve in the West, he expressed his pleasure at service in that section, but inquired how he was to raise his command, and for the first time learned that he had been nominated and confirmed as a general in the Army of the Confederacy." [38]

Robert E. Lee, a fifty-five-year-old professional soldier and the third highest ranking Confederate general, was also Jefferson Davis's friend. The president and Lee had been students together at West Point. While secretary of war, Davis had aided Lee's military career; Lee, in turn, had defended Secretary Davis against a newspaper critic. In 1861, Davis later stated, he had "unqualified confidence" in Lee, "both as a man and a patriot." Tactful, courteous, and modest, Lee proved repeatedly throughout the war that he knew how to get along with the president. Lee never demanded; he got what he wanted by subtle persuasion. He always referred to Davis as "Your Excellency." The president even believed that Lee cared nothing about rank: "he had been appointed a full general," recalled Davis, "but so wholly had his heart and his mind been consecrated to the public service, that he had not remembered, if he ever knew, of his advancement." [39]

The appointment of Lee was inextricably linked with that of Joseph E. Johnston, the fourth highest ranking Confederate general. Joe Johnston and Robert E. Lee were the same age; they were graduated from West Point in the same class (1829); they were both professional soldiers; they had served together in the Mexican War, where both had received the brevet rank of colonel for gallant conduct under fire. After the Mexican War, on the same date (March 3, 1855), both were promoted to lieutenant colonel and assigned to cavalry regiments—Lee to the Second Cavalry, Johnston to the First Cavalry. On June 28, 1860, Johnston left the cavalry to become the army's quartermaster general with the rank of brigadier general. Lee remained in the cavalry and was not promoted to the rank of full colonel until March 16, 1861. [40]

Thus, when the two men left the United States Army to join the Confederacy, Johnston, a brigadier general, outranked Lee, a colonel. Consequently, Johnston was shocked and angered to discover, when the list of Confederate full generals appeared, that his old friend and rival now outranked him. A proud man, Johnston believed that he had been treated unjustly by the president. Johnston recalled that he had not been Davis's choice for quartermaster general in 1860; Davis, then chairman of the Senate's Military Affairs Committee, had favored Sidney Johnston for the position. Now, it must have appeared to Joe Johnston, Davis was taking his revenge. Honor demanded a protest. In an angry letter to the president, Johnston argued that Confederate law guaranteed "that the relative rank of officers of each grade shall be determined by their former commissions in the U.S. Army." Since he was the highest ranking officer of the Old Army to join the Confederacy, it was unfair and illegal to appoint others above him. "I now and here declare my claim," he wrote, "that notwithstanding these nominations by the President and their confirmation by Congress, I still rightfully hold the rank of first general in the Armies of the Southern Confederacy." Davis considered the letter insubordinate; his reply was cold and brief: "I have just received and read your letter. . . . Its language is, as you say, unusual; its arguments and statements utterly one-sided, and its insinuations as unfounded as they are unbecoming." From that point on the men never trusted each other. In October 1863 a close observer noted: "the President detests Joe Johnston . . . and General Joe returns the compliment with compound interest. His hatred of Jeff Davis amounts to a religion. With him it colors all things." [41]

The president came to dislike and to mistrust the fifth highest ranking full general, Pierre Gustave Toutant Beauregard, as much or more than Joe Johnston. Beauregard was one of the bright young professional soldiers who joined the Confederacy. Forty-three years old when the war started, he had been graduated second in his class at West Point in 1838 and assigned to the elite engineering corps. During the Mexican War, while serving on General Winfield Scott's staff, he had received brevet promotions to captain and to major for gallant and meritorious conduct in battle. Beauregard became the Confederacy's first hero after Fort Sumter fell to his forces; he won additional fame at First Manassas. His high opinion of his own military ability and his jealousy of those generals above him in rank, especially Joe Johnston, caused problems. After the war Beauregard explained why he considered himself better qualified in 1861 for high command than Johnston: "Having been attached . . . to the staff of . . . General Scott, in the Mexican War, General Beauregard had taken a leading part in the reconnaissances and conferences that had led and determined the marches and battles of that campaign; and as to what was really essential in these respects to the command of an army he had a practical military experience beyond any opportunities of General Johnston." Beauregard, a vain man, could be haughty when he considered his prerogatives impinged. Soon after First Manassas he became engaged in a series of disputes with the administration over supplies, military law, and army command. For a time the president tried to be conciliatory, but gradually he grew impatient. In January 1862, after another argument between Beauregard and Davis, an observer in the War Department noted: "Beauregard has been ordered to the West. I knew the doom was upon him." [42]

Following the death of Sidney Johnston at Shiloh, Beauregard became commander of the western forces, but in June 1862 he left his headquarters in northern Mississippi without the president's permission. He merely informed the government that his health was bad and that he was going to Alabama to recover. "I desire to be back . . . to retake the offensive as soon as our forces shall have been sufficiently reorganized," he explained. "I must have a short rest." Davis jumped at this opportunity to appoint Braxton Bragg to the permanent command of the western department. Beauregard would never again command a major army. The president no longer trusted him. Davis later told another general: "Beauregard was tried as Commander of the army of the West and left it without leave, when the troops were demoralized and the country he was sent to protect was threatened with conquest." [43]

The sixth highest ranking general was Braxton Bragg, the man who replaced Beauregard as commander of the western department. Forty-four years old when the war began, Bragg too was a professional soldier but he had left the Old Army in 1856 to become a Louisiana sugarcane planter. He had served for nineteen years in the Third Artillery after being graduated fifth in his class at West Point in 1837. He had received three brevet promotions during the Mexican War for gallant conduct. At Buena Vista, he became a national hero when his battery stopped the final Mexican charge "with a little more grape." [44]

Bragg, it is often charged, received promotion to full general only because he and President Davis had long been friends. Such was not the case. One reason why Bragg had resigned from the United States Army was because he disliked Davis, who was then secretary of war. In 1855 Bragg informed his friend William T. Sherman: "To judge from high sounding words in reports and bills before Congress, Mr. Jeff. Davis intends to have an Army after his own heart (not a very good one by the way). We are all to be placed at his mercy, and to be rearranged to suit his pleasure and convenience." Bragg considered Davis "a good deal of the pettifogger & special pleader." Years later Sherman recalled that "Bragg hated Davis bitterly" for sending him to the frontier, "as Bragg expressed it 'to chase Indians with six-pounders [cannons]." [45]

Davis certainly never knew that for years Bragg had disliked and distrusted him. When the Civil War started, Bragg feared that he would be ignored by the Confederate president. Nor was Bragg reassured when Davis gave him command of forces near Pensacola, Florida, in 1861. Only after receiving extensive reports from people he trusted did Bragg become convinced that the president was not his enemy. In the spring of 1862 Congressman James L. Pugh, formerly a soldier at Pensacola, wrote that he "was delighted to find" in the Confederate capital "the highest confidence in my old Genl. Bragg. It gives me pleasure to assure you that no General in the army has more of public confidence and admiration. Your praise is on the lips of every man. . . . President Davis said that 'you had shown a most self sacrificing devotion to the cause, and was about the only General who had accomplished all you undertook.' " And Bragg's brother, who was a member of Davis's cabinet, noted that the president "spoke [favorably] of Gen'l Bragg—said he had put down drinking and that his had been the only well disciplined and managed army in the field. That he set a proper example to his men. In speaking of other Generals, their qualities &c, he [Davis] ranked him [Bragg] with Sidney Johns[t]on." Bragg owed his promotion to full general not to long-time friendship with the president, but to the reputation Bragg had gained as an organizer and administrator. When Bragg moved north to reinforce Sidney Johnston before Shiloh, Davis wrote his old friend: "General Bragg brings you disciplined troops, and you will find in him the highest administrative capacity." [46]

It is easy enough, using hindsight, to blame Jefferson Davis for appointing at the war's outset too many generals who would later prove to be less than outstanding soldiers, but such a judgment is unfair—a misuse of history. Before censuring Davis for not picking the right men to lead the Confederate armies, historians should ask themselves what, given the circumstances, Davis could have done differently. He had to pick some political generals; he understandably picked some friends. What obvious leaders did he overlook? The six men he promoted to full general were all experienced and distinguished soldiers. They were reputed to be the elite of the Old Army. Another man, less well acquainted with military affairs, might have selected different generals. But Davis simply could not. His own military experience and knowledge forced him to appoint the men he did to high rank. He had fought beside some of them, and, as secretary of war and as chairman of the Senate's Military Affairs Committee, he had helped to advance their careers. They were already, before the Civil War, his men. If, as has been charged, Davis's judgment of military ability left something to be desired; if he relied too heavily upon his youthful impressions of men; if he regarded criticism of his appointees as criticism of himself and stubbornly defended proved incompetents, it was because he was imprisoned by his own character and background. And so was the Confederacy.

If the Confederacy's leaders failed, it was in their selection of Jefferson Davis to lead the "Lost Cause." Once he became president the pattern of leadership was established. The major appointments to high positions, especially to high military positions, were his. He picked, assigned, and replaced. When the Provisional Congress chose the Confederacy's president, it indirectly chose its generals.

NOTES

1. Thomas Cooper DeLeon, *Four Years in Rebel Capitals: An Inside View of Life in the Southern Confederacy from Birth to Death* (New York, 1962), p. 54; Hudson Strode, *Jefferson Davis: American Patriot, 1808–1861* (New York, 1955); Francis B. Heitman, *Historical Register and Dictionary of the United States Army* (Washington, 1903), 1:358; Jefferson Davis to C. J. Wright, February 12, 1876 (copy), Jefferson Davis Papers, Library of Congress, Washington.

2. E. Merton Coulter, *The Confederate States of America, 1861–1865* (Baton Rouge, 1950), p. 24; Varina H. Davis, *Jefferson Davis . . . A Memoir* (New York, 1890), 2:392.

3. John J. Pettis to Jefferson Davis, December 20, 1859, John J. Pettis Papers, Chicago Historical Society; Bell I. Wiley, *The Road to Appomattox* (Memphis, 1956), pp. 6–7; *Montgomery Daily Post,* February 18, 1861; John B. Jones, *A Rebel War Clerk's Diary,* ed. Earl Schenck Miers (New York, 1958), p. 34.

4. A. L. Hull, ed., "Correspondence of Thomas Reade Rootes Cobb, 1860–1862," Southern History Association, *Publications* 11 (1907):147–85; Mary Boykin Chesnut, *A Diary from Dixie,* ed. Ben Ames Williams (Boston, 1949), p. 5; Wilfred Buck Yearns, *The Confederate Congress* (Athens, Ga., 1960), p. 31.

5. Hudson Strode, ed., *Jefferson Davis: Private Letters, 1823–1889* (New York, 1966), p. 124; Horace Montgomery, *Howell Cobb's Confederate Career* (Tuscaloosa, Ala., 1959), pp. 48–49; George W. Bagby's Notebook, March 1862, George William Bagby Papers, Virginia Historical Society, Richmond; Edward Younger, ed., *Inside the Confederate Government: The Diary of Robert Garlick Hill Kean* (New York, 1957), p. 34.

6. Charles Winslow Elliott, *Winfield Scott: The Soldier and the Man* (New York, 1937), p. 712.

7. Frank Vandiver, ed., *The Civil War Diary of General Josiah Gorgas* (University, Ala., 1947), p. 58; C. C. Clay to William L. Yancey [1863?], William L. Yancey Papers, Alabama State Archives, Montgomery.

8. *De Bow's Review* 34 (July–August 1864):102; Bell I. Wiley, ed., *Letters of Warren Akin, Confederate Congressman* (Athens, Ga., 1959), p. 75.

9. The best analysis of Davis's personality is in Wiley, *The Road to Appomattox,* pp. 1–42.

10. Mrs. Jefferson Davis to Mrs. Franklin Pierce [c. April 4] 1858, Franklin Pierce Papers, Library of Congress; Jefferson Davis to Franklin Pierce, September 2, 1859, *ibid.;* William B. Hesseltine, ed., *Three against Lincoln: Murat Halstead Reports the Caucuses of 1860* (Baton Rouge, 1960), p. 121; William Howard Russell, *My Diary North and South* (Lon-

don, 1863), 1:250; Wiley, ed., *Letters of Warren Akin*, p. 20; Jones, *Rebel War Clerk's Diary*, p. 41; Arthur James Lyon Fremantle, *The Fremantle Diary*, ed. Walter Lord (Boston, 1954), pp. 167–68. See also Justus Scheibert, *Seven Months in the Rebel States during the North American War, 1863*, ed. Wm. Stanley Hoole (Tuscaloosa, Ala., 1958), p. 128, and U.S. War Department, *The War of the Rebellion: A Compilation of the Official Records of the Union and Confederate Armies* (Washington, 1880–1901), Series 1, 5:829 (hereafter cited as *OR;* unless otherwise indicated all references are to Series 1).

11. Hesseltine, ed., *Three against Lincoln*, p. 23; Fremantle, *Diary*, pp. 170, 174; Albert T. Bledsoe to Jefferson Davis, November 12, 1862, Jefferson Davis Papers, Duke University, Durham, N.C.; Jones, *Rebel War Clerk's Diary*, pp. 17, 121, 202, 242, 433, 434, 447; William Brierly Memoir, 1864, William Brierly Papers, Chicago Historical Society.

12. Chesnut, *Diary from Dixie*, p. 285; DeLeon, *Four Years in Rebel Capitals*, p. 136; Ezra J. Warner, *Generals in Gray: Lives of the Confederate Commanders* (Baton Rouge, 1959), p. 225; Heitman, *Historical Register*, 1:751, 326; William W. Mackall to his wife [October 1862], William W. Mackall Papers, Southern Historical Collection, University of North Carolina, Chapel Hill; Grady McWhiney, *Braxton Bragg and Confederate Defeat*, vol. 1, *Field Command* (New York, 1969), pp. 179–80; Braxton Bragg to William T. Sherman, June 3, 1855, William T. Sherman Papers, Library of Congress.

13. John P. Dyer, *The Gallant Hood* (Indianapolis, 1950), p. 238; T. Harry Williams, *P. G. T. Beauregard, Napoleon in Gray* (Baton Rouge, 1955), pp. 157–58; Robert M. Hughes, *General Johnston* (New York, 1893), pp. 21, 25, 32, 144; Heitman, *Historical Register*, 2:26; Joseph E. Johnston, *Narrative of Military Operations*, ed. Frank E. Vandiver (Bloomington, Ind., 1959), pp. 186, 173; *OR*, 23, pt. 2:745.

14. Clifford Dowdey, ed., *The Wartime Papers of R. E. Lee* (Boston, 1961), pp. 589–90; Douglas Southall Freeman, *R. E. Lee: A Biography* (New York, 1935), 2:502–4, 512, 4:522.

15. Frank E. Vandiver, *Mighty Stonewall* (New York, 1957), pp. 7, 9, 17, 46, 48–55 *passim;* Lenoir Chambers, *Stonewall Jackson* (New York, 1959), 1:63, 71, 153–57 *passim*, 2:75–76; Thomas J. Jackson to his sister, January 1, 1848, April 27, December 3, 1849, September 3, 1850 (photocopies), Thomas Jonathan Jackson Papers, Library of Congress.

16. DeLeon, *Four Years in Rebel Capitals*, p. 123; *OR*, Series 4, 3:1184. The secretaries and their tenure were Leroy P. Walker, February 21–September 16, 1861; Judah P. Benjamin, September 17, 1861–March 18, 1862; George W. Randolph, March 18–November 17, 1862; Gustavus W. Smith (assigned temporarily), November 17–21, 1862; James A. Seddon, November 21, 1862–February 6, 1865; and John C. Breckinridge, February 6–April 26, 1865.

17. Jefferson Davis, *The Rise and Fall of the Confederate Government* (New York, 1958), 1:306, 307; Yearns, *The Confederate Congress*, p. 108; Haskell Monroe, "Early Confederate Political Patronage," *Alabama Review* 20 (1967):45–61; Hudson Strode, *Jefferson Davis: Confederate President, 1861–1864* (New York, 1959), p. 138; Davis to W. M. Brooks, March 13, 1862, in Dunbar Rowland, ed., *Jefferson Davis, Constitutionalist: His Letters, Papers and Speeches* (Jackson, Miss., 1923), 5:218.

18. Warner, *Generals in Gray*, pp. 212–13; Heitman, *Historical Regis-*

ter, 1:691; Braxton Bragg to John Bragg, June 28, 1852, John Bragg Papers, Southern Historical Collection, University of North Carolina; Jefferson Davis to Humphrey Marshall, October 6, 1862, in Rowland, ed., *Davis,* 5:348.

19. Warner, *Generals in Gray,* pp. 34, 306–7, 336–37, 48–49, 28–29, 31, 55, 89–90, 320–21, 284–85, 341–42.

20. *OR,* Series 4, 1:474–75; Warner, *Generals in Gray,* pp. 349–50; William L. Yancey and Clement C. Clay to Jefferson Davis, April 21, 1862, Yancey Papers.

21. Warner, *Generals in Gray,* pp. 89–90, 350, 240, 44–45, 248, 341–42; *OR,* 10, pt. 2:370–72; Alvy L. King, *Louis T. Wigfall, Southern Fire-eater* (Baton Rouge, 1970); William Y. Thompson, *Robert Toombs of Georgia* (Baton Rouge, 1966); Louis T. Wigfall to C. C. Clay, August 13, 1863, Clement C. Clay Papers, Duke University; Younger, ed., *Inside the Confederate Government,* p. 102; Allan Nevins, *The War for the Union* (New York, 1959–1971), 3:397.

22. Braxton Bragg to Samuel Cooper, July 28, 1861 (copy), William P. Palmer Collection of Braxton Bragg Papers, Western Reserve Historical Society, Cleveland; Younger, ed., *Inside the Confederate Government,* p. 87; Rowland, ed., *Davis,* 6:44.

23. Civil War Centennial Commission, *Facts about the Civil War* (Washington, 1960), p. 7; Ellsworth Eliot, Jr., *West Point in the Confederacy* (New York, 1941), pp. xii–xxxii *passim.*

24. Twiggs, who was seventy-one years old and a veteran of both the War of 1812 and the Mexican War, had been in the regular army for nearly half a century. He died in 1862. Loring, after volunteer service against the Seminole Indians, had been commissioned directly into the regular army in 1846 as a captain of mounted rifles. When he resigned to join the Confederacy, he was—at age forty-six—the youngest line colonel in the army.

25. Warner, *Generals in Gray,* pp. 312, 192, 49, 203–4; Heitman, *Historical Register,* 1:976, 642, 299, 625, 670, 826. Only four officers of field grade who left the Old Army in 1861 failed to become Confederate brigadier generals or higher in the first year of the war. These exceptions— William W. Mackall, Robert H. Chilton, Richard B. Lee, and Thomas G. Rhett—had been staff officers in 1861 and they continued as staff officers in the Confederate service. Apparently they were victims of Davis's opposition to high rank for staff. While secretary of war in the 1850s, Davis had proposed the abolition of permanent staff assignments. See Rowland, ed., *Davis,* 2:299–406.

26. Warner, *Generals in Gray,* pp. xix–xxiii.

27. Yancey to Davis, May 6, 1863, Yancey Papers; Dr. J. H. Claiborne to his wife, March 29, 1864, Dr. J. H. Claiborne Papers, University of Virginia, Charlottesville.

28. Davis to Yancey, June 20, 1863, Yancey Papers; Warner, *Generals in Gray,* pp. 75–76, 216–17, 242–43; Heitman, *Historical Register,* 1:383, 703, 796.

29. Warner, *Generals in Gray,* p. 120.

30. *Ibid.,* pp. 299–300; Charles L. Dufour, *Nine Men in Gray* (New York, 1963), p. 3; Richard Taylor, *Destruction and Reconstruction* (London, 1879), p. 19. For valuable statistical information on some of Davis's early appointments I am indebted to Bruce Nims, one of my former graduate students.

31. *OR*, 20, pt. 2:449; Manigault to Braxton Bragg, November 30, 1862, Palmer Collection of Bragg Papers.

32. Edmund Kirby Smith and John Bell Hood were full generals in the Provisional Confederate Army only, and Hood's appointment was temporary and never confirmed.

33. Warner, *Generals in Gray*, pp. xxiv–xxv, 62–63; Heitman, *Historical Register*, 1:326. Actually Cooper was only adjutant general of the United States Army.

34. Younger, ed., *Inside the Confederate Government*, pp. 87–88.

35. Davis, *Rise and Fall*, 1:308.

36. Warner, *Generals in Gray*, pp. 62–63.

37. Charles P. Roland, *Albert Sidney Johnston: Soldier of Three Republics* (Austin, 1964), pp. 12, 15, 45–46, 135, 137.

38. Heitman, *Historical Register*, 1:577–78; Roland, *Johnston*, pp. 3–259; Davis, *Rise and Fall*, 1:309.

39. Freeman, *Lee*, 1:55, 327, 360, 369; Dowdey, ed., *Wartime Papers of Lee*, pp. 589–90, 700; Davis, *Rise and Fall*, 1:340, 309. General Joseph Hooker reportedly said that Lee was "a courtier" with an "insinuating manner," who was "never much respected in the [United States] army." Mrs. John Hay, ed., *Letters of John Hay and Extracts from Diary* (Washington, 1908), 1:99, 100.

40. Heitman, *Historical Register*, 1:578, 625.

41. *OR*, Series 4, 1:605–8; Gilbert E. Govan and James W. Livingood, *A Different Valor: The Story of General Joseph E. Johnston, C.S.A.* (Indianapolis, 1956), pp. 32, 66–71; Hughes, *General Johnston*, pp. 33–34; Mary Boykin Chesnut, *A Diary from Dixie*, ed. Isabella D. Martin and Myrta Lockett Avary (Gloucester, Mass., 1961), pp. 248–49.

42. Williams, *Beauregard*, pp. 1–114; Heitman, *Historical Register*, 1:204; G. T. Beauregard, *A Commentary on the Campaign and Battle of Manassas of July, 1861, together with a Summary of the Art of War* (New York, 1891), pp. 44, 15–16; Jones, *Rebel War Clerk's Diary*, p. 65.

43. *OR*, 27, pt. 2:599; Williams, *Beauregard*, pp. 139–65; Jefferson Davis to E. Kirby Smith, October 29, 1862, Edmund Kirby Smith Papers, Southern Historical Collection, University of North Carolina.

44. McWhiney, *Bragg*, pp. 1–101; Heitman, *Historical Register*, 1:240.

45. Bragg to Sherman, February 5, March 15, 1855, William T. Sherman Papers, Library of Congress; William T. Sherman, *Memoirs* (Bloomington, Ind., 1957), 1:162.

46. Pugh to Bragg, March 16, 1862, Palmer Collection of Bragg Papers; Thomas Bragg Diary, January 8, 1862, Southern Historical Collection, University of North Carolina; *OR*, 7:912, 258; McWhiney, *Bragg*, pp. 154, 202–3.

CHAPTER VII

Who Whipped Whom?

Sometime after the Civil War an unreconstructed Rebel, Robert
Toombs, was arguing with a Federal army officer over the relative fighting qualities of Union and Confederate soldiers.

"Well, we whipped you," the exasperated officer finally told Toombs.

"No," Toombs retorted, "we just wore ourselves out whipping you." [1]

Although as a general Toombs left a great deal to be desired, he was
a perceptive military analyst. His statement that the Confederacy beat
itself may have been intended as a joke, but as an appraisal of how the
South lost the Civil War it was surprisingly accurate.

More than six hundred thousand Americans died in the Civil War, a
greater American mortality than in the two World Wars and the Korean
War combined. The charge of the British Light Brigade at Balaclava
(almost 40 percent of its men were shot in the "Valley of Death") has
symbolized needless sacrifice, but heavier losses were common during
the Civil War. Some sixty Union regiments lost more than half their
men in a single engagement, and at least 120 Union regiments sustained losses equal to the Light Brigade's. In eleven different campaigns
the Union suffered ten thousand casualties; over a thousand men were
killed or wounded in fifty-six different actions. At Gettysburg one of
every five Federal soldiers present was hit, and a Minnesota regiment
was decimated, losing 82 percent of its men.

Proportionally, Confederate losses were even greater. More than
eighty thousand Confederate soldiers fell in only five battles. At Gettysburg three of every ten Southerners present were hit; one North Carolina regiment lost 85 percent of its strength, and every man in one company was killed or wounded. In the first twenty-seven months of combat

the South lost 175,000 men.[2] This number exceeded the entire Confederate military service in July 1861 and the strength of any army Robert E. Lee ever commanded.

Losses were so staggering because officers on both sides fought by the books, and the books were wrong. All the official and unofficial tactical manuals insisted that bayonets would decide the outcome of battles and that troops should assault either in long lines or in massed columns.[3] Such assumptions were tragically in error, for by 1861 bayonets were obsolete weapons and played no significant role in the outcome of the Civil War. During the Virginia campaign of 1864, when there was more close combat than usual, 33,292 Federal soldiers were treated for bullet wounds but only 37 for bayonet wounds.[4]

Before the Civil War, bayonet attacks had been justifiable because the basic infantry firearm, the smoothbore musket, was highly inaccurate. A soldier might fire a smoothbore musket at a man all day from a distance of a few hundred yards and never hit him.[5] Nevertheless, field commanders of the early 1800s favored smoothbores over rifles for general infantry use. Rifles required too much time and effort to load because each bullet had to be slightly larger than the bore; otherwise, when the weapon was fired, the bullet would fail to spin through the barrel along the rifled grooves. These rifled grooves gave the rifle both its name and its superiority in range and accuracy over the smoothbore. Usually only special units such as the British sharpshooters at Waterloo were equipped with rifles, and then the men were also issued ramrods and mallets with which to hammer in their shots. Loading took two minutes.[6]

Tactics during the first half of the nineteenth century were designed to compensate for the smoothbore's inaccuracy and short range. Armies learned to perform series of stylized maneuvers and sometimes prepared for battle within a few hundred yards of each other. Soldiers fought in tight formations and fired in volleys. The usual battle alignment was two or three lines of infantry, armed with smoothbores and long bayonets, supported in the rear by artillery and on the flanks by cavalry. After the infantrymen had fired a volley, they advanced, elbow to elbow, at a trot. The defenders, who had time to fire only one or two volleys before the attackers reached their line, either repulsed the assault or retreated to reform and counterattack. Success in battle usually depended upon strict discipline and precise movements. If the infantrymen on either side broke, enemy cavalry dashed in from the flanks to slash at the retreaters with sabers. Most infantry attacks were checked

by artillery firing scattershot. Although an army might advance and re-
treat several times during a battle, it rarely suffered heavy losses.

Americans had used these conventional tactics successfully in the
Mexican War. At Palo Alto in 1846 Zachary Taylor formed his three-
thousand-man army in one long line. "The Mexicans immediately
opened fire upon us, first with artillery and then with infantry," wrote
an American officer. "At first their shots did not reach us, and the advance . . . continued. As we got nearer, the cannon balls commenced
going through the ranks. They hurt no one, however, . . . because they
would strike the ground long before they reached our line, and ricochet-
ted through the tall grass so slowly that the men would see them and
open ranks and let them pass. When we got to a point where the artillery could be used with effect, a halt was called, and the battle opened
on both sides." The Americans attacked; the Mexicans retreated, and by
nightfall Taylor's men occupied the Mexican position. American losses
were only nine killed and forty-seven wounded.[7]

Bayonet assaults in the 1860s were far more costly than ever before
because the smoothbore musket had been replaced by a better weapon.
The technological innovation that finished the smoothbore as the standard infantry arm was the development in the 1850s of the Minié
"ball." Neither Captain Minié's invention nor a ball, the projectile actually was an elongated bullet with a hollow base; it was small enough
to fit easily into the rifle's bore but would expand automatically when
fired and fit snugly into the rifled grooves. The Minié bullet made the
rifled muzzleloader a practical military weapon.

Both sides used a variety of small arms during the Civil War, but the
basic infantry weapon was the single-shot, rifled muzzleloader, either
the Springfield caliber .58, or the British Enfield caliber .577. The
Springfield rifle was fifty-six inches long and weighed nearly ten pounds
when fitted with its eighteen-inch triangular bayonet. All parts were in-
terchangeable. Between 1861 and 1865 over 1,600,000 of these rifles
were produced in the United States at a cost of $14.93 each. The En-
fields, which were more popular in the South, varied considerably in
length and bayonet type, but they all fired the same ammunition. Moreover, they were the equal of any Union rifle—so good, in fact, that
after the fall of Vicksburg General U. S. Grant rearmed some of his
Union regiments with captured Enfields.[8]

Compared with pre–Civil War shoulder weapons, the rifled muzzleloader was a firearm of deadly accuracy. It could be fired two or three
times a minute; it could stop an attack at up to four hundred yards; and

it could kill at a distance of one thousand yards. In October 1861 a Union soldier wrote his parents: "We went out the other day to try [our rifles]. We fired [from a distance of] 600 yards and we put 360 balls into a mark the size of old Jeff [Davis]." In contrast, some Illinois soldiers armed with smoothbore muskets fired 160 shots at a flour barrel 180 yards away. It was hit only four times.[9]

The rifle became the great killer of the Civil War. It inflicted 80 percent of all wounds and revolutionized tactics. Because of the rifle's range and accuracy, Civil War infantry assaults were always costly. For the first time in over a century defenders had the advantage in warfare. "One rifle in the trench was worth five in front of it," wrote General J. D. Cox. Perhaps Cox exaggerated a bit, but a few entrenched men armed with rifles *could* hold a position against great odds. The rifle and the spade had made defense at least three times as strong as offense.[10]

But no one knew this at the time. Shortly before the Civil War the army had decided to modify infantry tactics, because officers believed they could offset the rifle's range and accuracy simply by teaching soldiers to move more quickly in battle. "They are introducing the light infantry tactics this spring, a new thing," wrote Cadet Henry A. du Pont from West Point on March 28, 1857. "There are a great many very rapid movements in it, and many of them are performed in double quick time, that is running. Within the last week [Colonel William J.] Hardee [commandant of cadets and author of the new tactics book] has had the whole battalion going at double quick with the band. . . . It will take time for everyone to learn to keep step. I expect that they will almost run us to death when the board of visitors come." Two months later du Pont admitted that the new tactics were "no doubt better in some respects, that is to say that troops drilled to them would be more efficient, but they do not look so well, for it is impossible to attain . . . the same precision and accuracy with all this running and quick movements, as was possible under the old system, and besides it is much harder work." [11]

If the new tactics could have stressed dispersal as well as speed then attackers might have had a chance to overcome the advantage rifles had given defenders, but dispersal of forces was impracticable in the 1860s. In some ways the Civil War was a modern struggle: in minutes generals communicated with each other by telegraph over thousands of miles; trains quickly carried large armies great distances and piled mountains of supplies at railheads. But, in other ways, the war was strikingly antiquated: men walked or rode horses into battle, and their supplies followed in wagons. No telephone lines connected combat units with each other or with field headquarters; all messages went by courier on horseback. This traditional system of battlefield communication bound Civil War generals to close order formations. They had no choice; the dispersal of forces to avoid the rifle's firepower and accuracy would have made communication even more difficult and further weakened a commander's control of his men in battle. Even though they usually kept their troops in tight formations, Civil War commanders never completely solved the problems of battlefield communication and control. In the Wilderness in 1864 both Lee and Grant lost effective control of their armies after the action began.[12]

Except for the quicker movements required of troops, the new tactics were much like the old ones. Both emphasized close-order formations, and taught men to rely on the shock effect of bayonet assaults. A Prussian officer who visited the South in 1863 recalled that "there was diligent drilling in the camps according to an old French drill manual that had been revised by Hardee, and I observed on the drill field only linear formations, wheeling out into open columns, wheeling in and marching up into line, marching in line, open column marching, marching by sections, and marching in file. . . . The tactical unit in battle seemed to be the brigade. The drilling, according to my observation, seemed to be somewhat awkward. The cavalry drilled in a manner similar to ours, and the main emphasis was on a good jog, with loud yelling and shouting. The infantry also used this sound, the famous rebel yell, in bayonet attacks." [13]

The Confederate yell was intended to help control fear. As one soldier explained: "I always said if I ever went into a charge, I wouldn't holler! But the very first time I fired off my gun I hollered as loud as I could, and I hollered every breath till we stopped." Jubal Early once told some troops who hesitated to charge because they were out of ammunition: "Damn it, holler them across." [14]

Union soldiers studied the same manuals and practiced the same drills as the Confederates. "Every night I recite with the other 1st Sergts and 2nd Lieutenants," wrote a Union sergeant in 1862. "We shall finish Hardee's Tactics and then study the 'Army Regulations.' Theory as well as practice are necessary to make the perfect soldier." In 1863 a Union corporal explained that the noncommissioned officers of his company "have lessons in tactics every night at the Captains quarters to fit them to drill the privates in squads according to the book." Union General Marsena R. Patrick, a graduate of West Point, wrote on March 30, 1862, that "Although this is the Sabbath, I have been obliged to look over Tactics, Regulations etc. etc." The next day he described how he drilled his troops for combat: "Formed [them] in Mass—then in Column—then deployed by Battalion—in 4 lines, . . . and then handled them in masses almost exclusively. . . ." On April 1 he drilled his men "in Mass Movements some 2 or 3 hours," and on July 18 he wrote: "The Drills, for some time back, have been very interesting, as the men are beginning to see the value of them. . . ." [15]

After the war Union General William B. Hazen admitted that most Civil War battles were merely the formation of troops into lines to attack or to repel attacks. Almost any battle can serve as an example. "I saw our infantry make a charge [at Murfreesboro]," wrote a Confederate; "they got [with]in fifty yards of the yanks [before the Federals] fired a shot, when they poured the heaviest volley into them that I ever saw or heard." A Louisiana soldier wrote of the fight at Perryville: "The men stood right straight up on the open field, loaded and fired, charged and fell back as deliberately as if on drill."[16] At Shiloh the Confederates attacked by corps in four lines across a three-mile front. Such an arrangement of forces could result only in disorder and confusion, and within a few minutes after their first contact with the enemy the Southerners became hopelessly tangled, with corps, divisions, and brigades pell-mell in one battle line.[17] At Winchester in 1862 Richard Taylor's brigade attacked in long lines with the men elbow to elbow. As they advanced many fell and others wavered. "What the hell are you dodging for?" screamed Taylor. "If there is any more of it, you will be halted under fire for an hour." With Taylor leading the way, the brigade marched to within fifty yards of the enemy "in perfect order, not firing a shot." Taylor proudly reported that his men closed "the many gaps made by the [enemy's] fierce fire," and preserved "an alignment that would have been creditable on parade."[18] Two weeks later Taylor used a similar attack formation at Port Republic. These two battles cost him five hundred casualties and taught him nothing.

Many generals besides Taylor favored traditional weapons and tactics. Stonewall Jackson, often praised as a military innovator, was partial to bayonet assaults. General Alexander R. Lawton claimed Jackson "did not value human life. . . . He could order men to their death as a matter of course. Napoleon's French conscription could not have kept him supplied with men, he used up his command so rapidly." In little less than six months in 1862 Jackson's tactics cost the South over twenty thousand casualties—the equivalent of one entire army corps

—or almost twice the number of men under Jackson's command when the campaign began.[19] Jackson was so committed to conventional offensive tactics that he once actually requested that some of his troops be equipped with pikes instead of muskets. Pikes, he explained, should be "6 or more inches longer than the musket with the bayonet on, so that when we teach our troops to rely upon the bayonet they may feel that they have the superiority of arm resulting from its length." Apparently Lee saw nothing wrong with such a request; he approved it and ordered Josiah Gorgas, chief of ordnance, to send pikes to Jackson. Gorgas sent muskets instead.[20]

One Confederate general even considered the bayonet too modern and "inferior to the *knife*," because Southerners "would require long drilling to become expert with the [bayonet] . . . , but they instinctively know how to wield the bowieknife." General Henry Wise, a former governor of Virginia, scoffed at both new weapons and new tactics. He insisted "it was not the improved *arm,* but the improved *man,* which would win the day. Let brave men advance with flint locks and old-fashioned bayonets, . . . reckless of the slain, and he would answer for it with his life, that the Yankees would break and run." [21]

Wise's views were extreme, but even the highest ranking officers failed to recognize the limitations of traditional arms, formations, and services. Winfield Scott predicted at the outset that the war would be won by artillery. He was wrong, of course; only about 10 percent of all Civil War casualties were caused by artillery fire.[22] In February 1862, Joseph E. Johnston, commander of Confederate forces in Virginia, wrote Adjutant General Samuel Cooper that "we should have a much larger cavalry force. The greatest . . . difficulty, in increasing it, is said to be the want of proper arms. This can be easily removed by equipping a large body of lancers." Johnston claimed lances "would be formidable . . . in the hands of new troops, especially against the enemy's . . . artillery." [23] Cooper wisely ignored Johnston's suggestion; cavalry armed with sabers or lances were no match for artillery or infantry in the 1860s.

No one guessed just how much the rifled musket had diminished the importance of cavalry and artillery. At first cavalry officers trained their troopers to charge infantry and artillery. A Union private recalled a drill in December 1861 where infantry regiments fired blank shots at each other and "a squadron of cavalry dashed around . . . and charged down on them with the wildest yells." Another Union infantryman wrote in 1862: "We had our first Brigade drill day before yester-

day. . . . The Cavalry charged down on us and for the first time I saw
something that looked like fighting. . . . It was a beautiful sight, and our
officers expressed themselves well satisfied with the drill." One soldier
described how his regiment formed a hollow square to repel cavalry
charges: "When they charge us with wild yells (some of them get awfully
excited, so do the horses), it takes some nerve to stand against them, although it is all a sham. But we have found out one thing—horses cannot
be driven onto fixed bayonets and I dont believe we shall be as afraid of
the real charge if we ever have to meet one in the future. We are learning
a good deal, so are the Cavalry." [24]

But cavalry generals on both sides learned their lessons slowly. "Not
until the closing days of the war did we wake up to what our experience
. . . ought to have taught us," confessed James H. Wilson. When
Philip H. Sheridan took command of the Army of the Potomac's cavalry in 1864 he proposed to concentrate it to fight the enemy's cavalry,
but George Meade objected. Sheridan recalled that "my proposition
seemed to stagger General Meade," who "would hardly listen . . . , for
he was filled with the prejudices that, from the beginning of the war,
had pervaded the army regarding the . . . cavalry. . . ." Until his
death J. E. B. Stuart held the archaic and romantic view that the "duty
of the cavalry after battle is joined is to cover the flanks to prevent the
enemy from turning them. If victorious, it improves the victory by rapid
pursuit. If defeated, it covers the rear and makes vigorous charges to
delay the advance of the enemy—or in the supreme moment in the crisis
of battle . . . the cavalry comes down like an avalanche upon the . . .
troops already engaged, with splendid effect."[25]

A number of bloody failures often occured before even the more astute cavalry commander learned he could no longer use pre–Civil War
tactics successfully. The charge of the Fifth U.S. Cavalry at Gaines's
Mill in June 1862 was an excellent example of the frequent misuse of
horsemen. This regiment lost 60 percent of its troopers in a saber attack
on Confederate infantry and artillery. One of the attackers, Private
W. H. Hitchcock, recalled the action: "We dashed forward with a wild
cheer, in solid column of squadron front; but our formation was almost
instantly broken. . . . I closed in to re-form the line, but could find no
one at my left, so completely had our line been shattered by the mus-
ketry fire in front. . . ." At this point Hitchcock's horse veered off to
the rear. "I dropped my saber," Hitchcock admitted, "and so fiercely
tugged at my horse's bit as to cause the blood to flow from her mouth,
yet could not check her." Finally he gained control of his mount,

"turned about and started back. . . . The firing of artillery and infantry . . . was terrific," he remembered. "None but the dead and wounded were around me. It hardly seemed that I could drive Lee's . . . veterans alone, so I rode . . . off the field." Nearly 250 men had galloped into action; only about 100 returned.[26]

After such tragic experiences many horsemen and their commanders became so gun-shy that General John A. Logan allegedly offered a reward for a dead cavalryman, Federal or Confederate. And one of Sherman's soldiers wrote in 1863: "We have considerable cavalry with us, but they are the laughing stock of the army and the boys poke all kinds of fun at them. I really have as yet to see or hear of their doing anything of much credit to them." [27] Despite such derision, cavalrymen performed many creditable services: they were excellent couriers, scouts, and raiders; when necessary, they dismounted and fought as infantry. But Civil War horsemen were no longer effective as a shock force in assaults. They were too vulnerable to accurate rifle fire.

Unlike the modifications in cavalry tactics, changes in Civil War artillery tactics were less marked. Artillery remained primarily a defensive weapon throughout the war, for it lacked the range, precision, or elevation needed to cover assault troops in that critical area just in front of the enemy's line. Civil War guns were usually incapable of providing what is now called effective preparation, or softening up the enemy, for an assault.

Nevertheless, some generals attempted to use artillery as an offensive weapon, and almost invariably they failed. Before Pickett's charge at Gettysburg, 150 Confederate guns pounded the Union line without doing much damage. The Federals merely dug in and waited for the bombardment to end; they suffered very few casualties from artillery fire. In his assault on the Federal left at Murfreesboro, John C. Breckinridge placed his batteries between two lines of infantry and ordered them to join the attack. He ignored a young artillery officer's warning that such an arrangement of guns would cause confusion and misdirection of fire. As the Confederate gunners advanced, sandwiched between the infantry lines and unable to find clear fields of fire, they hit some of the southern infantrymen. Federal shells disabled several Confederate guns and three were captured when the attack failed.[28]

Though relatively ineffective as an offensive weapon, artillery was a most important adjunct to the infantry on defense. At Malvern Hill the Federals massed over two hundred guns to stop what could have been a breakthrough; at Gettysburg twenty-five cannon along Plum Run held the Union line without infantry support; at Atlanta only twenty-nine guns checked twelve thousand Confederates; and at Murfreesboro fifty-eight pieces of artillery helped disrupt Breckinridge's assault. Used on defense, artillery was deadliest in precisely those areas offensive artillery could not reach. When infantry assault columns got within four hundred yards, the defenders loaded their guns with scattershot that decimated closely bunched infantry.[29]

Attacks on strongly posted batteries rarely succeeded and nearly always penalized the attackers heavily. A Confederate diarist wrote of his brigade's attempt to take some Federal guns at Spotsylvania in 1864: "After being subjected to a heavy artillery fire for some time we were ordered . . . to charge the enemy. We charged them. . . . Our loss [was] heavy. We fell back. . . ." Perhaps General D. H. Hill left the best description of the Confederate attack on the Union line at Malvern Hill. "I never saw anything more grandly heroic," he wrote. "As each brigade emerged from the woods, from fifty to one hundred guns opened upon it, tearing great gaps in its ranks. . . . Most of them had an open field half a mile wide to cross, under the fire of field-artillery . . . and . . . heavy ordnance. . . . It was not war—it was murder." [30]

When the struggle began, neither the North nor the South was prepared for war, much less for murder. There were no strategic plans ready; indeed, it was uncertain which side would be the invader. President Lincoln and Secretary of War Simon Cameron, who had no military experience, gladly relegated the awesome responsibility of strategic planning to Winfield Scott, hero of two previous wars. "General Scott seems to have *carte-blanche,*" noted an observer in May 1861. "He is, in fact, the Government. . . ." [31]

Yet Scott failed to inspire confidence. He was seventy-five years old and a semi-invalid. State Senator Alexander K. McClure and Governor Andrew Curtin of Pennsylvania, who saw Scott the morning after Fort Sumter fell, concluded "that the old chieftain had outlived his . . . usefulness, and that he was utterly unequal to the appalling task he had accepted." After the Pennsylvanians had left Scott's office Curtin threw up his hands and exclaimed: "My God, the country is at the mercy of a dotard." A few days later, when the governor of Iowa called, Scott dodged any discussion of strategy, reminisced instead about his service in the War of 1812, and then fell asleep in his chair. But Scott may have put on a senile act to disarm nosey politicians, for President Lincoln only half jokingly told a visitor: "Scott will not let us outsiders know anything of his plans." [32]

Scott revealed his scheme in May. He told the president the best way to defeat the Confederacy was to encircle it, and then divide it by means of a naval blockade and a drive down the Mississippi River. Such action, Scott believed, would make it possible "to envelop the insurgent States and bring them to terms with less bloodshed than by any other plan." Cut off from the outside world, the Confederacy would slowly strangle and die as if caught in the grip of a giant anaconda.[33]

The "Anaconda" plan proved that Scott could still view military problems realistically, but that he misunderstood the nation's temper. He knew the Union was unprepared for an immediate offensive, and that no major action should be taken until a large army of regulars and three-year volunteers had been assembled and trained. His mistake was in assuming that the people would wait. William T. Sherman recalled: "Congress and the people would not permit the slow and methodical preparation desired by General Scott." Northerners demanded action; Scott's policy was too conservative, too cautious. Sherman observed in late June how Scott "seemed vexed with the clamors of the press for immediate action, and the continued interference in [military] details by the President, Secretary of War, and Congress." Secretary of the Navy Gideon Welles admitted that he disapproved of Scott's plan as "purely defensive." Welles wrote in his diary that "instead of halting on the borders, building intrenchments . . . we should penetrate their territory." [34] The cry "On to Richmond!" soon became too insistent for Lincoln to ignore. He realized that, whatever its military merits, Scott's plan was politically inexpedient. So on June 29, 1861, the President and his cabinet overruled the old general's objections to an immediate offensive. Thence the Union would follow an offensive strategy aimed at the occupation and conquest of the South.[35]

At first the Confederacy planned to fight a defensive war. President Jefferson Davis explained that "the Confederate Government is waging this war solely for self-defence, . . . it has no design of conquest or any other purpose than to secure peace and the abandonment by the United States of its pretensions to govern a people who have never been their subjects and who prefer self-government to a Union with them." [36]

The South's decision to fight a defensive war was sound; in fact, it was the only tenable military policy the government could have followed. The North had greater resources and a three-to-two military manpower advantage over the South. An offensive strategy would almost certainly exhaust the Confederacy more quickly than the Union because an invasion takes more men and resources than a defense. As a rule, defense is the most economical form of warfare. Civil War defenders enjoyed even greater advantages than usual because tactics lagged behind military technology. The rifled muzzleloader gave the defense at least three times the strength of the offense; theoretically the Confederates could have stayed in entrenchments and killed every man in the Union army before the South exhausted its own human resources.[37]

But the Confederacy flung away its great advantage because southern sentiment overwhelmingly favored an invasion of the North. Confederate Secretary of State Robert Toombs announced in May 1861 that he was for "taking the initiative, and carrying the war into the enemy's country." He opposed any delay. "We must invade or be invaded," he said. In June 1861 the famous Confederate war clerk John Jones wrote in his diary: "Our policy is to be defensive, and it will be severely criticized, for a vast majority of our people are for 'carrying the war into Africa' without a moment's delay. The sequel will show which is right, the government or the people. At all events, the government will rule."

Jones was wrong; the government did not rule. Just after First Manassas in July 1861, Davis indicated in a public speech that he was ready to abandon his defensive strategy. "Never heard I more hearty cheering," recorded Jones. "Every one believed our banners would wave in the streets of Washington in a few days; . . . that peace would be consummated on the banks of the Susquehanna or the Schuylkill. The President had pledged himself . . . to carry the war into the enemy's country. . . . Now . . . the people were well pleased with their President." Although Davis called his new policy defensive-offensive, it was in fact an offensive strategy, for the president held a view best described by one of today's clichés: the best defense is a good offense. In September 1862, Davis wrote the commanders of the South's two largest armies that "we [must] . . . protect our own country by transferring the seat of war to that of [the] . . . enemy . . . the sacred right of self defence demands that if such a war is to continue its consequences shall fall on those who persist in their refusal to make peace." Davis concluded his instructions with an order that Confederate armies "occupy the territory of their enemies and . . . make it the theatre of hostilities." [38]

The substitution of an offensive for a defensive strategy early in the war probably doomed the Confederacy. Southern leaders could have enjoyed all the moral and military advantages of defenders. Instead they chose to be aggressors. Confederate forces attacked in eight of the first twelve big battles of the war, and in these eight assaults 97,000 Confeder-

ates fell—20,000 more men than the Federals lost in these same battles.[39] President Davis's cult of the military offense bled the South's armies to death in the first three years of combat. After 1863 the
Confederates attacked less often. Attrition forced them to defend; they
had spent too much of their limited manpower in unsuccessful offensives. Even so, Confederate generals attacked in three of the last ten
major campaigns of the war.[40]

A close examination of two battles indicates in some detail how so
many men were lost. Both Stone's River and Chickamauga are examples of sustained Confederate attacks, and an analysis of regimental
losses in each battle reveals a high degree of correlation between assaults and casualties. Because the Federals were on the defense in both
battles they suffered relatively fewer casualties except in those units
that were outflanked or surrounded. It is significant that half of the most
battered Union regiments incurred their highest casualties when they attacked or counterattacked.[41] At Stone's River the Fifteenth Indiana lost
130 of its 440 men in a single bayonet charge, and the Thirty-fourth Illinois and the Thirty-ninth Indiana each sustained 50 percent casualties
in a counterattack. In still another attempt to check the Confederate advance a brigade of regulars charged into a dense cedar grove and lost
500 men in about twenty minutes. The Sixteenth and Eighteenth U.S.
Infantry regiments, which formed the center of this assault group, lost
456 men from a combined total of 910.[42] At Chickamauga the Eighty-
seventh Indiana suffered over 50 percent casualties in one charge across
an open field, and three Illinois regiments—the Twenty-fifth, Thirty-
fifth, and Thirty-eighth—together with the Twenty-sixth Ohio, tried to
dislodge part of Bushrod Johnson's Confederate division from the crest
of a hill. The attack failed, and cost the Federal regiments 791 of their
1,296 men.[43]

Confederate losses were even more exceptional. Of the eighty-eight
Confederate regiments present at Stone's River, twenty-three suffered
over 40 percent casualties. Moreover, 40 percent of the infantry regimental commanders were killed or wounded, and in several regiments
every field officer was lost. Eight of the twenty Confederate brigades
that fought at Stone's River sustained more than 35 percent casualties,
and 25 percent of the infantry brigade commanders were killed or
wounded.[44]

Reckless assaults accounted for most Confederate casualties. At
Stone's River the First Louisiana charged across an open field. "Our
loss was very severe at this place," wrote the commander. The regiment

lost 7 of its 21 officers and nearly 100 of its 231 men.[45] Attacks made by other Confederate units were just as costly. Colonel J. J. Scales, commander of the Thirtieth Mississippi, was ordered to charge and capture several Federal batteries. Five hundred yards of open ground "lay between us and those . . . batteries," wrote Scales. "As we entered [this field] a large body of [Union] infantry in addition to the Batteries on my flanks and front rained their leaden hail upon us. Men fell around on every side like autumn leaves and every foot of soil over which we passed seemed dyed with the life blood of some one or more of [my] gallant [men]. . . . Still no one faltered, but the whole line advanced boldly and swiftly to within seventy-five yds. of the battery when the storm of death increased to such fury that the regt. as if by instinct fell to the ground." This single charge cost the Thirtieth Mississippi half of its 400 men.[46] A young soldier in the Twenty-fourth Alabama recalled how his regiment made three desperate charges at Stone's River and that each time 30 or 40 of his comrades fell.[47] The commander of the Twenty-sixth Alabama reported the Federal fire so heavy that 38 of his men defected during the first thrust.[48]

It takes courage to charge at any time, but it is almost unbelievable what some units endured. General James R. Chalmers's brigade of Mississippians hit the strongest part of the Union line at Stone's River. This in itself was in no way remarkable, but half the men in the Forty-fourth Mississippi Regiment went into battle armed only with sticks and most of the Ninth Mississippi's rifles were still too wet from the previous night's rain to fire. Nevertheless the men charged.[49]

As the Mississippians faltered, General Daniel S. Donelson's brigade of Tennesseeans came up. No unit on either side fought any harder than this brigade; it dashed itself to bits against the Union center in the Round Forest. One of Donelson's regiments lost half its officers and 68 percent of its men; another lost 42 percent of its officers and over half its men. The Eighth and Sixteenth Tennessee regiments spent several hours and 513 of their combined total of 821 men in brave but unsuccessful efforts to break the Federal line.[50]

Sometime in the early afternoon two fresh Confederate brigades tried where Chalmers's and Donelson's men had failed. Generals John K. Jackson and Daniel W. Adams led their men across a field thick with bodies. Both of Jackson's two furious assaults aborted. In an hour of combat he lost more than a third of his men, including all his regimental commanders. One of his regiments, the Eighth Mississippi, lost 133 of its 282 men. Adams had no more success than Jackson, though his men made what one Federal called "the most daring, courageous, and best-executed attack . . . on our line." Adams was wounded and his brigade, caught in a cross fire, retreated. One of his units, the Thirteenth and Twentieth Consolidated Louisiana Infantry, entering the fight with 620 men, lost 187 on the afternoon of December 31, and another 129 in an attack two days later.[51]

Confederate losses at Chickamauga were even more severe than at Stone's River. At least twenty-five of the thirty-three Confederate brigades present lost more than a third of their men, and incomplete returns indicate that at least forty-two infantry regiments suffered over 40 percent casualties. Nearly half of all regimental commanders and 25 percent of all brigade commanders were killed or wounded.[52]

Just as at Stone's River the heaviest losses at Chickamauga occurred when units assaulted strong Union positions. General Lucius E. Polk's brigade of about 1,400 men attacked Kelly's field salient twice on September 20. The first attack, checked by heavy guns and musket fire, cost the Confederates 350 casualties in about ninety minutes. In the second attack the brigade lost 200 men. In an assault against the Federal position on Horseshoe Ridge the Twenty-second Alabama lost 55 percent of its men, and two battalions of Hilliard's Legion lost nearly 60 percent of their effectives in an attack on Snodgrass Hill, where the Federals had thrown up breastworks.[53]

Bloody battles like Stone's River and Chickamauga took the lives of the bravest southern officers and men. Relatively few combat officers went through the conflict without a single wound, and most of those who did could claim, as did General Reuben L. Walker—who participated in no less than sixty-three battles—that "it was not my fault." Only three of the eight men who commanded the famous Stonewall Brigade survived the war. What happened to the commanders of one regiment is told in a bare sketch penned by semiliterate Bartlett Yancey Malone, who "was attached to the 6th N. C. Regiment . . . which was commanded by Colonel Fisher who got kild in the first Manassas Battel. . . . And then was commanded by Colonel W. D. Pender untell [his promotion; he was subsequently killed in battle]. . . . And then Captain I. E. Av[e]ry . . . was promoted to Colonel and . . . in command untell . . . the day the fite was at Gettysburg whar he was kild. And then Lieut. Colonel Webb taken command." [54]

Casualty lists prove that generals often led their men into action. Of all Confederate generals 55 percent (235 of 425) were killed or wounded in battle.[55] Thirty-one generals were hurt twice, eighteen were wounded

three times, and a dozen were hit four or more times. Clement A.
Evans, William ("Extra Billy") Smith, and William H. Young were
wounded five times. Young was hit in the shoulder and had two horses
shot from under him at Murfreesboro; he was hit in the leg at Jackson,
in the chest at Chickamauga, in the neck and jaw at Kennesaw Mountain, and again in the leg at Allatoona, where another horse was shot
from under him and he was captured. John R. Cooke, William R.
Terry, and Thomas F. Toon were wounded seven times, but the record
seems to have been set by William Ruffin Cox, who joined the Second
North Carolina Infantry as major in 1861 and fought through the war
with the Army of Northern Virginia. He was wounded eleven times.

Twenty-one of the seventy-seven Confederate generals who were
killed or mortally wounded in battle had been shot at least once before
they received their fatal injuries. Some of them had been hit two or
more times. William D. Pender survived three wounds before a shattered leg killed him at Gettysburg. Stephen D. Ramseur recovered from
wounds received at Malvern Hill, Chancellorsville, and Spotsylvania,
only to die at Cedar Creek.

More generals lost their lives leading attacks than in any other way;
70 percent of the Confederate generals killed or mortally wounded in action fell in offensives.[56] In a single charge against Federal fortifications
at Franklin in 1864, six Confederate generals were killed or mortally
wounded—John Adams, John C. Carter, Patrick R. Cleburne, States
Rights Gist, Hiram B. Granbury, and Otho F. Strahl.

Precisely why the Confederates attacked so often is unclear. Professors David Donald and T. Harry Williams think Jomini's theories of
war contributed to Confederate defeat.[57] At first both Union and Confederate generals followed the strategic and tactical concepts, which
they had learned at West Point, of this famous European military
writer. Southerners continued to fight as Jomini suggested, argues Donald, because they were unlucky enough to win most of the first battles
and saw no reason to change their outdated methods of warfare until it
was too late. Northerners began to abandon Jomini's concepts and to in-
novate after they were defeated in the early campaigns.

Perhaps Southerners attacked more frequently at first because of what
Thomas Livermore called "the greater impetuosity of the Southern temperament." Union General Winfield Scott, himself a Virginian, understood this temperament. He predicted that Southerners were too
undisciplined to fight a defensive war. They "will not take care of things,
or husband [their] . . . resources," said Scott. "If it could all be done

by one wild desperate dash [then southerners] . . . would do it, but [they cannot] . . . stand the long . . . months between the acts, the waiting." Livermore pointed out that "Southern leaders were, at least up to 1864, bolder in taking risks than their opponents, but also that they pushed their forces under fire very nearly to the limit of endurance." [58]

Whatever the reason, Confederate leaders ignored the casualty lists and continually mutilated their armies. Throughout the war Jefferson Davis favored offensive operations, and five of the six men who at one time or another commanded the South's two largest armies were as devoted to aggressive warfare as was Davis. Albert Sidney Johnston, P. G. T. Beauregard, Braxton Bragg, John B. Hood, and Robert E. Lee all preferred to be on the offensive; of the major field commanders, only Joseph E. Johnston really enjoyed defense. "What we have got to do must be done quickly," said Sidney Johnston. "The longer we leave them to fight the more difficult will they be to defeat." Beauregard, who helped Sidney Johnston plan the bloody assault at Shiloh, favored a Confederate invasion of Maryland in 1861, and in 1862 he wrote, "I desire to . . . retake the offensive as soon as our forces . . . have been sufficiently reorganized." [59] Bragg, who objected to trenches because he believed they destroyed an army's aggressiveness, attacked in three of the four major battles he directed. [60]

Hood, who took command of the Army of Tennessee after Joe Johnston's removal, was the general most committed to assault tactics. In fact, his only qualification for army command was his reputation as the hardest hitter in the Confederacy. Everyone knew Hood would attack Sherman's army; that was why he had been given command. To prevent defeat at this time the Confederacy certainly needed a military miracle. Johnston did not believe in military miracles, but Davis and Hood did. So Davis appointed Hood to high command, and Hood—a gambler and a visionary, a man unaware of just how little he knew—wagered the lives of his men that he could beat the Federals by repeated attacks. Johnston's defense of Atlanta in May and June 1864 cost the Federals five thousand more men than the Confederates lost. Hood lost eleven thousand more men than Sherman in operations around Atlanta from late July to early September 1864. [61]

Lee, too, liked to attack. He often suggested offensives to the president and urged other generals to be aggressive. In May 1862, a month after what Lee called the Confederate "victory of Shiloh," he advised Beauregard to invade Tennessee. [62] When Lee assumed command of

Confederate forces in Virginia in June 1862, he promptly abandoned a defensive strategy and launched two offensives—one by Jackson in the Valley and Lee's own Seven Days campaign against McClellan. President Davis's wife recalled: "General Lee was not given to indecision, and they have mistaken his character who supposed caution was his vice. He was prone to attack. . . ." [63] At Gettysburg, when James Longstreet advised Lee to move his army around the Federal left flank, select a strong position, and wait for Meade to attack, Lee announced that "if he is there to-morrow I will attack him." To which Longstreet replied, "If he is there to-morrow it will be because he wants you to attack." [64]

Though Lee was at his best on defense, he adopted a defensive strategy only after attrition had deprived him of the power to attack. His brill'ant defensive campaign against Grant in 1864 made the Union pay in manpower as it had never paid before. But the Confederates adopted defensive tactics too late; Lee started the campaign with too few men, and he could not replace his losses as could Grant. [65]

Even after the Wilderness campaign Lee still wanted to launch another offensive. He continued to hope that he could maneuver Grant out into the open and attack him. In May 1864, Lee wrote Davis: "[Grant's] position is strongly entrenched, and we cannot attack it with any prospect of success without great loss of men which I wish to avoid if possible. . . . my object has been to engage him when [his army is] in motion and . . . I shall continue to strike him whenever opportunity presents itself." Just two weeks before he surrendered, Lee lost 3,500 men in an assault on the Federal fortifications at Petersburg. "I was induced to assume the offensive," Lee explained to Davis, "from the belief that the point assailed could be carried without much loss." [66] As it happened, Lee's push failed to break the Union line, and the Confederates lost three times as many men as the defenders.

Perhaps the best way to illustrate the advantage defenders enjoyed over attackers is by a comparison of casualties. In half the twenty-two major battles of the Civil War the Federals attacked. They lost 119,000 men when they assaulted and 88,000 when they defended—a difference of 31,000 men. The Confederates lost 117,000 men when they attacked, but only 61,000 when they defended—a difference of 56,000 men, or enough to have given the South another large army. Every time the Confederates attacked they lost an average of 10 more men out of every 100 engaged than the Federal defenders, but when the Confederates defended, they lost 7 fewer men out of every 100 than the Union attackers. [67]

Bismarck is reputed to have said that fools learn from their own mistakes, but that he preferred to learn from the mistakes of others. The Confederacy failed because its leaders made the same mistakes time and again. "The reb[e]ls," observed a Union private in 1863, "fight as though a mans life was not worth one sent or in other words with desperation; or like Gen. Lafeyet [sic] said to Washington, there is more *dogs* where them came from." [68] By 1865 southern military leaders had exhausted their human resources. In attacking when they should have defended, they had, in Toombs's apt phrase, simply worn themselves out trying to whip the Yankees.

NOTES

1. Pleasant A. Stovall, *Robert Toombs* (New York, 1892), p. 322.

2. William F. Fox, *Regimental Losses in the American Civil War, 1861–1865* (Albany, 1889), pp. 47, 554, 22; Thomas L. Livermore, *Numbers and Losses in the Civil War in America: 1861–65* (Bloomington, Ind., 1957), pp. 63–64, 140–41.

3. See Winfield Scott, *Infantry Tactics* (New York, 1861); William J. Hardee, *Rifle and Light Infantry Tactics* (Philadelphia, 1861); Silas Casey, *Infantry Tactics* (New York, 1862); George B. McClellan, *Manual of Bayonet Exercise: Prepared for the Use of the Army of the United States* (Philadelphia, 1862); and John H. Richardson, *Infantry Tactics, or, Rules for the Exercise and Manoeuvres of the Confederate States Infantry* (Richmond, 1862).

4. Among the works that explain how new weapons outdated Civil War tactics, I have found most useful J. F. C. Fuller, *The Generalship of Ulysses S. Grant* (New York, 1929), pp. 57–62, and "The Place of the American Civil War in the Evolution of War," *Army Quarterly* 26 (1933):316–25; G. F. R. Henderson, *The Civil War: A Soldier's View,* ed. Jay Luvaas (Chicago, 1958), pp. 197–224; Bruce Catton, *America Goes to War* (New York, 1958), pp. 14–20; and John K. Mahon, "Civil War Infantry Assault Tactics," *Military Affairs* 25 (1961):57–68.

Moreover, though I disagree with some of their conclusions, numerous authors have influenced my thought on the relationship of tactics and weapons to strategy and command. I am particularly indebted to Bruce Catton, "The Generalship of Ulysses S. Grant," in *Grant, Lee, Lincoln and the Radicals: Essays on Civil War Leadership,* ed. Grady McWhiney (Evanston, Ill., 1964), pp. 3–30; David Donald, *Lincoln Reconsidered* (New York, 1956), esp. chap. 5; Douglas S. Freeman, *R. E. Lee* (New York, 1935), and *Lee's Lieutenants* (New York, 1942–44); Archer Jones, *Confederate Strategy from Shiloh to Vicksburg* (Baton Rouge, 1961); Charles P. Roland, "The Generalship of Robert E. Lee," in *Grant, Lee, Lincoln,* pp. 31–71; Kenneth P. Williams, *Lincoln Finds a General* (New York, 1949–59); T. Harry Williams, *Lincoln and His Generals* (New York, 1952), and *Americans at War* (Baton Rouge, 1960); and Frank E. Vandiver, *Rebel Brass* (Baton Rouge, 1956).

5. Ulysses S. Grant, *Personal Memoirs* (New York, 1885), 1:95.

6. T. H. McGuffie, "Musket and Rifle," *History Today* 7 (1957):475.

7. Grant, *Personal Memoirs,* 1:94–96.

8. Arcadi Gluckman, *United States Muskets, Rifles and Carbines* (Harrisburg, 1959), pp. 229–44; Francis A. Lord, "Strong Right Arm of the Infantry: The '61 Springfield Rifle Musket," *Civil War Times Illustrated* 1 (1962):43; Jac Weller, "Imported Confederate Shoulder Weapons," *Civil War History* 5 (1959):170–71, 180, 158.

9. Quoted in Bell I. Wiley, *The Life of Billy Yank: The Common Soldier of the Union* (Indianapolis, 1951), p. 63; Fritz Haskell, ed., "Diary of Colonel William Camm," *Journal of the Illinois State Historical Society* 18 (1926):813.

10. Jacob D. Cox, *Atlanta* (New York, 1909), p. 129; Fuller, *Generalship of Ulysses S. Grant,* pp. 361, 367.

11. Stephen A. Ambrose, ed., "West Point in the Fifties: The Letters of Henry A. du Pont," *Civil War History* 10 (1964):306–7.

12. Bruce Catton, *A Stillness at Appomattox* (New York, 1955), pp. 64–65.

13. Captain Justus Scheibert, *Seven Months in the Rebel States during the North American War, 1863,* ed. William Stanley Hoole (Tuscaloosa, Ala., 1958), pp. 37–38.

14. Quoted in Bell I. Wiley, *The Life of Johnny Reb: The Common Soldier of the Confederacy* (Indianapolis, 1943), pp. 71–72.

15. Quoted in Wiley, *Life of Billy Yank,* p. 50; David S. Sparks, ed., *Inside Lincoln's Army: The Diary of Marsena Rudolph Patrick* (New York, 1964), pp. 62–63, 108.

16. Henderson, *The Civil War,* p. 207; Robert W. Williams, Jr., and Ralph A. Wooster, eds., "With Terry's Texas Rangers: The Letters of Dunbar Affleck," *Civil War History* 9 (1963):311–12; E. John Ellis to his mother, October 21, 1862, E. John, Thomas C. W. Ellis and Family Papers, Louisiana State University, Baton Rouge.

17. U.S. War Department, *The War of the Rebellion: A Compilation of the Official Records of the Union and Confederate Armies,* 128 vols. (Washington, 1880–1901), Series 1, 10, pt. 1:392–95, 463–66; pt. 2:387 (hereafter cited as *OR;* unless otherwise indicated all references are to Series 1).

18. Richard Taylor, *Destruction and Reconstruction* (New York, 1879), p. 58; John H. Worsham, *One of Jackson's Foot Cavalry* (New York, 1912), p. 87.

19. Mary Boykin Chesnut, *A Diary from Dixie,* ed. Ben Ames Williams (Boston, 1949), p. 330. The campaigns and Jackson's losses were 2,095 in the Valley, 6,700 during the Seven Days, 1,365 at Cedar Mountain, 4,629 at Second Bull Run, and 6,095 in the Maryland campaign. Robert Underwood Johnson and Clarence Clough Buel, eds., *Battles and Leaders of the Civil War* (New York, 1887–89), 2:300–301, 315–16, 496, 500, 601–2.

20. *OR,* 12, pt. 3:842.

21. John B. Jones, *A Rebel War Clerk's Diary,* ed. Earl Schenck Miers (New York, 1958), p. 3.

22. Philip H. Sheridan, *Personal Memoirs* (New York, 1888), 1:355; L. Van Loan Naisawald, *Grape and Canister . . . the Field Artillery of the Army of the Potomac* (New York, 1960), p. 535.

23. Johnston still thought enough of lances after the war to include a

copy of his proposal in the appendix of his *Narrative of Military Operations* (Bloomington, Ind., 1959), p. 479.

24. Quoted in Wiley, *Life of Billy Yank,* pp. 51–52.

25. James H. Wilson, "The Cavalry of the Army of the Potomac," *Papers of the Military Historical Society of Massachusetts* 13 (1913):85; Sheridan, *Personal Memoirs,* 1:354–56; William W. Blackford, *The War Years with Jeb Stuart* (New York, 1945), p. 26.

26. W. H. Hitchcock, "Recollections of a Participant in the Charge," in *Battles and Leaders,* 2:346.

27. Quoted in Wiley, *Life of Billy Yank,* p. 327.

28. Henry J. Hunt, "The Third Day at Gettysburg," in *Battles and Leaders,* 3:372–74; E. Porter Alexander, "The Great Charge and Artillery Fighting at Gettysburg," in *Battles and Leaders,* 3:363–65; *OR,* 20, pt. 1:759–61.

29. Mahon, "Civil War Infantry Assault Tactics," pp. 66–67; Williams, *Lincoln Finds a General,* 4:278, 281.

30. Entry of May 12, 1864, Charles M. Walsh Diary, owned by Mr. and Mrs. John K. Read, Norfolk, Va.; Daniel H. Hill, "McClellan's Change of Base and Malvern Hill," in *Battles and Leaders,* 2:391–95.

31. Edwin M. Stanton, quoted in George Ticknor Curtis, *The Life of James Buchanan* (New York, 1883), 2:548.

32. Alexander K. McClure, *Recollections of Half a Century* (Salem, Mass., 1902), pp. 205–6; Charles Winslow Elliott, *Winfield Scott: The Soldier and the Man* (New York, 1937), p. 724; George William Curtis, ed., *The Correspondence of John Lothrop Motley* (New York, 1889), 2:143.

33. *OR,* Series 3, 1:148–49, 177–78, 250.

34. Elliott, *Winfield Scott,* pp. 722–23; William T. Sherman, *Memoirs* (Bloomington, Ind., 1957), 1:178, 179; Howard K. Beale, ed., *Diary of Gideon Welles* (New York, 1960), 1:84, 242.

35. John G. Nicolay and John Hay, *Abraham Lincoln: A History* (New York, 1904), 4:323.

36. Dunbar Rowland, ed., *Jefferson Davis, Constitutionalist: His Letters, Papers and Speeches* (Jackson, Miss., 1923), 5:338.

37. Over two million men enlisted in the Union Army, but Thomas Livermore estimated that only about 1,556,000 Northerners and about 1,082,000 Southerners actually served as long as three years in either army. *Numbers and Losses,* p. 63.

38. Jones, *A Rebel War Clerk's Diary,* pp. 18, 27, 36; Rowland, ed., *Jefferson Davis,* 5:339.

39. The first twelve major campaigns of the war, those in which the total casualties exceeded six thousand men, were Shiloh, Fair Oaks, the Seven Days, Second Bull Run, Antietam, Perryville, Fredericksburg, Stone's River, Chancellorsville, Vicksburg, Gettysburg, and Chickamauga. The Confederates clearly assumed the tactical offensive in all these battles except Antietam, Fredericksburg, and Vicksburg. Both sides attacked for a time at Shiloh and Second Bull Run, so one is counted here as a Confederate attack and the other as a Union attack. Livermore, *Numbers and Losses,* pp. 140–41.

40. The last ten campaigns in which the total casualties in each exceeded six thousand men were Chattanooga, the Wilderness and Spotsylvania, Johnston's Atlanta campaign (which included the battles of Buzzard's Roost, Snake Creek Gap, New Hope Church, and Kenesaw Mountain),

Hood's Atlanta campaign (which included the battles of Peach Tree Creek, Atlanta, July 22 and 28, and Jonesborough, August 31 and September 1), Cold Harbor, Petersburg, Winchester, Cedar Creek, Franklin, and Appomattox. The Federals took the tactical offensive in all of these actions except Hood's Atlanta campaign, Cedar Creek, and Franklin. Livermore, *Numbers and Losses,* pp. 140–41.

41. I am grateful to Thomas M. Baumann, one of my former graduate students, who helped me to establish regimental numbers and losses at Stone's River and Chickamauga.

42. *OR,* 20, pt. 1:495–96, 305–6, 314–15, 319–21, 325–26, 394–95, 401–3.

43. *Ibid.,* 30, pt. 1:1058–59, 427–30, 529–31, 521–22, 654–58, 590, 839–40, 173, 174.

44. *Ibid.,* 20, pt. 1:676–81, 693, 758, 780, 852, 855, 875, 900; unpublished reports in the William P. Palmer Collection of Braxton Bragg Papers, Western Reserve Historical Society, Cleveland.

45. Report of Capt. Taylor Beatty, First Louisiana Infantry, Palmer Collection of Bragg Papers.

46. Report of Lt. Col. J. J. Scales, Thirtieth Mississippi Infantry, Palmer Collection of Bragg Papers.

47. Charles T. Jones, Jr., "Five Confederates: The Sons of Bolling Hall in the Civil War," *Alabama Historical Quarterly* 24 (1962):167.

48. Report of Lt. Col. N. N. Clements, Twenty-sixth Alabama Infantry, Palmer Collection of Bragg Papers.

49. Reports of Maj. J. O. Thompson, Forty-fourth (Blythe's) Mississippi Infantry, and Lt. Col. T. H. Lyman, Ninth Mississippi Infantry, Palmer Collection of Bragg Papers. Thompson reported: "During the night of Friday [December] 26 all guns in the hands of Blythe's Regiment were taken from them and distributed among the regiments of Chalmers' Brigade. The Sunday morning following we were furnished with refuse guns that had been turned over to the Brigade ordnance officer. Many of these guns were worthless. . . . Even of these poor arms there was not a sufficiency and after every exertion on my part to procure arms, one half of the Regt. moved out with no other resemblance to a gun than such sticks as they could gather."

50. *OR,* 20, pt. 1:710–12, 714–18, 543–46.

51. *Ibid.,* pp. 838–39, 841–42, 795–99; Alexander F. Stevenson, *The Battle of Stone's River* (Boston, 1884), p. 113.

52. *OR,* 30, pt. 2:11–532.

53. *Ibid.,* pp. 176–78, 336–37, 424–29.

54. James I. Robertson, Jr., *The Stonewall Brigade* (Baton Rouge, 1963), p. 243; William Whatley Pierson, Jr., ed., *Whipt 'Em Everytime: The Diary of Bartlett Yancey Malone* (Jackson, Tenn., 1960), p. 28.

55. These figures are based upon data taken from Ezra J. Warner, *Generals in Gray* (Baton Rouge, 1959), and Mark Mayo Boatner, III, *The Civil War Dictionary* (New York, 1959).

56. Only 23 percent of these seventy-seven generals were killed while on defense; 7 percent died in ways that can be classified as neither offense nor defense. Stonewall Jackson and Micah Jenkins, for example, were accidentally killed by their own men, and John H. Morgan was killed by Union cavalrymen after he was surprised while asleep in a private home.

57. Donald, *Lincoln Reconsidered,* pp. 82–102; T. Harry Williams,

"The Military Leadership of North and South," in *Why the North Won the Civil War,* ed. David Donald (Baton Rouge, 1960), pp. 23–47.

58. Chesnut, *A Diary from Dixie,* Williams, ed., p. 245; Livermore, *Numbers and Losses,* p. 71.

59. *Confederate Veteran* 3 (1895):83; Jones, *A Rebel War Clerk's Diary,* p. 54; *OR,* 17, pt. 2:599.

60. In April 1863, President Davis's military aide wrote: "General Bragg says heavy intrenchments demoralize our troops." *OR,* 23, pt. 2:761. And a member of Bragg's staff wrote in his diary about the same time: "The Engineers are busy in strengthening the field works around Tullahoma. Gen. Bragg has never shown much confidence in them—Murfreesboro for example." George W. Brent Diary, April 13, 1863, Palmer Collection of Bragg Papers.

61. Livermore, *Numbers and Losses,* pp. 119–21, 122–26.

62. *OR,* 10, pt. 2:546.

63. Varina H. Davis, *Jefferson Davis . . . A Memoir* (New York, 1890), 2:318–19.

64. James Longstreet, *From Manassas to Appomattox,* ed. James I. Robertson, Jr. (Bloomington, Ind., 1960), p. 358.

65. A recent study estimates that Grant lost about fifty thousand men between the Wilderness and Cold Harbor, about the number Lee started the campaign with. Clifford Dowdey, *Lee's Last Campaign* (Boston, 1960), p. 299.

66. Douglas S. Freeman and Grady McWhiney, eds., *Lee's Dispatches to Jefferson Davis* (New York, 1957), pp. 183–84, 341–42.

67. These computations are based upon figures given in Livermore, *Numbers and Losses,* pp. 140–41.

68. Quoted in Naisawald, *Grape and Canister,* p. 536.

CHAPTER VIII

Reconstruction and Americanism

Until thirty years ago scholars agreed that the decade following the
Civil War was a tragic era, especially in the South, where carpetbaggers, Negroes, and renegade scalawags instead of "decent white men"
ruled. Reconstruction, it was argued, "reduced [the South] to the very
abomination of desolation." "It was the most soul-sickening spectacle
that Americans had ever been called upon to behold," wrote John W.
Burgess in 1902. "Every principle of the old American polity was here
reversed. In place of government by the most intelligent and virtuous
part of the people for the benefit of the governed, here was government
by the most ignorant and vicious part of the population for the benefit,
the vulgar, materialistic, brutal benefit of the governing set." [1]

Today most historians still consider the postwar period a tragic one,
but usually for a different reason. Products of an age that is not shocked
by Negro suffrage, they are inclined to deny that Reconstruction was an
unmitigated disaster for the South. Revisionists have taught them to see
some evidence of democratic advance in the achievements of the Republican Reconstruction regimes in the fields of public education and
internal improvements. [2]

But the democratic advance seems to many a modern eye to have
been painfully limited and compromised. The real tragedy, in this revisionist view, was that the national reconstruction program was only in-
sincerely democratic. It gave the black man nominal political power
without giving him economic power, and so condemned him to virtual

reinslavement. The tragedy of Reconstruction was that it did not really reconstruct.

One may well puzzle over this peculiar Reconstruction that did not reconstruct, with its peculiar Southerners (presumably feudal-minded racists) who accepted more colorblind democracy than they could have been expected to, and who would have accepted more than they were forced to, and with its peculiar Yankees (presumably democratic idealists) who abandoned all too quickly any effort to make colorblind democracy stick. If one puzzles long enough, he may begin to perceive that these Southerners and these Northerners were acting in peculiarly similar ways. He may begin to suspect that Reconstruction was not so peculiar after all, that it may not have been so tragic after all—except as a reflection of the contradictions of Americanism.

Today most Americans are remarkably alike. Their values and aspirations are similar. With few exceptions, they believe in democracy, progress, success, universal education, equal opportunities for all citizens, Mother, God, and country. Their tastes in literature, art, music, food, drink, clothing, houses, furniture, automobiles, and entertainment vary only slightly. According to the Kinsey reports even their sex lives are similar.

American society is so mobile that economic, social, or intellectual status is frequently difficult or impossible to determine. Salesmen dress like celebrities. Cadillacs are accessible to plumbers. By following advice readily available in newspapers and magazines garbage collectors can learn to dress, talk, and even smell like bankers. A coal miner can fly to South Bend for a football game between Pitt and Notre Dame and, if his fingernails are clean, be mistaken for an industrialist. Fashion journals tell secretaries how to outdress executives' daughters. For a nominal price every American can obtain a product that allegedly retards tooth decay. Twenty-four solid hours of odorless armpits are denied no one.

Such opportunities did not always obtain. Nor did such homogeneity. In colonial America a man's class could be recognized by his dress and, as late as 1815, gentlemen still wore ruffles and silk stockings. Nineteenth-century technological developments, however, soon allowed the poor to ape the rich. The presidency of James Monroe marked the end of an era. He was the last chief executive to wear a wig. By the end of the antebellum period nearly all Americans dressed alike.

Aiding technology in effecting this revolution were two of the most pervasive themes in American history: the ideology of progress and the

democratic dogma. Brought to the colonies by Europeans, both doctrines were subtly shaped by Americans and have enjoyed almost
universal approval since the Jacksonian period. The majority of Americans, without having heard of the Enlightenment, accepted unquestion-
ingly the belief that men and institutions (especially American men
and institutions) could attain here on earth a state of perfection once
thought possible only for Christians in a state of grace, and for them
after death. Not to believe in both material and individual progress
quickly became un-American. By hard work any man could become
successful. The newer religions even promised earthly salvation for the
most miserable sinner. A man born in a log cabin could become president.
Indeed, for a time, it was hard for a man not born in a log cabin to become president.

Complementing the ideology of progress was the liberating tendency
of American democracy. To develop their talents, it was argued, men
must be free from traditional restraints. They must have freedom to get
ahead, to make something of themselves, to start a new business, religion, or political party. But democracy was also a leveling process. If
the race to perfection was to be run fairly the participants must start together. Men must have equal opportunities.

Combined, the progressive and democratic doctrines have encouraged
(among other things): the accumulation of wealth, westward expansion,
"manifest destiny," emigration from Europe, extension of the suffrage,
political demagoguery, "common man" culture, crime and violence, religious diversity and religious conformity, erosion of the family unit,
sundry reform movements, and technological developments.

One of the great myths of history is that somehow the South escaped
the intellectual forces that shaped American thought and action. Tied to
slavery from colonial times until 1865, Southerners supposedly developed a separate nationalism, glorified and practiced the plantation ideal
and its concomitant philosophy of aristocracy and white supremacy. Democracy and progress found no supporters in the Old South, it is alleged; even the failure to win independence in the 1860s scarcely
changed the Bourbon attitude of white Southerners, who continued to
exploit the Negro and to follow a reactionary policy of racial discrimination.

Such assertions distort the past. Democracy developed in the South as
it did in other parts of America. Southerners were likewise as devoted
as other Americans to progress, especially material progress. The whole
colonial experience of Southerners was one of improving themselves by

acquiring farms near the Atlantic coast, or by moving westward. The westward trek of Southerners continued throughout the antebellum years. Like their Yankee cousins, southern migrants were men on the make, driven to the frontier by the ideology of progress and the liberating theme of democracy. They knew that in America individual progress was measured in dollars and cents, and they had faith in their ability to succeed in the virgin land beyond the Appalachians. The industrious and lucky ones were not disappointed. Aided by technological discoveries that improved agriculture, transportation, and manufacturing, many Southerners prospered during the antebellum period. Particularly in the lower South, cotton was a great democratizing influence before 1860. It could be cultivated profitably on a few acres by one man, or on large plantations by many slaves. Men could climb to riches over bales of cotton.[3]

Southerners joined other Americans in the Jacksonian rebellion against entrenched privilege. In fact, Andrew Jackson received some of his largest majorities in the South, where popular culture, universal suffrage for white males, and other leveling developments also won victories. Before the Civil War southern "men of the people" like W. R. W. Cobb, Alabama's "friend of the poor against the rich," who sang such original compositions as "Uncle Sam is rich enough to give us all a farm," were unbeatable politicians. According to recent studies, by 1860 white Southerners enjoyed a large measure of political, social, and economic democracy.[4]

If most Southerners believed in progress and democracy, why were blacks denied liberty and equality in the Old South? Part of the answer is that throughout the nineteenth century there was an aberration in the thinking of all white Americans about black men. Nowhere is this better demonstrated than in the diaries and letters of Union soldiers.[5] Although considered human, "colored" peoples (such as Negroes, Indians, and Orientals) were regarded as inferiors by most Americans. Ironically, Americans believed in equality, but they also believed that some men were more equal than others. This perversion of the doctrine of equality was more apparent in the South because of its large Negro population, but it also existed in the North.

Knowing that few Yankees practiced equalitarianism, Southerners nevertheless had an uneasy conscience. True, they sought religious, philosophical, scientific, historical, and sociological justification for slavery. But many Southerners were too American to be convinced by their own arguments. One thing they did know, however: slavery was

profitable. Without slaves, Southerners were certain they would fall behind the rest of America in the progressive race. As businessmen, they
did not want to lose their investments or gamble with the uncertainties
of a free labor supply. They were as grasping as their northern kinsmen.
The indulgent master, the fabled southern planter of cavalier extrava-
gance, existed more in the minds of romantics than in fact. Plantation
mansions were exceptions in the architectural pattern of the Old
South; [6] most planters lived in rather crude houses and enjoyed few luxuries. None was as wealthy as the richest Northerners. Southern slaveholders were not knights of some nineteenth-century Round Table, but
men of the marketplace. Intellectually, their culture was as sterile as the
dreary romances their wives and daughters read. Planters damned the
dry or rainy weather when they met and talked about the price of staples, land, and slaves, not about the philosophy of Plato or Aristotle.
Clearly, antebellum Southerners were men of progress. They favored
better methods of cultivation, improvements in transportation and technology, and higher profits. "No class of people in the world are so dependent on Science . . . as the planters," wrote a slaveholder in 1859.[7]

The great majority of Southerners owned no slaves (nearly three-
fourths of all free Southerners had no connection with slavery through
either family ties or direct ownership), yet even these nonslaveholders
had practical, thoroughly American reasons for defending the "peculiar
institution" to the end. Owning slaves was the way to wealth and success in the antebellum South, and men who owned none hoped to acquire human chattels someday. In a real sense, emancipation would
endanger their chance of success. Thus, Southerners faced an intellectual
dilemma: how to be progressive and democratic and yet at the same
time dominate the Negro.

Ironically, one reason why Southerners lost their struggle to preserve
slavery was because they were too democratic. "Universal suffrage—
furloughs & whiskey, have ruined us," wrote a high ranking Confederate general.[8] The extreme liberty practiced by states' rightists, the frequently malicious criticism of civil and military officials by the
unmuzzled Confederate press, the lack of discipline in the army (fostered by the election of numerous officers), and the high rate of deser-
tion by soldiers and disaffection by civilians contributed more to the destruction of the Confederacy than stronger northern armies. Superior to
the South in resources, the North could afford democracy. Lacking a
distinct nationalism, the South could not.

Throughout their entire history down to Appomattox, then, Southerners had shown an unshakable devotion to both democracy and material progress, and—in case of conflict between the two—a disposition to bend their democratic ideals to accommodate their progressive appetites. But were the Yankees so different? While marching to "The Battle Hymn of the Republic" it had been easy for them to picture the Civil War as a struggle between their own democratic idealism and the South's materialistically based racism. But Appomattox was not the end of the story; in a sense it was but the prelude to its climactic and most revealing phase. For in the sequel of Reconstruction white Northerners and white Southerners discovered a spiritual brotherhood that, however unedifying to a later generation, resulted in a durable reunion. In this spiritual brotherhood material progress took precedence over democracy.

Southerners opened the drama of Reconstruction by manifesting a disposition—such was the paradoxical situation created by defeat—to accept a large measure of democratization, including a goodly dose of colorblind democracy, in order to get back on the progress road. "The war being at an end, . . . and the questions at issue . . . having been decided, I believe it to be the duty of every one to unite in the restoration of the country, and the reestablishment of peace and harmony," wrote General Robert E. Lee. "By doing this and encouraging our citizens to engage in the duties of life with all their heart and mind . . . our country will not only be restored in material prosperity, but will be advanced in science, in virtue and in religion." [9]

Southerners were so eager for a share in American material prosperity that they complied with every demand made upon them for readmission to the Union. Arguing that actually they had never been out of the Union, they renounced secession, abolished slavery, repudiated the Confederate debt, and—as a result of demands by such determined congressional leaders as Thaddeus Stevens and Charles Sumner—even temporarily consented to try Negro suffrage. "I was not disappointed at the result of the war," wrote a Georgian. "Thad. Stevens would be as safe here as in Pennsylvania," said a Virginian. "Should you visit Mississippi I would be pleased to have you at my house," a stranger informed Senator John Sherman.[10] James L. Alcorn, a former brigadier who had suffered financial ruin during the war, admitted: "you were right Yankee! You have established your power; . . . we are and ever have been in the Union; secession was a nullity. We will now take the oath to support the Constitution and laws of the United States. . . ." [11] As proof of his sincerity, Alcorn became the Republican governor of Mississippi in 1869 and a Republican member of the United States Senate in 1871. He also recouped his financial losses and increased his property holdings.

Of course not all Southerners were as easily reconstructed as Alcorn. Many able men were disenfranchised and prohibited from holding office. Some, like Judah P. Benjamin, left the South and found economic opportunities abroad. Edmund Ruffin, one of the most determined secessionists, committed suicide; John J. Pettus, Mississippi's war governor, spent the remaining two years of his life as a disillusioned recluse.

But Ruffin and Pettus were exceptions. Eventually only 71 of the 656 prominent Confederates who lived long enough to make postwar readjustments "failed to recover a substantial portion of the position and prestige they had enjoyed at the Confederacy's peak." [12] Denied the right to hold public office, Jefferson Davis sought to rehabilitate himself economically. For a time he served as president of a life insurance company. When it went bankrupt, he tried to start a steamship line. Only after repeated economic failures did he devote himself to glorifying the Old South and the Lost Cause.

A number of leaders joined the carpetbag and Negro governments and returned to power sooner than others. In Mississippi Albert G. Brown, a former governor, advocated political expediency and submission to Radical Reconstruction. By 1868 such prominent Alabama Democrats as Lewis E. Parsons, Alexander McKinstry, Judge Samuel F. Rice, and Alexander White had joined the Republican party. Motivated partly by personal political ambition, they also believed that as Republicans they could best help their own as well as their state's economic recovery. General William C. Wickham, of Virginia, endorsed the Republican party less than a month after Appomattox. He soon became president of the Virginia Central Railroad, and three years later president of the Chesapeake and Ohio. In New Orleans, General James Longstreet actually led an army of black men against Confederate veterans. His reward was lucrative posts from successive Republican administrations. James L. Orr, of South Carolina, marched into the National Union Convention in 1866 arm in arm with a Massachusetts general. When President Andrew Johnson's candidates lost the fall congressional elections, however, Orr changed his allegiance to the victorious Radicals. In North Carolina, James G. Ramsey, Richmond M. Pearson, and General Rufus Barringer were early advocates of Negro suffrage and industrialization. General George Maney, of Tennessee, became president of the Tennessee and Pacific Railroad and a Republican.

It is obvious that not all scalawags were renegade "poor whites." Many of them were former Whigs, seeking a new political home. Others were simply trying to adjust to the new order or to get ahead politically and financially.[13] That they were not always concerned with the means by which success was obtained is illustrated by the case of Josephus Woodruff. A native South Carolinian, Woodruff deserted the Democratic party to become clerk of the state senate, and to ensure that his company received all the state's official printing business. In 1874 he confided to his diary a conversation in which the influential black legislator Robert Smalls "said if anyone was to offer him $50,000 to vote against me he would indignantly decline." Woodruff replied that he "was pleased to hear it, but would be glad to see the offer made and accepted, and the amount equally divided between us." Three years later Smalls was convicted of having accepted a $5,000 bribe from Woodruff to vote for a printing bill.[14]

The Radical regimes in the South lasted only a few years, however, and many scalawags either lost their positions of power and privilege or in order to save them were forced to become Democrats. After abandoning the Republican party Joseph E. Brown not only weathered investigations of his honesty, but remained one of the most powerful politicians in Georgia and one of the leading industrialists in the South. Generals P. G. T. Beauregard and Jubal A. Early had yielded to the blandishments of the Republican supported Louisiana Lottery Company and received substantial sums for presiding over the drawings. "Ever since Longstreet feathered his nest, there has been an itching about Beauregard's stern for a similar application, and, to those who know him, it was evident time would find him in the radical camp," wrote an impoverished Confederate general.[15] Yet both Beauregard and Early managed to retain their posts after the Democrats returned to power in Louisiana.

Without consistent Federal support, torn by internal conflicts within their own state parties, and hurt by a nationwide depression, Republican officeholders were driven from the South in the 1870s. Charged with fraud and corruption, they were ousted by pragmatic Democrats who did not shrink from using violence, intimidation, and stuffed ballot boxes.

The Radical Reconstruction experiment failed for a number of reasons, but foremost perhaps was northern disillusionment with blacks. "In spite of all their efforts, the abolitionists . . . failed to create widespread determination in any part of the nation to grant to the freedmen social or political or economic equality," writes a perceptive scholar.[16] For the most part Negro suffrage was a political expedient endorsed by northern voters only because politicians "waved the bloody shirt." Senator T. O. Howe wrote in 1875 that the Civil War was not "fought for the 'nigger' " and the Negro was not "the end and aim of all our effort." [17] James H. Paine tried to insert a promise of suffrage for southern blacks into the platform of the Wisconsin Republican Convention in 1875, but the delegates voted overwhelmingly against his proposal.[18]

When Northerners discovered that former Confederates would defend Yankee railroad and industrial interests as vigorously as they fought Yankee armies, the Negro vote became less important. "There can be no way so sure to make the late rebels of the South loyal men and good citizens," declared the New York *Commercial and Financial Chronicle* in 1865, "as to turn their energies to the pursuits of peace, and the accumulation of wealth." [19] By the 1870s Southerners had proved that they were willing to help bring the American dream of a materialistic utopia to fulfillment. Newspapers throughout the South reflected and helped shape their reader's enthusiastic devotion to material progress. "Country papers gave those patron saints of the New South . . . a wide reading public. Liberal news space was devoted to excerpts from the *Manufacturer's Record*. In many areas . . . there was something of religious fervor in the numerous editorials on immigration and on exploitation of land, timber, and mineral resources. Since 1867 country editors have told their readers that they were living in a land of golden opportunity. Their section . . . needed only population, capital, industry, and mechanical knowledge to make it wealthy." [20]

The struggle for power in the South, as well as in the rest of the country, during the Reconstruction period should not be treated as a contest between the forces of good and evil. Rather it should be considered as an encounter between rival economic interests seeking exclusive privileges and trying to control the various states through two different political parties. After 1868 financiers, not radicals, dominated southern politics. According to Horace Mann Bond "the Louisville and Nashville Railroad, the Alabama and Chattanooga Railroad, . . . the banking houses of the Cookes, of Russell Sage, of the Morgans and the Drexels, loom more significantly in Alabama Reconstruction than do the time-honored figures of the history books." In the struggle for state bonds and land grants, Democrats supported the L. & N., whose president was backed by August Belmont, national chairman of the Democratic party and the American agent for the Rothschilds. In turn, Republicans supported the A. & C., which had the backing of Russell Sage, Henry Clews, and William D. ("Pig Iron") Kelley. Initially, the L. & N. got the upper hand, but after Republicans took over the state the A. & C. put pressure on them to eliminate the L. & N. During the depression of the 1870s, however, the A. & C. went bankrupt, and when the Democrats returned to power in 1874 the L. & N. was assured of success.[21]

In Virginia, railroad promoters also played an important role in the state's reconstruction. One of the leading figures in this struggle for power was General William Mahone, who in order to protect his railroad interests successively shifted his political allegiance from the Radicals, to the Conservatives (Democrats), to the Readjusters.[22] Even General Robert E. Lee, who was named president of the Valley Railroad a few months before his death in 1870, succumbed to the promotion fever.

By the time the Reconstruction experiment ended Southerners were again thoroughly Americanized. Every southern state was controlled by businessmen or the friends of business.[23] The dream of an industrial millennium captivated nearly every mind. "The South found her jewel in the toad's head of defeat," said the most famous southern apostle of progress.[24] The Lost Cause was not forgotten, but the Yankee was forgiven. Instead of lynching Congressman Lucius Q. C. Lamar for eulogizing Charles Sumner, Mississippians made him a United States Senator.

Though the Negro once again was relegated to a subservient position in the South, he too pursued the goal of material progress. Booker T. Washington, the most famous Southerner of his day, advised his people: "Cast down your bucket where you are—cast it down in making friends in every manly way of the people of all races by whom we are surrounded. Cast it down in agriculture, mechanics, in commerce, in domestic service, and in the professions. And in this connection it is well to bear in mind that whatever other sins the South may be called to bear, when it comes to business, pure and simple, it is in the South that the Negro is given a man's chance in the commercial world." [25] If Washington's thoroughly American and materialistic plan to raise his race to equality was not entirely successful, it was nevertheless applauded by white Southerners.

Twentieth-century international developments have helped shape a New Reconstruction program. Today many Americans, aware that their future prosperity as well as the fate of their country may well be determined by an overwhelmingly "colored" world, insist that national survival depends upon practicing colorblind democracy. A number of white Southerners recognize the logic of this argument, but most of them are still too American either to endorse racial equality or to renounce their democratic pretenses. Like most Americans, they boast of being common men while they admire elitism. They see no inconsistency between the doctrine of personal equality and the selecting of beauty queens. They admire the queen of England more than the wife of their own chief executive. They send their children to schools that do not educate so they will not be maladjusted in a society that reveres television and movie stars. They suspect that integration is a diabolical scheme to destroy not only their present social and economic status but their chance of future success. The white ladies of Montgomery, Alabama, who chauffered their bus-boycotting maids to and from work are merely comfort-loving Americans, not integrationists.

Aware that white Northerners also indulge in democratic hypocrisy, white Southerners fear that they will be jim-crowed by other Americans if racial equality is practiced in the South. Subconsciously, Southerners realize that the genius of America is inequality. They will accept colorblind democracy only if convinced that the alternative is loss of status and the chance of future success. Briefly this was the situation during the Old Reconstruction, when the white Southerner was ready to acquiesce in Negro suffrage; and now the New Reconstruction seems to promise a similar but more lasting acquiescence in a limited amount of school desegregation. The great segregationists' bastion at Little Rock fell because those ultratypical Americans, the members of the Downtown Businessmen's Association, held racial exclusiveness less dear than the good name and the continued growth and prosperity of their fair city. For Governor Faubus's constituents, like other Southerners and other Americans, were more devoted to the ideology of material progress than to either racial superiority or the democratic dogma.

NOTES

1. John W. Burgess, *Reconstruction and the Constitution, 1866–1876* (New York, 1902), pp. 296–97, 263–64. Some additional examples of this view of Reconstruction are William A. Dunning, *Reconstruction, Political and Economic, 1865–1877* (New York, 1907); James Ford Rhodes, *History of the United States from the Compromise of 1850 . . .* (New York, 1906), vols. 5–7; Walter L. Fleming, *The Sequel of Appomattox* (New Haven, 1921); Claude G. Bowers, *The Tragic Era* (Boston, 1929); and E. Merton Coulter, *The South during Reconstruction, 1865–1877* (Baton Rouge, 1947).

2. See such important revisionist writing as Francis B. Simkins and

Robert H. Woody, *South Carolina during Reconstruction* (Chapel Hill, 1932); W. E. Burghardt Du Bois, *Black Reconstruction* (New York, 1938); C. Vann Woodward, *Tom Watson, Agrarian Rebel* (New York, 1938); Alrutheus A. Taylor, "Historians of the Reconstruction," *Journal of Negro History* 23 (1938):16–34; Horace Mann Bond, *Negro Education in Alabama* (Washington, 1939); Roger W. Shugg, *Origins of Class Struggle in Louisiana* (Baton Rouge, 1939); Francis B. Simkins, "New Viewpoints of Southern Reconstruction," *Journal of Southern History* 5 (1939):49–61; Howard K. Beale, "On Rewriting Reconstruction History," *American Historical Review* 45 (1940):807–27; T. Harry Williams, "An Analysis of Some Reconstruction Attitudes," *Journal of Southern History* 12 (1946):469–86; Vernon L. Wharton, *The Negro in Mississippi, 1865–1890* (Chapel Hill, 1947); Thomas B. Alexander, *Political Reconstruction in Tennessee* (Nashville, 1950); and C. Vann Woodward, *Reunion and Reaction* (New York, 1951).

3. Charles S. Sydnor, *The Development of Southern Sectionalism, 1819–1848* (Baton Rouge, 1948), p. 14.

4. Fletcher M. Green, "Democracy in the Old South," *Journal of Southern History* 12 (1946):3–23; Frank L. Owsley, *Plain Folk of the Old South* (Baton Rouge, 1949), pp. 133–49.

5. Bell I. Wiley, *The Life of Billy Yank: The Common Soldier of the Union* (Indianapolis, 1951), p. 109.

6. James C. Bonner, "Plantation Architecture of the Lower South on the Eve of the Civil War," *Journal of Southern History* 11 (1945):370–88.

7. Braxton Bragg to Edward G. W. Butler, December 27, 1859, Edward George Washington Butler Papers, Duke University, Durham, N.C.

8. Bragg to Mrs. Bragg, April 8, 1862, William K. Bixby Collection of Braxton Bragg Papers, Missouri Historical Society, St. Louis.

9. Douglas S. Freeman, *R. E. Lee: A Biography* (New York, 1935), 4:220–21.

10. J. G. Randall, *The Civil War and Reconstruction* (Boston, 1937), pp. 694–95.

11. P. L. Rainwater, ed., "Letters of James Lusk Alcorn," *Journal of Southern History* 3 (1937):209.

12. William B. Hesseltine, *Confederate Leaders in the New South* (Baton Rouge, 1950), p. 16.

13. David Donald, "The Scalawag in Mississippi Reconstruction," *Journal of Southern History* 10 (1944):447–60; Thomas B. Alexander, "Whiggery and Reconstruction in Tennessee," *ibid.*, 16 (1950):291–305.

14. R. H. Woody, ed., "Behind the Scenes in the Reconstruction Legislature of South Carolina: Diary of Josephus Woodruff," *Journal of Southern History* 2 (1936):91, 235 n.

15. Braxton Bragg to William Preston Johnston, July 3, 1873, Mrs. Mason Barret Collection of Albert Sidney and William Preston Johnston Papers, Tulane University, New Orleans.

16. Merton L. Dillon, "The Failure of the American Abolitionists," *Journal of Southern History* 25 (1959):176.

17. William B. Hesseltine, "Economic Factors in the Abandonment of Reconstruction," *Mississippi Valley Historical Review* 22 (1935):209.

18. Helen J. and Harry Williams, "Wisconsin Republicans and Reconstruction, 1865–70," *Wisconsin Magazine of History* 23 (1939):22.

19. Hesseltine, "Economic Factors in the Abandonment of Reconstruction," p. 192.

20. Thomas D. Clark, "The Country Newspaper: A Factor in Southern Opinion, 1865–1930," *Journal of Southern History* 14 (1948):8.

21. Horace Mann Bond, "Social and Economic Forces in Alabama Reconstruction," *Journal of Negro History* 23 (1938):290–348.

22. Nelson M. Blake, *William Mahone of Virginia: Soldier and Political Insurgent* (Richmond, 1935), pp. 70–195.

23. C. Vann Woodward, *Origins of the New South, 1877–1913* (Baton Rouge, 1951), pp. 1–22.

24. Henry W. Grady, "The New South," in *The Literature of the South,* ed. Richmond Croom Beatty *et al.* (Chicago, 1952), p. 492.

25. Booker T. Washington, "Speech at the Atlanta Exposition," *The Negro Caravan,* ed. Sterling A. Brown *et al.* (New York, 1941), p. 674.

CHAPTER IX

The Ghostly Legend
of the
Ku Klux Klan

The concept of the South as a distinct region of the United States is largely based on a series of legends little changed by the researches of the realists. Among these persistent stereotypes are the myths about the Suwannee River, Kentucky colonels, beaux and belles under the moonlight, the inability of the white man to work under the August sun, and the success of the planters' sons and daughters in avoiding toil. The Negro as the central character of southern history has inevitably evolved into the most distinctive participant in the southern legend.

In the imaginings of the South's numerous storytellers the Negro takes two forms—the Good Darky and the Bad Negro. The former is represented as bowing at the proper time and always agreeing with his reputed betters. He is characterized as slow, easygoing, unadapted to severe climates, irresponsible, good-natured, mercurial, and naturally fond of sweet taters, possum, and the banjo. The Good Darky is supposed to be so congenitally superstitious that the stratagems of all the schoolma'ams from Cape Cod to Philadelphia do not dispel his delusions. In the legend he is so persistently under the influence of nightly apparitions that the mere mention of a ghost makes him shake as actively as Stepin Fetchit under the influence of an arctic breeze.

This concept of the Good Darky is no small factor in explaining one

of the significant facts of American history: the survival of the southern
view of life and thought despite the setbacks of the Civil War and Reconstruction. Thereby does the South live as a cultural entity. Fantastic
as this attitude may appear to the objective observer, it is a means
through which the white man asserts his superior caste status. It gives
even the lowly poor white a chance to laugh at a creature adjudged
meaner than the poor white himself. It allows the southern mind to float
back to the "good old days" before the war with illusions of "mint
juleps," "grand balls," "gracious ladies," and loyal slaves suited to the
interests of leisure-class idealism.

Of equal importance in the white man's mind is the legend of the
Bad Negro. He is characterized as a huge brute with a large, flat nose
and lust-crazed eyes. Of necessity, he is arrogant, untrustworthy,
sneaky, and vicious. His primary interest is the deflowerment of white
ladies and the murder of former masters. This creation was expressed in
The Clansman and other writings of the Reverend Thomas Dixon, Jr.,
of North Carolina.[1] Dixon's imaginings as projected in the film *The
Birth of a Nation* were imposed upon the popular mind with such compelling effectiveness that race riots were narrowly averted. Indirectly
the concept of the black hands around the white throats of southern
maidens gave all true sons of Dixie a creature to hate and to fear.

The Good Darky and the Bad Negro have become a main convention
of southern literature. It has its kindliest expression in the winsome cre-
ations of Irwin Russell. It has its most sinister expression in the fulmi-
nations of Dixon. The attempt in the 1920s of the white South Carolinians DuBose Heyward and Julia Peterkin to endow the Negro with the
varied emotions of normal men was only temporarily successful. Their
writings have been followed by a return to type: the humorous, mercurial fellow of Roy Octavus Cohen; the credulous preacher of *Green
Pastures;* the kowtowing servitors of *Gone with the Wind.* Such Negroes
figure in books of non-Southerners; they appear in the works of serious
historians; [2] and they have become too precious a part of the southern
legend to be rejected wherever the South is esteemed.

Such beliefs concerning the Negro culminate in the southern conception of the Ku Klux Klan of the Reconstruction period. The mythology
surrounding the magic letters *KKK* is still vivid in the minds of the
southern people eighty years after the organization's supposed death.
The ride of the hooded knights under a mythical Forrest and a mythical
Gordon is considered as real as the ride of Confederate cavalrymen behind the real Nathan B. Forrest and the real John B. Gordon. Southern-

ers hold to the aberration that the sole purpose of the Ku Klux Klan was to prevent the rape of southern womanhood, to reestablish white supremacy, and to drive infamous carpetbaggers back to their northern homes. The degree to which the authors [McWhiney and Simkins; see Notes] believe this to be untrue is set forth elsewhere.[3]

An explanation of the full scope and purpose of the Ku Klux Klan awaits the critical appraisal of the historian; such an ambitious task is beyond the limits of this essay. Its sole objective is to question the legend that ghostly affectations were an important means of effecting the Klan's ambitions.

The great body of literature about the hooded order is loaded with assertions about knights in ghostly disguise using weird demonstrations as a certain method of effecting the return of the blacks to their traditional position of subordination. Such behavior is presented as a vivid example of the black man's inherent tendency to be superstitious as opposed to artificially imposed urges of the Negro to seek political and social equality. The first Klansmen, says Susan L. Davis, a historian sympathetic to the Klan, "rode slowly through the streets of Pulaski [Tennessee] waving to the people and making grotesque gestures, which created merriment to the unsuperstitious, and to the superstitious, great fear." Elaborating, this interpreter of the motives of the actors in the Ku Klux drama emphasizes how idle Negroes thought they had seen ghosts and hastily returned to their former masters asking for work.[4]

John C. Lester and Daniel L. Wilson, two of the original members of the dreaded organization, loosely assert that the Klan "swept noiselessly by in the darkness with gleaming death's-heads, skeletons, and chains" striking "terror into the hearts of the evil-doer." [5]

"Pretty soon," says Stanley F. Horn, the organization's most comprehensive historian, "the Ku-Klux were being referred to generally as the 'ghosts of the Confederate dead,' and a Negro preacher in Tennessee electrified his congregation by telling them that he had seen one of the spirits rise from the grave of a murdered Confederate soldier who was buried near his church." Not satisfied with this test of the reader's credulity, Horn relates the story of a Klansman drinking a bucket of water to the utter horror of his Negro host. " 'That's good,' he would say, smacking his lips. 'That's the first drink I've had since I was killed at the Battle of Shiloh; and you get mighty thirsty down in Hell!' " [6] Already this story had been related, with implied endorsement of its authenticity, by Walter L. Fleming, the most careful of the southern historians of Reconstruction.[7]

These and other interesting cases of blacks quailing before ghosts are based on the recollections of the white Klansmen themselves or on hearsay recorded by willing retailers of a myth too precious not to be accepted. They form a part of the specious data that fit too well in the pattern of the Negro legend to be questioned by any but the most outlandish historian. Davis gives no proof that it was the "grotesque gestures" of the first Klansmen that created "great fear" among "the superstitious" and caused them to return to their traditional tasks. Lester and Wilson do not bother to give proof that their death's-heads, skeletons, and chains were the cause of the terror they say their cavalcade of disguised horsemen inspired. Horn fails to give the direct testimony of the Negro preacher or even so much as this preacher's name for the assertion that this black believed he had seen spirits rising from the grave of a Confederate soldier. Horn's and Fleming's story about the heavy-drinking visitor from hell is obviously based on the testimony in 1871 of Joseph H. Speed of Marion, Alabama, before the committee of Congress that was then investigating the activities of the Klan. Speed's recollections have the value of being nearly contemporary, but they were based on hearsay and are not substantiated by the testimony of the heavy-drinking Klansman or of the horrified Negro.[8]

That the Ku Klux Klan fulfilled its historic mission of frightening Negroes is not to be denied; indeed Fleming cannot be successfully challenged when he asserts that the hooded order was crucial in restoring white supremacy in a number of states.[9] But there are other explanations aside from rationalizations about ghostly blandishments that can be used to explain this denouement. Let it be remembered that there were other organizations of southern white men as effective as the Klan in forcing the Negro into social and political subordination: the Pale Faces and the Knights of the White Camelia in Louisiana, the White Brotherhoods in Mississippi, and the Red Shirts in South Carolina. The members of these organizations wore no disguises and about their memory cling no ghostly legends. They accomplished their purpose by violence or threats of violence. They, the historians tell us, rode about the country brandishing weapons and frequently using them. Obviously the Negroes were frightened into submission.

Is this not also true of the Ku Klux raiders? Is it not reasonable to assume that the "superstitious" blacks were realists enough to be terrorized by the weapons hidden beneath the ghostly robes of the Klansmen rather than by ghostly decorations of which the robes were a part? That the Klansmen used the methods of violence as extensively as any of the other white terroristic organizations is attested by the number of crimes they committed. Their woundings, murders, whippings, and even rapes became so widespread that responsible leaders of white opinion became alarmed and ordered the hooded order disbanded.

The most reliable way to approach the problem of whether or not Negro victims of the Klan were frightened by its ghostly affectations is to let these victims speak for themselves. They do this to the number of 167 in confessions embodied in the thirteen volumes of testimony taken in 1871–1872 by a committee of Congress investigating the activities of the Klan. The validity of this evidence has been attacked on the ground that it came from an illiterate group who inherited mendacious habits from slavery and who were black stooges mouthing the sentiments of the white politicians who put them on the witness stand. The answer to this challenge is suggested by Homer C. Hockett, a critic of historical evidence, when he says that a contemporary account, given by a naive person, is more likely to be accurate than a partisan memoir.[10] In other words, there is reason to believe that these Negroes, because they were uneducated and unsophisticated, would not have been ashamed to confess their belief in the efficacy of ghosts as would have been people better educated and more sophisticated. They had no motive while being questioned by congressional investigators for exercising their supposed proclivity for lying. They were perhaps under obligation to their Republican mentors to assert that Democratic violence was visited upon them; but they were under obligation to no one to assert that they did not believe in ghosts. What they said or did not say on this point was seemingly spontaneous, the outpouring of their hearts. This was something of no immediate concern to the practical politicians of both parties on the investigating committee.

The congressional committee questioned the 167 subjects of Ku Klux visitations concerning their names, places of residence, political affiliations, political activities, and the ways in which witnesses said that they were approached by the Klansmen. In all cases those questioned said that they were ordered to stay out of politics and to conform in other respects to the southern white's conception of proper social behavior for Negroes. As a means of enforcing their wishes the white visitors in all cases used or threatened violence. This behavior was likely to take forms as far removed from the gentle actions of ghosts as earthly conduct can be. This meant beatings, woundings, and killings with clubs and guns wielded by men too real to have been regarded as grave-dwellers. "They said they wanted him (my horse) for a charger to ride to hell. I tell it to you just like they repeated it to me," stated Joseph Gill, a Negro of Huntsville, Alabama, in explaining how so-called ghosts addressed him in the unmistakable tones of living ex-masters of slaves. This black knew that his white neighbors were doing the talking.[11]

It is significant that in not one of the confessions of the Negro victims of the Klan did the investigating committee ask the Negroes if they believed their Klan visitors were ghosts. This is true despite the fact that the victims admitted that the visitors often called themselves ghosts and often dressed accordingly.

Why was this question not asked? It was because such an inquiry would have appeared obviously stupid when addressed to persons who were able to prove that the fear of actual physical violence was the only reason they were frightened by their Klan visitors. Had this not been true, the Democratic members of the congressional committee would not have lost the opportunity to defend the thesis that the Klan accomplished its glorious purpose by nothing less harmful than ghostly affectations. Thereby the Klan could have been freed of the stigma of violence, and the desire of the American people to laugh at the supposedly credulous Negro could have been gratified. But this golden opportunity to explain the effectiveness of the Klan in the nonviolent terms of ghostly apparitions did not come until public opinion had time to envelop the Klan in the haze of the Negro legend.

Many Ku Klux raiders claimed they came from hell or wore disguises designed to create that illusion. The fact that this contention was not believed is proved by the ability of a goodly number—36 of the 167—of the witnesses testifying before the congressional committee to identify by name one or more members of each of the attacking parties.

William Coleman, a Negro farmer of Macon, Mississippi, gave a typical demonstration of ability to identify the alleged ghosts. He was asked by the chairman of the congressional committee if those who had whipped him were disguised. After an affirmative answer, the next question was: "Did you know any of them?"

Answer: Of course I did. I ought to know them, my neighbors; and I knocked off the faces and horns fighting, and then they knocked down the one that I ran between his legs; when they struck him, his horns and everything flew about; of course I knowed him. I don't know as I would know his ashes, unless I saw him burned.

Question: Did you see that they had horns?

Answer: They had horns on them.

Question: They said they rode from Shiloh?

Answer: They said they rode from Shiloh in two hours and come to kill me.

Question: Did they say they were the spirits of the Confederate dead?

Answer: They didn't tell me nothing about spirits. They said they come from Shiloh but said nothing about spirits.[12]

Hampton Hicklin of York County, South Carolina, clearly proved that he did not believe that the disguises of his attackers were effective in creating the desired illusion:

Question: All had on disguises?

Answer: Yes, sir.

Question: What sort?

Answer: They had on these false faces and white covers.

Question: Were their heads covered?

Answer: No, sir, their heads were not covered, but their faces were. I could see their hair.[13]

One of the clearest proofs of a victim being able to identify elaborately disguised attackers was the testimony of Lucy McMillan, a forty-five-year-old widow of Spartanburg District, South Carolina. Concretely did she describe the ghostly disguises: "They had just such cloth as this white cotton frock made into old gowns; and some had black faces, and some red, and some had horns on their heads." With equal emphasis did she prove that the harm they did was that of real men: "I was afraid of them; there was so much talk of Ku-Klux drowning people, and whipping people, and killing them. My house was only a little piece from the river, so I laid out at night in the woods. The Sunday evening after Isham McCrary was whipped I went up, and a white man, John McMillan, came along and said to me, 'Lucy, you had better stay at home, for they will whip you anyhow.' I said if they have to, they might whip me in the wood, for I am afraid to stay there. Monday night they came in and burned my house down; I dodged out alongside of the road not far off." Clearly did she prove that she was able to identify her visitors: "I saw them. I was sitting right not far off, and as they came along the river I knew some of them. I knew John McMillan, and Kennedy McMillan, and Billy Bush, and John Hunter. They were all together. I was not far off, and I saw them." In explaining how she knew them, she said: "They came a-talking and I knew their voices." [14]

Although many of the Klan's victims were not able to identify their disguised assailants, they could dispel the make-believe. Joseph Gill who had been whipped by Klansmen at Briar Forks in Madison County, Alabama, in 1868 gave detailed proof of this fact. The Klansmen, he told the congressional committee, "had gowns on just like your overcoat, that came down to the toes, and some would be red and some black, like a lady's dress, only open before. The hats were made of paper, and at the top about as thick as your ankle; and down around the eyes it was bound around like horse-covers, and on the mouth there was hair of some description, I don't know what. It looked like a mustache, coming down to the breast, and you couldn't see none of the face, nor nothing; you couldn't see a thing of them. Some of them had horns about as long as my finger, and made black." But when Joseph Gill was asked to give names, he gave the following perplexed reply: "Oh, you are too hard for me, sir. I can't tell that. I couldn't see their faces to tell who they were." [15]

The secrecy on which the ghostly make-believe was based was at times carelessly betrayed. Joseph Davis, a Negro of Columbus, Mississippi, was in 1871 forced to accompany local Klansmen on several raids.[16] Christina Page of Columbia, South Carolina, was hired to make disguises for Jim Rodger and John Gist, members of the local Klan den.[17] The list of such testimonies can be extended indefinitely as a means of cutting deeply into the hypothesis of the supernatural effectiveness of the Ku Klux Klan. Occasionally blacks caused amusement by the manner in which they saw through the ghostly. "Had they disguises on?" asked the members of the congressional committee. Lydia Anderson of Macon, Mississippi, replied: "Yes, sir; they all wore dresses." [18]

Why did the Klansmen wear disguises if, as we claim, these habiliments were not effective in frightening the Negroes? An adequate explanation is that disguises were used to conceal identity in the desperate business of lawlessness and crime in which the Klansmen were engaged. These costumes afforded convenient concealment for weapons; the more elaborate the disguise the more effective was the concealment of the personal characteristics of the night riders. Cherishing the well-known inability of the white man to understand the Negro as well as the Negro understands the white man, the whites perhaps in many cases were foolishly convinced that they were deceiving their black victims. Moreover, Southerners, like other Americans, black and white, were fond of ritual and costume as a means of creating collective enthusiasm. This mummery manifests itself in numerous other secret organizations such as the Odd Fellows, the Masons, and the Knights of Columbus. Members of these organizations wear costumes as elaborate as those of the Klansmen without any desire to create the superstitious illusions. The original Klansmen of Pulaski said that their purpose in founding their organization was the delight of masquerading before their girl friends, their mothers, and each other.

Can it not be concluded that the supposed ghostly effectiveness of the Klansmen was an afterthought invented to fit into the white man's inherited stereotype of the American Negro? Such a concept survives because it fits so well into the conventional assumption that the Negro is a superstitious creature believing in ghosts in general and especially believing in them at the time the Ku Klux Klan was creating a momentous crisis in the black man's career. But the hollowness of this supposition is indicated by the fact that it was not claimed by contemporaries and not admitted by the black victims.

NOTES

This, my first graduate seminar paper, was written in the summer of 1950 at Louisiana State University for Professor Francis B. Simkins. After Doc, as his students affectionately called him, had read the paper, that wonderfully stimulating and kind man invited me to discuss it with him at a campus café. I recall that he paid for our iced tea with the most crumpled dollar bill I had ever seen, which he finally found, after a lengthy search, deep in one of his pockets. He told me that he liked my paper (its thesis probably appealed to his iconoclastic nature; the unusual always delighted him), but he explained—tactfully, to avoid hurting my feelings—that my "effort" needed revision before an editor would consider it for publication. When I expressed fear that I lacked the skill to make a significant improvement in what I had done, Doc offered to become my coauthor. I accepted, and one hot day our collaboration began. Under the shade of a great live oak (neither faculty offices nor the library were air conditioned then), Doc rewrote our piece; he scratched out my awkward and amateurish words, moved sentences about, and added colorful phrases. What he did amazed and pleased me. He turned a rough draft into an article. More important to me, he explained why he thought certain words or phrases belonged or did not belong here or there; graciously he asked—and always got—my approval of each change. It seems to me, looking back, that I learned a good bit about writing that day.

1. Thomas Dixon, Jr., *The Clansman* (New York, 1905), *The Traitor* (New York, 1907), *The Leopard's Spots* (New York, 1902), *The Fall of a Nation* (New York, 1916), and *The Black Hood* (New York, 1924).

2. Claude G. Bowers, *The Tragic Era* (Cambridge, 1929), pp. 306–7; Walter L. Fleming, ed., *Documentary History of Reconstruction* (Cleveland, 1906), 2:447–48.

3. Francis B. Simkins, "The Ku-Klux Klan in South Carolina, 1868–1871," *Journal of Negro History* 12 (1927):606–47.

4. Susan L. Davis, *Authentic History of the Ku-Klux Klan, 1865–1877* (New York, 1924), p. 8.

5. John C. Lester and Daniel L. Wilson, *Ku-Klux Klan* (Nashville, 1884), p. 98.

6. Stanley F. Horn, *Invisible Empire* (Boston, 1939), pp. 18–19.

7. Walter L. Fleming, *The Sequel of Appomattox* (New Haven, 1919), p. 254.

8. U. S. Congress, *Report of the Joint Select Committee to Inquire into the Condition of Affairs in the Late Insurrectionary States,* 42nd Cong., 2d sess. (Washington, 1872), 8:432 (hereafter cited as *Ku Klux Reports*).

9. Fleming, *Sequel of Appomattox,* pp. 291–92.

10. Homer C. Hockett, *Introduction to Research in American History* (New York, 1948), p. 91.

11. *Ku Klux Reports,* 9:813.

12. *Ibid.,* 11:483–84.

13. *Ibid.,* 5:1567.

14. *Ibid.,* 4:604–5.

15. *Ibid.,* 9:813–14.

16. *Ibid.,* 12:810.

17. *Ibid.,* 4:1142.

18. *Ibid.,* 11:510.

CHAPTER X

The Meaning of Emancipation

No period of American history was more promising or more disillu-
sioning to the Negro than the last forty years of the nineteenth century.
In 1860, nearly 90 percent of America's four and a half million Negroes were slaves. Of those who were free the vast majority were sec-
ond-class citizens, even in the North. Usually only the most menial jobs
were open to them. They were segregated; they were forbidden to migrate from state to state. Hardly any of them could vote. They were
barred from jury duty and from the witness stand. The federal government seemed oblivious to their condition. As a free Negro remarked:
"Under the Constitution and Government of the United States, the colored people are nothing and can be nothing but an alien, disfranchised
and degraded class." In 1854, Abraham Lincoln admitted that he objected to social and political equality for Negores. "My own feelings
will not admit of this," he said, "and if mine would, we well know that
those of the great mass of white people will not."

During the Civil War period, this prejudice against Negroes appeared
to change. By 1870, every black had been emancipated and given full
citizenship. Not only could he travel freely about the country; he could
vote and hold public office. No state or local government post in the
South was beyond his grasp. For forty-three days, Louisiana had a
black governor; in other states, Negroes served as lieutenant governors,
supreme court justices, secretaries of state, superintendents of public education, legislators, treasurers, sheriffs, and city councilmen. Between

1869 and 1877, sixteen Negroes sat in the Congress of the United States. Such a change in the Negro's status suggests that white Americans were adopting the view expressed by Senator Charles Sumner in 1866—that a "man, of whatever country or race, whether browned by equatorial sun or blanched by northern cold, is with you a child of the Heavenly Father, and equal with you in all the rights of Human Nature."

But Sumner's hopes were premature. By the beginning of the twentieth century, colorblind democracy was a mockery in America. The Negro was one of the most discriminated-against men in all Christendom. Systematically, he had been stripped of nearly all his rights; even his freedom had been circumscribed. He had been relegated to a subservient position in society, disfranchised throughout most of the South, and deserted by both the federal government and the United States Supreme Court. He was being lynched, vilified, and exploited; he was jim-crowed nearly everywhere.

What happened to the Negro between 1860 and 1900 is clear; why it happened is often misunderstood. It seems paradoxical that a nation so apparently committed to liberty and democracy would give the Negro a large measure of equality and then take it from him. The reason is rather simple, but it can be explained best by reviewing some post–Civil War history.

Most Negroes were unprepared for freedom in 1865. Few of them understood its meaning. "One say dis, an' one say dat, an' we don't know," an old Negro told a reporter. "After freedom a heap of people . . . went roaming round like wild, hunting cities," recalled a former slave. Many Negroes flocked to military camps seeking aid. Some freedmen actually refused to be free. They were accustomed to slavery; they were frightened and uncertain about a new way of life. "Freedom wasn't no different," said John McCoy. "I works for Marse John just the same for a long time. He say one morning, 'John, you can go out in the field iffen you wants to or you can get out iffen you wants to, cause the government say you is free. If you wants to work I'll feed you and give you clothes but can't pay you no money. I ain't got none.' Humph, I didn't know nothing what money was, nohow, but I knows I'll get plenty . . . to eat, so I stays till Old Marse die and Old Miss git shut of the place." Adeline White remembered that when "Master called us up and told us we was free, some rejoiced so they shouted, but some didn't, they was sorry. . . . I wouldn't leave my white folks. . . . I worked on for them as long as I was able to work and always felt like I belonged to 'em, and, you know, after all this long time, I feel like I am theirs."

Soon many Negroes discovered that their freedom was limited. The government "left the freedman in a [bad] condition," said the distinguished Negro leader Frederick Douglass. "It felt that it had done enough for him. It had made him free, and henceforth he must make his own way in the world. . . . He was free from the individual master, but the slave of society. He had neither money, property, nor friends. He was free from the old plantation, but he had nothing but the dusty road under his feet. . . . He was . . . turned loose, naked, hungry, and destitute to the open sky."

In August 1865, a group of disgruntled freedmen resolved by a vote of 700 to 200 that in three months of freedom they "had discovered that the prejudices of color were by no means confined to the people of the South, but . . . that it was stronger and more marked against them in the strangers from the North." They also agreed "that negroes no more than white men, can live without work, or be comfortable without homes . . . , and that . . . their true happiness and well-being required them to return to the homes which they had abandoned in a moment of excitement, and to go to work again under their old masters."

Only the exceptional freedman escaped economic bondage. Most Negroes returned to work under their old master or some new master. If the freedman could have elected his occupation, he probably would have been a planter or a businessman. Though some of the most economically successful freedmen were artisans, most blacks rejected the mechanical trades. In 1890, less than 5 percent of all Negroes were employed in the trades. This was a natural reaction against the manual labor they had performed as slaves. Like the whites they aped in dress and manners, Negroes sought high-status employment. Their prejudices, together with those of the whites, helped fix the freedman's status. Moreover, Negroes who tried to start a business were handicapped by inexperience and inadequate capital. A Freedmen's Bureau official recounted the failure of a mercantile partnership. In 1866, four South Carolina Negroes established a store. It "was a single room in a deserted hotel, and the entire stock in trade might have been worth forty dollars. On this chance of business four families proposed to live. By the time the United States license of twenty dollars, the town license of five dollars, and certain other opening expenses had been paid, the liabilities of the firm were nearly sufficient to cover its assets." Within three weeks, two of the partners quit the business, and two others were taken in. Being ignorant of the revenue law, the freedmen formed a new partnership and were taxed for a new license. This mistake was disastrous; the business dissolved. Apparently, only one of the partners made any money from the enterprise. He sold some borrowed equipment used to start the store and absconded with the cash.

Most freedmen remained in the South, working as field laborers or sharecroppers. Usually they received only a subsistence income. Over 82 percent of all southern Negroes lived in rural areas in 1900, yet only 25 percent of these owned their own farms. At the same time, 63 percent of all southern white farmers owned their land. If a Negro managed to acquire a farm, it seldom exceeded forty acres, and he had to scratch hard to survive. He might own a cow, a few pigs, and some chickens; his farm equipment probably consisted of a ramshackle wagon, a plow, a few hoes, an ax or two, and some shovels. Very likely, his home was an unpainted, box-shaped structure of boards nailed vertically to a frame and covered with clapboards.

If not a farmer, the freedman probably was a servant. Domestic service, like agriculture, required limited skills; also, it fitted into the white man's conception of a Negro's occupation. Nearly a third of all Negroes were domestic servants in 1890.

Because the freedman was poor, ignorant, and unsophisticated, white men used him. He became their tool. When they needed his support, they wooed him; when they did not, they ignored him. Republicans as well as Democrats, Northerners as well as Southerners, viewed the Negro through self-interested eyes. How he could help them was far more important than how they could help him.

In 1865, Republicans vacillated on the question of Negro suffrage. A few men defended the justice of giving the black man the ballot. Other men, like George Templeton Strong, feared that "the average field hand would use political power as intelligently as would the mule he drives." A New York editor asked: "Are we expected in the light of the intelligence of the century, to believe that any body of men, be they the Congress of the United States or a body of mythological gods, can, by a simple legislative feat, lift the negro from barbarism to the summit of civilization?"

The answer to this question was that Republicans believed they could stay in power only by enfranchising and controlling the freedmen. "We need their aid," insisted a Boston editor. "We cannot expect to carry the country through the difficulties of the next twenty years without the effective assistance of Southern colored men."

Expediency, more than morality, dictated Republican policy toward the Negro. "I have never insisted," said Congressman Thaddeus Stevens, "that the franchise should be unjustly regulated so as to secure a Republican ascendancy but I have insisted and do insist that there can be no unjust regulation of that franchise which will give to any other party the power of governing." Denouncing the Democrats as the immigrant's party, Senator Ben Wade told Ohioans that Negroes were better qualified to vote than Irishmen. "I think I could easily convince any man," added Elizur Wright, "that it will probably make a difference of at least $1,000,000,000 in the . . . national debt, whether we reconstruct on the basis of loyal . . . black votes, or on white votes exclusively. . . . I am not disputing about tastes. A negro's ballot may be more vulgar than his bullet [but] . . . the question . . . is how . . . to protect my property from taxation; and I am sure . . . the victories of 1865 [will be] thrown away . . . if . . . the government allows 4,000,000 of black population to continue disfranchised."

By 1868 the Republicans had made southern Negroes voters. At first, they voted Republican almost without exception. The chief persuasive agency was the Union League. In some southern states, nearly every Negro was a member, and every member was oath-bound to vote Republican. "That's the party of my color," said a freedman. In Mississippi the Republicans could count on 90 percent of the Negro vote.

Occasionally, the vote was used for the Negro's benefit; often, it was not. Fraud and corruption characterized many of the South's Republican regimes. One Republican governor, whose annual salary was $8,000, made over $100,000 during his first year in office. Another governor received over $40,000 in bribes. A free restaurant for state legislators cost South Carolina taxpayers $125,000. Over $300,000 was spent on legislative supplies and incidentals in one session.

Even when the freedman held high office, he seldom profited from the corruption around him. He was more the dupe than the scoundrel. Thousands of Negroes voted without knowing the names of the candidates. Enterprising Republicans sold Alabama Negroes pictures of General Grant for $2.00 each, and told them federal troops were in the South to see that all Negroes voted for him. In Florida a white Republican, who campaigned for office by kissing Negro babies, told the voters that "Jesus Christ was a Republican."

Not all Negroes were fooled. "What we call a carpet-bagger is a man who comes here . . . to occupy public position . . . and then leaves the state when he has made his money," said a Louisiana Negro. "They will associate with the negro, because they want to use him and get his vote;

but as soon as they get his vote they don't care about him. They want to make money out of him and get a position."

The Republicans also followed a policy of expediency in the North. Until the adoption of the Fifteenth Amendment in 1870, only six northern states allowed the Negro to vote. In fact, the Fifteenth Amendment was intended to ensure Republican political control in the South rather than to enfranchise the northern Negro. He was given a few political sops, but Republicans generally held the color line. In 1871 a white mob killed a Negro school principal in a Philadelphia election riot. "We have always known that there was a sentiment in the North strongly opposed to Negro suffrage," complained a black journalist. "This has never been a secret."

Of course, Republicans had no patent on expediency. Probably most white Southerners agreed with the South Carolinian who said: "For one I will never consent that when I approach the ballot-box a son of Africa shall stand by my side as my equal." But southern Democrats, like Republicans, needed the Negro's vote.

The freedman's low economic position made him particularly susceptible to Democratic persuasion. President Andrew Johnson had predicted in 1865 that former slaveowners eventually would control the freedman's ballot. In 1868 a Georgia Republican wrote the national party secretary: "The Negroes are too dependent upon their employers to be counted upon with certainty. They are without property, and cannot sustain themselves . . . without being fed by their Masters; they are without education or sufficient intelligence to appreciate the power the Ballot gives them, add to which a system of intimidation persistently practiced by the Rebels . . . , and you have a mass of poverty, ignorance, stupidity, and superstition under the influence of fears both real and imaginary, to organize and control, upon whom little reliance can be placed."

Conservative white Southerners gradually drove a wedge between the Negro and the Republican party. In March 1867, General Wade Hampton, formerly one of the South's wealthiest men, addressed a crowd of Negroes celebrating their enfranchisement at Columbia, South Carolina. Insisting that former slaveowners were the freedmen's best friends, Hampton promised to respect the Negro's right to vote. He explained his motives in a private letter: "but one hope is left to us and that is to direct the Negro vote. . . . If we cannot direct the wave it will overwhelm us. Now how shall we do this? Simply by making the Negro a Southern man, ... a Democrat."

The Hampton plan was adopted throughout the South. In April 1867 a group of white Alabamians passed the following resolution: "We find nothing in the changed political condition of the white and black races in the South that ought to disturb the harmonious relations between them; that we are ready to accord to the latter every right and privilege to which they are entitled under the laws of the land; that we sincerely desire their prosperity and their improvement . . . ; that we are their friends, both from gratitude for their fidelity in the past . . . and because our interests in the future are inseparably connected with their well-being." Where persuasion failed, pragmatic Democrats used violence, fraud, and intimidation to capture the Negro vote and to destroy the Republican regimes.

By 1877 the conservatives had won. All attempts to keep the southern Negro voting Republican had been abandoned. Northerners had discovered that former Confederates would defend Yankee economic interests as vigorously as they had attacked Yankee armies. Besides, conservative white Southerners had the Negro's vote in their pocket. They did not eliminate the Negro from public life; they merely controlled and manipulated him.

The Negro reemerged as an important political figure in the South during the Populist period. At first, small farmers and their friends tried to win him away from the conservative Democrats. Needing the Negro's support, the Populists preached class unity. They pointed out how farmers of both races had been hurt by depressions, mortgage foreclosures, high taxes, excessive freight rates, and the increased cost of farm machinery. Leaders like Tom Watson defended Negro speakers, and encouraged black and white farmers to unite against concentrated wealth and conservative politics. The Democrats reacted with violence and intimidation. Race riots developed, and more than a dozen Negro Populists were murdered. While posing as defenders of white supremacy, the Democrats used Negro votes to beat the Populists. In the election of 1892, Populists carried every Alabama county except those twelve where Negroes constituted more than two thirds of the population. But the Democrats won the election by getting overwhelming majorities in the twelve Black Belt counties. In states where the elections were in doubt, the Democrats imported Negro voters. The Democratic vote in one Louisiana parish exceeded the total population of the parish.

The fury of the agrarian revolt convinced both Populists and Democrats that Negro voters were dangerous. No longer could they be allowed to hold the balance of political power; they must be deprived of the ballot. Mississippi led the way in 1890. Other states followed; and by the end of the nineteenth century, almost all southern Negroes had been disfranchised and barred from public office. The number of Negro legislators in South Carolina declined from eight in 1886 to none in 1900.

Anti-Negroism became a basic plank in every southern politician's platform. Mississippi's "Great White Chief," James K. Vardaman, always dressed in white and rode about the state in a wagon drawn by white oxen. He symbolized white supremacy. A contemporary said Vardaman "stood for the poor white against the Negro—those were his qualifications as a stateman." Tom Watson, formerly a defender of Negroes, made his peace with the Georgia Democrats and turned Negrobaiter. Senator Benjamin R. Tillman, the hero of South Carolina's "wool hat" and "one-gallus" boys, became the most famous anti-Negro orator of his time. In 1900, he boasted in the United States Senate: "We took the government away [from the Negro]. . . . We stuffed ballot boxes. We shot them. We are not ashamed of it." Tillman believed that dropping the caste barrier would cause the disappearance of the Caucasian, the "highest and noblest of the five races," in an orgy of miscegenation. He considered racial amalgamation the greatest of social crimes. What the Negro really wanted, Tillman insisted, was to kill all white men, marry white women, and use white children as servants. He admitted that Negroes were not baboons, but he claimed some of them were "so near akin to the monkey that scientists are yet looking for the missing link."

By 1900 there was ample proof that most Northerners had deserted the Negro. Large audiences applauded Tillman everywhere he spoke in the North. In 1886 a group of New England Negroes declared: "the colored citizen is discriminated against in so many depressing and injurious manners not withstanding the letter of the law. . . . No distinction is made as to intelligence, character, deportment or means among the colored people." In 1889 editor Henry W. Grady charged that in the North six times as many blacks as whites were in jail (1 of every 466 Negroes was behind bars); in the South only four times as many blacks as whites were in prison (1 of every 1,865 Negroes). "If prejudice wrongs [the Negro] in Southern courts," said Grady, "the record shows it to be deeper in Northern courts." Sophisticated Americans interpreted Darwin's theories as scientific justification for white supremacy. Moreover, the imperialism of the 1890s had brought over eight million additional "colored" people under American control. This "varied assortment of inferior races," said a northern journal, "of course, could not be allowed to vote." The Republican party no longer sought black voters. It was unnecessary; no matter what Republicans did, they could count on the Negro's vote. Northern Negroes had no other political home. In 1885 a Negro editor lamented: "No one black man in New York State enjoys the respect or confidence of the Republican politicians. . . . And this may apply to the colored leaders throughout the country in their relations to the politicians of the National Republican party."

Frustration drove Negroes in various directions. Isaiah T. Montgomery, a black Republican delegate to the Mississippi constitutional convention of 1890, favored the disfranchisement of over 123,000 Negroes. He thought such action would ease racial tension and improve state government. A young black intellectual, W. E. Burghardt DuBois, turned to historical scholarship. His purpose was to contribute "to the scientific study of slavery and the American Negro." In 1896, he published the first of his many monographs. T. Thomas Fortune, an editor, attempted to organize a black national federation (the Afro-American National League) in 1887. He hoped to unite Negroes outside the existing political parties and to use their strength to improve their status. But the Negro was unprepared educationally or financially to follow Fortune's program. Moreover, Fortune weakened his plan by suggesting that Negroes unite with poor whites. He failed to realize that race lines were more important than class lines to most white Americans.

Nineteenth-century Americans were not colorblind enough to accept racial equality. From 1860 to 1900, most Negro leaders based their plea for civil rights upon the theory of human equality expressed in the Declaration of Independence. Their argument was logical, but essentially naive. Because most Americans gave lip service to the Declaration of Independence, Negroes made the mistake of assuming that white Americans meant what they said. They did not. Most Negroes misjudged the amount of democratic hypocrisy in America. They did not understand that white Americans who believed in equality also believed that some men were more equal than others.

Only one of the many nineteenth-century plans to improve the Negro's status seemed completely realistic. It was proposed by Booker T. Washington, the most famous Negro of his time. Instead of demanding social and political equality, he advised Negroes to strive for economic independence. "I plead for industrial education and development for the

Negro not because I want to cramp him," said Washington, "but because I want to free him. I want to see him enter the all-powerful business and commercial world." Some of his ideas were outmoded—artisanship and small farming were no longer sure ways to economic independence in an industrial age—but Washington understood the whites better than most blacks did. He recognized that white opposition could doom any program for the Negro's improvement. Washington's proposal was ingeniously subtle. It appeared moderate enough for whites, North and South, to applaud. Yet, actually, it was revolutionary in a thoroughly American and materialistic way. Washington knew that Americans measured progress in dollars. He was aware that greenbacks could not erase the color line, but he believed they could shade it. He realized that if racial prejudice ever weakened, rich blacks had a better chance than poor blacks of being accepted as equals by white Americans.

CHAPTER XI

Rustic Radicalism

In November 1912, 1 of every 14 Louisiana voters cast a ballot for a party supposedly dedicated to destroying the southern way of life. Despite the fact that a native Southerner, Woodrow Wilson, was the presidential candidate of the Democratic party, 5,249 Louisianians voted for Eugene V. Debs, the Socialist candidate. Debs ran ahead of William H. Taft, the Republican candidate, by nearly 1,500 votes.[1] Louisiana ranked nineteenth in the nation in Socialist votes and gave Debs a higher percentage of votes than his home state of Indiana. At no other time in the history of the state was such a sizable Socialist vote polled.[2] Clearly, such a vote appears strange in Louisiana and suggests several questions. First of all, who were these supporters of Debs? In what sections of the state did they live? What did they do for a living? And, most important of all, why were they voting for the Socialist party?

A few of Louisiana's geographic characteristics must be kept in mind when considering the Socialist vote. Lying entirely within the Gulf Coastal Plain and shaped like a boot, Louisiana has both very rich and very poor soil. Along the banks of the several rivers that flow through the state is found the alluvial plain, the most fertile soil in Louisiana. The widest strip of alluvial soil is, of course, along the Mississippi River. Entering from opposite directions at the northern top of the boot, the Red and Mississippi rivers join about halfway down the state and consequently extend the alluvial plain over a greater area in the southern part of Louisiana. Prairies and marshes are also found in the southern part of the state. The more elevated areas east and west of the alluvial plain are known as the uplands and consist of three main divisions: the uplands of the Florida parishes, north of Lake Pontchartrain

and east of the Mississippi; the west Louisiana uplands, west of the Red
and Calcasieu rivers; and the north Louisiana uplands, a wedge-shaped
area lying roughly between the Red and Ouachita rivers. Rolling hill
country, thick with pine forests, characterizes the upland regions, where
the land is far inferior to the rich soil of the alluvial plain.[3]

It was in these upland areas that the Socialist voters lived; nearly 70
percent of the Socialist vote came from hill parishes in 1912.[4] Vernon
Parish, in the heart of the yellow pine region, gave Debs 33.8 percent
of its total vote and nearly elected a Socialist school board.[5] In Winn
Parish 35.4 percent of the voters went for Debs, and the Socialists
elected a school board member and a police juror, as well as the town
of Winnfield's entire slate of municipal officials.[6] In Grant Parish 29
percent of the vote was polled by the Socialist; La Salle, Caldwell, West
Carroll, Bienville, Natchitoches, Red River, Franklin, and Calcasieu
parishes all contributed 14 percent or more of their vote to Debs.[7]

The Socialists made their poorest showing in the southern part of the
state and in the alluvial parishes. Debs did not receive a single vote in
the parishes of Cameron, Madison, Tensas, West Baton Rouge, and
West Feliciana, and he received less than 2 percent of the total vote in
Saint Mary, Saint Bernard, Saint James, Saint Helena, East Carroll,
Pointe Coupee, Plaquemines, LaFourche, East Feliciana, Iberville, and
Assumption parishes.[8] Not even in New Orleans did the radicals do
well. Debs received only 2.1 percent of the total vote, and the Socialist
candidate for mayor, George F. Weller, polled only 712 votes, losing to
the Democrat Martin Behrman by over 26,000 votes.[9] The Socialist
candidates for the New Orleans commission council were defeated by
even greater majorities than Weller.[10]

None of the three Socialists who ran for Congress was elected. But in
the upland Eighth District J. R. Jones, a veteran Socialist campaigner,
polled 1,734 votes; his Democratic opponent, J. B. Aswell, got 6,033.[11]

Actually, the Socialist strength was located in almost exactly the
same parishes as was the Populist strength in the 1890s.[12] It was in
Winn Parish that the Louisiana People's party was organized and had
its greatest strength;[13] Vernon, Bienville, Grant, Caldwell, Natchitoches,
Red River, and Calcasieu parishes were also strongholds of populism.[14]
But even more significant is the fact that the Populists and the Socialists
both showed weakness in the same parishes. Tensas, Saint Bernard,
Saint James, Saint Mary, Plaquemines, Assumption, Pointe Coupee,
East Feliciana, and Iberville parishes all contributed but few votes to
the Populists.[15] As was the case with socialism, "Populism never gained

Some Comparisons between Strong and Weak
Populist-Socialist Areas

	Percent of farms over 1,000 acres	Percent of population Catholic	Average value of farm property	Percent of population Negro	Percent of voting age illiterate		Percent voting	
					White	Total	Populist 1892	Socialist 1912
Upland parishes								
Vernon	0.1	0.0	$ 1,524	21.4	7.9	15.1	53.2	33.8
Winn	0.2	0.2	1,253	21.4	9.7	17.3	76.6	35.4
Grant	0.2	0.8	1,713	30.5	11.0	23.4	42.4	29.0
Caldwell	0.6	0.0	1,685	40.3	6.3	17.7	31.7	20.7
Bienville	0.1	0.0	1,381	43.5	4.1	22.8	26.8	14.0
Alluvial parishes								
Tensas	1.8	1.3	2,073	91.5	1.5	59.2	0.0	0.0
St. James	5.0	53.5	15,530	57.2	21.3	40.4	0.0	1.0
St. Charles	5.3	37.4	6,910	60.0	25.7	43.5	0.0	7.6
St. Bernard	3.4	26.1	8,586	46.5	28.4	38.7	0.0	0.4
Plaquemines	3.2	39.1	6,052	54.7	20.5	39.5	0.0	1.1

much of a foothold in the cotton parishes of the delta, or in the sugar parishes."[16]

The Populist-Socialist strongholds, in comparison with the parishes where the Populist-Socialist vote was the lowest, had: (1) a smaller percentage of farms over one thousand acres and consequently fewer powerful landowners; (2) fewer Catholics (in some parishes there were none); (3) a smaller percentage of Negro population; (4) less illiteracy; and (5) lower value of farm property.[17]

Because the Populists' and the Socialists' strength and weakness are found in virtually the same areas, it appears possible that socialism in Louisiana was merely a continuation of the Populist movement that largely died in 1900 [18] and that the Socialist voters of 1912 were generally the same men who voted the Populist ticket in 1892 and 1900. With a few important exceptions, this seems to be true. To be sure, the strength of populism and socialism came from rural people, although each appealed to both farmer and industrial laborer alike.[19] But the Socialists—in Louisiana, at least—were neither led nor supported by successful farmers or planters (men of substantial landed property) as the Populists were,[20] and the appeal of Socialists to the skilled workers of the American Federation of Labor went unheeded.[21] One will look in vain to find a man of the standing of Populist Donelson Caffery, Jr., among the Louisiana Socialists. It is also doubtful that the Socialists would have formed a fusion with the Republican party in Louisiana as the Populists did before they joined the Democrats in 1896.[22]

After the Populist party broke on the silver issue in 1896 and ceased to exist in Louisiana after 1900, the only choice its rural supporters seemed to have was to follow their planter leaders back into either the Democratic or Republican parties. This, however, offered no relief.[23] Conservative governors and legislators controlled by businessmen and lumber barons continued to rule the state.[24] Had there been a Jeff Davis, Tillman, or Vardaman in Louisiana in the first two decades of the twentieth century the discontented might have turned to him. But no spellbinding demagogue promising reforms appeared; twenty-eight years elapsed between the death of the Louisiana People's party and the election of a strong man. The discontented farmers did not wait. Without a leader and with their previous protest movement dead, some turned to socialism.[25]

In addition to this core of former Populist farmers there was another group that followed the Socialist banner in Louisiana—the unskilled lumber workers, unknown as followers of populism. There was also a

small body of strictly Marxian Socialists (found almost entirely in New
Orleans) who originally controlled the party in Louisiana, but they were
more devoted to discussion than to action and by 1912 the farmers and
lumber workers had taken over the party.[26] What success the Socialists
had in Louisiana resulted from the temporary alliance between the oppressed farmers and the lumber workers.[27]

The oppressed farmers were the first important Socialist converts, but
their support was not gained immediately. In fact, the first evidence of
socialism in Louisiana—the 995 votes cast for Debs in 1904—showed
the party to be strongest in the southern and alluvial parishes; Orleans
Parish alone contributed 48.2 percent of the total state Debs vote.[28]

The New Orleans Socialists lacked unity and were soon hopelessly
divided. By 1906 the more radical element among the New Orleans Socialists championed the cause of the Industrial Workers of the World
—a union that appealed to the unskilled worker and advocated direct
economic action in preference to political action.[29] Contemptuous of the
milder members of the party, whom they called Yellows and said were
"ballot-happy," the IWW supporters (they were known as Reds) invited Daniel De Leon, the leader of the Socialist Labor party and a
member of the IWW, to speak in New Orleans under the auspices of
the Socialist local. The Yellows were enraged and cancelled De Leon's
invitation. In the schism that followed the Reds quit the party to devote
their time to IWW activities, leaving the Yellows in control of the New
Orleans local.[30]

Despite the setback in New Orleans, Socialist gains in the November
election of 1908 were surprising. Besides contributing 2,538 ballots to
Debs's total, Socialists cast many votes for minor offices. The Socialist
strength, however, was shifting away from New Orleans and southern
Louisiana. The hill parishes of the northcentral and western parts of
the state were rapidly becoming the stronghold of socialism in Louisiana.[31]

As the movement spread into the uplands it began to assume many of
the social aspects of populism. "Feeling it our duty to do something for
the cause, the young people . . . have given a box supper . . . and
made $12.50," wrote two girls from Bentley, Louisiana. Although they
confessed that "none of us are members of the Socialist party . . . we
believe and are doing all we can to keep the good work going on." [32]
Encampments were numerous—some lasting for over a week at a time
—and there was much enthusiasm. "Comrades at Verda, Lofton and
Georgetown, Louisiana, will build brush arbors and have a speaker

every week during the summer," it was reported. In one period of three months twenty locals, with a total membership of 361, were organized. Women took an active part and one, a Miss Nellie Zey, was added to the list of Socialist speakers.[33]

An ever-increasing mass of Socialist literature aided the work of the organizers. Books, pamphlets, magazines, and newspapers expounding the virtues of the coming millennium were widely distributed. The most often read publications, according to contemporary observers, were the *Appeal to Reason,* the *National Rip-Saw,* and the *International Socialist Review.*[34] Two Socialist journals were published in Louisiana: *The Forum* was started at Dodson, Winn Parish, in 1909, and the *Toiler* was begun at Leesville in Vernon Parish at about the same time.[35]

While the Yellows continued to dominate the New Orleans branch of the party and to advocate only political action, the upland Socialists, who were gradually taking over the party outside New Orleans, tended to blend the radicalism of the Reds with their ruralism—sometimes advocating direct economic action, sometimes advocating political action as well.[36] By 1910 J. W. Barnes, Louisiana's representative at the Socialist Congress in Chicago, reflected the Reds' influence by concluding that industrial unionism "is the only thing that will solve the race problem of the South." [37] In November J. R. Jones, a Red, challenged Congressman A. P. Pujo for his seat, but only in the upland and timber areas of the Seventh District did Jones show strength, receiving but 706 votes to his opponent's 7,393. Other Socialist candidates in the Fourth and Fifth Congressional Districts did even worse, getting votes only in upland and lumbering parishes.[38] When Debs stopped in Louisiana in 1911 on his nationwide speaking tour, 3,500 people heard him in New Orleans—even the Reds turned out, although they took no part in the program.[39]

The dissension between the rural Reds and the Yellows was revealed in the April 1912 election. The Socialist ticket did not receive a single vote in New Orleans, even though the city had the largest Socialist local in the state. Being predominantly Yellows, the New Orleans Socialists refused to support the Red ticket headed by the candidate for governor, J. R. Jones, a card-carrying member of the IWW. (At this time the Reds in New Orleans were having nothing to do with political action.) In the entire state Jones received only 984 votes. L. E. Hall, the Democrat, got 50,581, and even the Republican candidate got five times as many votes as did the Socialist. Only in Vernon and Winn parishes did Jones demonstrate strength.[40] For the state legislature, Socialist candidate J. J. Cryer of Vernon Parish was defeated 1,147 to 369, and in

Winn Parish H. T. Nichols, another Socialist, lost 880 to 385 for the same office.[41]

The upland farmers were largely responsible for what votes the Socialists received in April; indeed, the New Orleans Yellows had deserted the state party, and as yet the lumber workers had not contributed in any sizable degree to the Socialist vote.[42]

When, in May 1912, the Socialist national convention met to choose a candidate for president, there was much tension among the delegates. The sharp dissension between Reds and Yellows that had been mounting throughout the country since the formation of the IWW now threatened to divide the party just as it had in Louisiana. On the fifth day, the report of the Committee on Labor Organizations and their relations to the Socialist party was read before the convention. "Astonishment showed on every face and then followed a tumultuous yell as the convention woke up to the fact that a bitter fight had been diverted," for the report proved to be a compromise. The committee suggested that "all labor organizations . . . throw their doors wide open to the workers" and emphasized the "vital importance of the task of organizing the unorganized, especially the immigrants and the unskilled laborers." Tom Hickey, a Red from Texas, got the floor and declared that "the impossible has happened. . . . the entire labor movement, economic and political, will stand together unified." [43]

The Yellows, however, were not entirely satisfied. When the Constitutional Committee read the Socialist platform a Yellow moved that Section Six be amended to read: "Any member of the party who opposes political action or advocates sabotage or other methods of violence . . . shall be expelled from the party." This was an open attack upon the IWW policy of direct economic action and a fight was on. For hours the amendment was debated—sometimes with logic and calm but mostly with passion and malice. At last, Victor L. Berger, a Yellow, got the floor and announced: "We have a number of men who use our political organization . . . as a cloak for what they call direct action, for I.W.W.-ism, sabotage and syndicalism." Expressing his opposition to "the bomb, the dagger and every other form of violence," Berger suggested that those who sang " 'Hallelujah, I'm a Bum' . . . start a 'Bum' Organization of their own. . . . I am ready to split right here." The split, however, did not occur. In the roll call that followed, Louisiana's lone delegate to the convention, J. R. Jones, cast his vote (along with the other Reds) against inserting the word *sabotage,* but the amendment carried.[44]

The final order of business was the nomination for president. The

Reds for the most part backed Debs, and, though the Yellows tried hard to prevent it, he was nominated.[45]

Despite their bitterness over the sabotage clause, the Reds were delighted that the Socialist party had officially recognized labor organizations. They could now, as their leader Big Bill Haywood remarked, "go to the working class . . . to the black men . . . to the disfranchised white men . . . the striking lumber workers . . . and carry them the message of Socialism . . . from the Socialist platform." There was still some unity within the party; indeed, Haywood believed the recognition of labor organizations to be "the greatest step that has been taken by the Socialist party . . . it unites every worker." [46] But would this unity withstand a practical test? Could the lumber workers in Louisiana be allied with the Socialists?

To some extent, the Louisiana lumber workers were temporarily allied with the Socialists. But the alliance was uncertain—the policy of the lumber operators and the position of the workers did much to prevent unity. The congressional policy of opening to speculators the public lands in the southern states during the Redeemer period resulted in wholesale exploitation of natural resources; not the least ravaged were the vast forests of Louisiana.[47] Along with the immense power and exhaustive methods of these exploiters came the wretched existence of the lumber workers.

Although lumbering in the South was not so important a source of employment as agriculture, in many states such as Louisiana, where 60 percent of all industrial wage-earners were lumbermen,[48] it was the only important industry. Because the lumber industry offered a source of income—when sometimes the farms did not—there was often a shifting back and forth between workers on the farms and workers in the forests or sawmills.[49] Indeed, lumber workers might be sons or relatives of farm owners or even the hard-pressed farm owner himself who was forced to supplement his income by working in the lumber industry.[50] There were, however, many lumber workers who knew no other occupation and who constantly moved about, living in lumber camps and having little contact with the farms.

Living conditions at the lumber camps were described by union agitators as deplorable.[51] Even an official spokesman for the lumber operators admitted: "It is the rule, not the exception, to employ practically anyone who applies for work. . . . the working force was usually honeycombed with loafers, floaters, worthless relatives, favorites, diseased men, the wornout and decrepit, inexperienced men in advanced age, etc." [52]

The workers, it was charged, were not paid in cash, but in scrip negotiable only at the company store. Here prices were from 20 to 50 percent higher than at independent stores, sometimes from 77 to 100 percent above wholesale cost, according to a contemporary worker.[53] It was alleged that certain mill owners deliberately cultivated the "narcotic drug habit among the workers," selling cocaine, morphine, and heroin at the company store. "These workers," stated one observer, "moved about from camp to camp" but, since only the mill owners would supply them with drugs, "never got away from the district." [54]

Claims were also made that disease and vice flourished in the lumber camps. Bill Haywood, after visiting Louisiana, wrote that "the companies had women who lived in the camps. . . . the men moved from camp to camp, staying perhaps a few months, perhaps a couple of years, but the women stayed in the shacks and took the newcomers as husbands for the duration of their stay in that camp." [55]

Living conditions, pay, and hours were the greatest causes of complaint, but rarely, if ever, were these grievances openly expressed. Minor strikes and unorganized walkouts, lasting only a few hours or a few days, were the only overt expressions of discontent before union activity began. On June 14, 1902, six hundred employees of the Ruddock and Louisiana Cypress Saw Mill Company in Calcasieu Parish demanded a reduction of the working day from eleven to ten hours. When the company refused, the mill hands united and walked out. A few days later the workers of the Lutcher Sawmill Company, about forty miles north of New Orleans, presented the same demands and got the same answer.[56] Both companies, however, gave in five days later and the laborers went back to work.[57]

Again in 1907 there was a mild strike in western Louisiana and eastern Texas, centering around Lake Charles, but the manifestation of discontent lacked leadership and organization—despite the contention that it was IWW inspired.[58] The strike accomplished nothing,[59] and at this time the Southern Lumber Operators Association was formed.[60] This organization was destined to deal the workers' union heavy blows in the years to follow.

The union movement began in earnest in 1910 when Arthur Lee Emerson formed the Brotherhood of Timber Workers.[61] Emerson and a fellow organizer, Jay Smith, traveled through the timber region, securing a few days' work in each camp, enlisting black as well as white members. Though a native of Tennessee,[62] Emerson had made trips to the west coast where, working as a lumberjack, he perceived the difference in the wage scale and living standard of the organized workers of the West and the unorganized laborers of the South. Immediately upon his return to Louisiana he began to organize the workers, and—according to a contemporary account—the union soon grew to thirty thousand members.[63]

What one observer called the Louisiana Lumber War began on May 17, 1911, when the lumber operators decided they could force the dissolution of the union by cutting down mill operations to four days a week.[64] Eleven Louisiana mills employing three thousand men were closed immediately. At Carson, states a biased account, the mills were shut down and some four hundred families were ordered to vacate the company houses.[65] At all mills, members of the union were discharged as fast as they were discovered.[66]

Ironclad oaths and "yellow dog" contracts were a prerequisite to employment everywhere.[67] These highhanded tactics of the lumber operators were not popular even with the nonunion men, and many workers refused to sign. One rustic Louisianian said in regard to signing the oath, "only a low-life lickskillet would do such a thing. . . . I would live on wild plants that grow in the hills before I would sign." [68]

The attempt to crush the union backfired on the operators, for the Brotherhood of Timber Workers emerged from the first struggle of the lumber war considerably strengthened. The union men mapped out a series of demands that included a minimum wage of two dollars for a ten-hour day; bimonthly payment in lawful United States currency; freedom to trade in independent stores; reasonable rents; revision of doctors' and hospital fees; improvements in camps and towns; disarming and discharge of company guards; and the right of free speech and assembly.[69]

On October 31, 1911, the Southern Lumber Operators Association met in New Orleans to discuss reopening the mills.[70] Some mills were subsequently opened with slightly higher wages and a ten-hour day granted, but the lockout at many mills continued until February 1912.[71] This prolonged lockout caused many unemployed workers to turn to the union for relief, and a contemporary claims that the wife of one idle lumberjack told her husband: "Get out of this house and join the union, or I'll leave it, and try to find a man to live with." [72]

During this period the Brotherhood sent three delegates to the convention of the Industrial Workers of the World. "For the first time in an I W W convention there were fraternal delegates from the South," remarked B. H. Williams in reporting on the convention. "These were the representatives of the Brotherhood of Timber Workers, who," he continued, "in only a few short months of experience in unionism have developed splendid fighting qualities in their combat with the lumber trust in Arkansas, Louisiana and Texas." [73]

Despite the sending of delegates to the convention, the Brotherhood of Timber Workers had not yet joined the IWW. Desiring to effect consolidation, Big Bill Haywood, recognized leader of the Wobblies— as IWW members were called—journeyed to Alexandria, Louisiana, for the Brotherhood's second annual convention on May 6, 1912. Haywood met privately with Arthur Emerson before the convention and, with the help of Covington Hall, a native Louisianian who was already a member of the IWW, convinced Emerson that his union should join the direct actionists. [74]

Emerson had no trouble convincing his men, who, besides voting to join the IWW, evidenced other signs of radicalism. Negro union men had been segregated in another building when the convention began, but after appeals by both Haywood and Hall the white delegates allowed the blacks to assemble in the same building, although the Negroes were compelled to sit at the opposite side of the room. Granting to women the right to hold membership in the Brotherhood was a more radical move. With their membership went the right to vote on any decision concerning the union. [75] The convention ended with great hopes for the future, and agitation following the Alexandria meeting was vigorous. Strikes were planned on a scale never before dreamed of in the South, while renewed effort was made to enlist farmers in the union cause. [76]

Haywood returned to Louisiana on July 1 to persuade the lumber workers to vote for Debs. Since as early as 1909 local Reds like J. R. Jones had tried to convert the lumber workers to socialism without much success. After hearing Jones speak to a group of lumber workers a small capitalist wrote, "those who work hard and get little are too ignorant to understand Socialism and are violently opposed to it. . . . Jones gave them an intelligent lecture but the boss told them it was all foolishness and they believed the boss." [77] Now, Big Bill was trying to accomplish what Jones had failed to do: make Socialist voters out of the lumber workers. Haywood and Emerson spoke at mass meetings throughout the timber district, endorsing both the IWW and the Socialist party, but confining themselves mostly to tirades against the lumber industry and its owners. [78]

The rapidly mounting tension between the union and the owners reached the explosive point on Sunday, July 7, 1912, when Emerson led a crowd of union men and women to the sawmill town of Grabow to hold a "speaking." A few weeks before, the union men at Grabow had gone out on strike. The town, owned by the Galloway Lumber Company and protected by armed guards, was believed by the union men to be an excellent place for a group of discontented radicals to meet. Most of the residents were strikebreakers, and Emerson hoped to persuade these newly arrived workers to join the union and to aid the strike. Emerson had hardly begun to speak when a shot was fired. A battle followed in which three men—two union members and a Burns detective —were killed and forty-eight persons were wounded.[79]

That night over a thousand men gathered in the town of DeRidder, where Emerson and his followers had gone after the encounter. Many demanded that Emerson lead them in an attack on surrounding towns, and, although he refused, "at midnight . . . the streets were filled with people and . . . serious trouble was likely to break out at any minute." [80] State troops were ordered to the area; the next day Emerson was arrested for murder, and two weeks after the incident twenty-three union men were in jail at Lake Charles.[81]

The timber workers and many of the farmers of the area were disgruntled over Emerson's arrest, for the Grabow affair looked to them like an attack upon the union men. Their attitude was not changed when, on July 23, a grand jury indicted Emerson and eight other members of the Brotherhood of Timber Workers for murder, but released John and Paul Galloway, owners of the mills at Grabow, without charges.[82] Repercussions followed. The mill workers at Bon Ami, heretofore nonunion in sentiment, threatened a general walkout unless Emerson was released. Mass meetings were held in New Orleans and Leesville. In New Orleans a crowd of 2,500 assembled in Lafayette Square. For the first time in years Socialist Yellows and Reds put aside their differences and protested against the treatment of the union men.[83] In the western and central upland parishes Reds worked hard to consolidate the farmers and laborers of all races and national origins. Covington Hall tells of the bravest man he ever met, a lumberjack with nine children who was willing to strike in an attempt to effect Emerson's release if the union would only guarantee food for his children. If Hall is to be believed, some degree of class solidarity was awakened by the arrest of the union men. "We farmers and workers will have to stick together," said one Negro farmer. And he pledged that "so long as I have a pound of meat or a peck of corn, no man, white or colored, who goes out in this strike will starve, nor will his children." [84]

Hall also saw a great opportunity for the Socialist party in the coming election. He implored the party to take advantage of the unity between the farmers and workers of western Louisiana. "The Socialist Party has a splendid chance, I think, to carry the seventh and perhaps one other congressional district of Louisiana in the coming election, if speakers, backing the timber workers, are thrown in here at once and the union aided in its fight," wrote Hall.[85]

"Goaded into action by Haywood," the national Socialist party's Executive Committee did appeal for funds to assist the timber workers. But that was all. Even though the party had officially recognized labor organizations at the national convention, the Yellows, who controlled the party, saw little advantage in supporting a group of ignorant, lawless lumberjacks at the expense of possibly losing votes among the respectable elements of the country in the November election.[86] Hall asked for speakers, but none was sent. Passing through Lake Charles on his way to a Yellow reception in New Orleans, Eugene V. Debs did not even so much as get off the train, much less endorse the lumberjacks' stand or visit their jailed comrades.[87] The IWW, however, was quite willing to aid the Brotherhood.[88]

The trial of the nine men charged with murder began on October 8, 1912.[89] Three days before, in a drastic effort to "knock all of the fight" out of the union, the lumber operators closed the American Lumber Mill at Merryville in Calcasieu Parish, leaving one thousand union men out of work.[90] Possibly this act would have defeated the Brotherhood, but, with the IWW on the scene, a bevy of agitators from all over the country flocking to the area, and a defense fund of $10,000, this action did little more than increase the workers' hatred. It was rumored that the laborers of western Louisiana had stated that if Emerson and the other men were convicted, "We are marching on Lake Charles, and burning sawmills and lumber piles as we come. . . . God Almighty will see more sawmill managers, gunmen-deputy sheriffs and Burns detectives hanging to trees in western Louisiana and eastern Texas than He saw in one place in His life!" [91]

The trial ended on October 31 with a verdict of not guilty, and despite the national party's general coolness to the efforts of the union, socialism was temporarily strengthened by the union victory. Mrs. Ira Dunn of Aloha, Louisiana, reported just before the election that "people are interested in Socialism more than ever, and I have great hopes for our local now." [92] One of the union men who got out of jail in time to vote reported that many workers and farmers were casting their ballots for the Socialists because of the solidarity caused by the Grabow incident.[93]

On November 4, 1912, the lumber workers and their farmer friends went to the polls and gave Debs the largest vote a Socialist was ever to receive in Louisiana.[94] But the 5,249 votes the Louisianians had given Debs, although noteworthy, represented only a small percentage of the potential Socialist vote. The migratory workers, the lowly rednecks who constantly moved from lumber camp to lumber camp and were thus disfranchised by the very nature of their work, were the untapped reservoir of any future radical success. But these men were in search of immediate gains—their faith lay only in more pay, shorter hours, and better working conditions. And the militant economic actions of the Industrial Workers of the World appealed more to these simple men than did the political action preached by the Socialists.

After 1912 socialism rapidly declined in Louisiana. The vote dropped from 5,249 in 1912 to 292 in 1916.[95] Subscriptions to the *Appeal to Reason* in Louisiana fell from 6,500 in 1912 to 3,000 less than a year later.[96]

There are several reasons for this decline. Possibly the unwillingness of the Socialist party and the IWW to cooperate after 1912 is foremost. But the prosperity produced by World War I also contributed to the decline of socialism in Louisiana—as it did throughout the country—and the obscurity of the Socialist candidate for president in 1916, Allan Benson, certainly did not aid the party. Moreover, the impermanency of anything radical in the South must be considered. Rarely has social change been effected rapidly in a section with such strong racial and sectional prejudices. The failure of the Socialist party and especially the failure of the Industrial Workers of the World to recognize this axiom is no less important. Covington Hall believed that when the IWW refused to incorporate the sharecroppers into its organization it was doomed to failure in the South. He knew that industrial organization could not take place in an agrarian society where IWW organizers were likely to denounce a union man's "parents and kinsmen as exploiters of labor" simply because they owned small farms and had a hired hand or two.[97]

For a brief time the aggressive tactics of the IWW appealed to the Louisiana lumber workers, and after 1912 political action and the Socialist party were pushed into obscurity. But an organization built on undisciplined "I'm-a-Bum-ism," as the Wobblies were, had little chance of long-range success. They were able to create enthusiasm for a short time, but the average worker, no matter how inspired by agitation or how impassioned by hatred of existing conditions, did not want to be a "bum." As soon as his conditions began to improve, the southern laborer—like all American laborers—aspired to new heights; he took up the customs, manners, and dress of his reputed betters and set out to become a member of the now-cherished plutocracy he once so violently hated.

The combination of prosperity and witch hunting brought about by World War I was devastating to radicalism in Louisiana. In addition to this, there was dissension already within the Socialist ranks, and also the determined effort of the lumber industry to crush unionism.

The lumber operators completely destroyed the union just before the outbreak of World War I by their tactics of blacklisting, lockouts, iron-clad oaths, and the importation of Negroes from plantation areas to act as strikebreakers.[98] The use of strikebreakers was quite effective because few of these Negroes knew what a union was, and any thought they might have entertained about joining was weighed heavily against the constant surveillance of "nigger-killing" deputy sheriffs.

A thorough analysis of the Negro's role in the radical movement would be desirable but is almost impossible because of the absence of reliable evidence. In passing, however, it might be noted that the Socialist party (in Louisiana as elsewhere) was not so enthusiastic about having Negro comrades as was the IWW.[99] Indeed, "a permanent colored organizer" was employed in the South by the IWW,[100] and when over a thousand lumber workers struck at Merryville, Louisiana, in 1912 because fifteen employees of the American Lumber Company had been "blacklisted . . . for testifying for the defense in the famous Grabow trial," Negroes were among the strikers. An agitator reported that "although not one of these fifteen [blacklisted workers] was a Negro, our colored fellow-workers showed their solidarity by walking out with their white comrades." Despite the fact that this writer believed "a better understanding exists now between the white and black . . . than I thought possible in such a comparatively short time," he was forced to admit that most of the scabs were Negroes.[101] Hall was willing to admit, too, that the lumber operators discredited the union by charging them with trying to organize the blacks against the whites. In any case, the Merryville strike was a failure. And after the defeat of this last large-scale effort of the Louisiana lumber workers the union rapidly disintegrated.[102]

With the return of prosperity and the taming of the organized lumber worker, the Louisiana Socialist party died a natural death. Ample proof that socialism was finished in Louisiana came in 1917 when the once-popular J. R. Jones ran for district attorney in the Seventh Judicial District and got two votes.[103] This was formerly a strong Socialist area.

The rustic radicals of the forest and the redneck pea pickers of the hill country rose again to follow protest programs; but these programs —heavily veiled with demagoguery—claimed no Socialist backing, for, just as one New Orleans paper accurately predicted, the Louisiana Socialists' objectives would never be attained unless the party came out "under another name, and with different captains in the vanguard." [104] Was "share-the-wealth-ism" that other name and Huey Long the "different captain"?

NOTES

1. *Report of the Secretary of State to His Excellency the Governor of Louisiana, 1914* (Baton Rouge, 1914), unnumbered folded page opposite 226.

2. It should be noted that Oklahoma gave the Socialists a higher percentage of votes than any other state in 1912; 1 of every 5 Oklahomans cast a ballot for Debs. Certain other southern states too, besides Louisiana, contributed a considerable number of Socialist votes. In Texas 1 vote of every 11 went to the Marxist; in Florida 1 of 10; and in Arkansas 1 of 14. (A study of the Socialist movement in each of these states might aid in a better understanding of not only the rise and ultimate decline of the party in the South but also of whatever legacy, if any, the movement left.) Most southern states, however, had relatively few Socialist voters. For example, only 1 voter in 30 was a Socialist in Mississippi, 1 in 70 in Tennessee, 1 in 117 in Georgia, 1 in 237 in North Carolina, and 1 in 306 in South Carolina. Alexander Trachtenberg, ed., *The American Labor Year Book, 1917–1918* (New York, 1918), p. 338, and William E. Walling *et al.*, eds., *The Socialism of To-day; a Source-book of the . . . Socialist and Labor Parties of All Countries* (New York, 1916), pp. 194–95.

3. Work Projects Administration, *Louisiana* (New York, 1945), pp. 7–8.

4. *Report of the Secretary of State . . . 1914*, p. opp. 226.

5. Socialist candidates ran in three wards. In Ward 5 the Socialist lost by a vote of 150 to 134; in Ward 4, where two Socialists were candidates, they were defeated by votes of 136 to 104 and 134 to 102; in Ward 3 the Socialist lost 72 to 26. (The vote is given in the *Baton Rouge New Advocate*, November 27, 1912, but without party designation. I am indebted to B. J. Glasscock, a former Socialist candidate for public office, of Leesville, Louisiana, who in a personal interview on November 25, 1950, matched the men with their party in this race.)

6. *Report of the Secretary of State . . . 1914*, p. opp. 226; *Girard (Kansas) Appeal to Reason*, November 16, 1912; *Baton Rouge New Advocate*, November 27, 1912.

7. *Report of the Secretary of State . . . 1914*, p. opp. 226.

8. *Ibid.*

9. *New Orleans Times-Democrat*, November 7, 1912; *New Orleans Picayune*, November 7, 1912.

10. *Baton Rouge New Advocate,* November 25, 1912.

11. *Report of the Secretary of State . . . 1914,* pp. 196–204. The Eighth District included the parishes of Avoyelles, Grant, Rapides, Natchitoches, Winn, Sabine, La Salle, and Vernon.

12. *Ibid., 1902,* pp. 562, 564; *Ibid., 1914,* pp. 162–63.

13. Melvin Johnson White, "Populism in Louisiana during the Nineties," *Mississippi Valley Historical Review* 5 (1918–1919):5.

14. *Ibid.,* p. 15.

15. *Report of the Secretary of State . . . 1902,* pp. 562, 564; *Ibid., 1914,* pp. 162–63.

16. White, "Populism in Louisiana during the Nineties," p. 15.

17. The parishes used for these generalizations are the five that, in three different elections, were among those with the largest percentages of both Populist and Socialist votes (Winn, Vernon, Grant, Caldwell, and Bienville) and are compared with the five that, in the same three elections, had the fewest Populist and Socialist votes (Tensas, Saint James, Saint Charles, Saint Bernard, and Plaquemines). The table on page 163 is computed from *Thirteenth Census of the United States, 1910: Population* (Washington, 1913), 2:778–89; *Thirteenth Census . . . Statistics for Louisiana,* pp. 622–27; *Report of the Secretary of State . . . 1902,* pp. 562, 564, and *ibid., 1914,* pp. 162–63.

18. White, "Populism in Louisiana during the Nineties," p. 19; Lucia E. Daniel, "The Louisiana People's Party," *Louisiana Historical Quarterly* 26 (1943):1138.

19. C. Vann Woodward, *Origins of the New South, 1877–1913* (Baton Rouge, 1951), pp. 253–54; David A. Shannon, "The Socialist Party before the First World War: An Analysis," *Mississippi Valley Historical Review* 38 (1951–1952):280.

20. White states that of the 18 Populists elected to the Louisiana legislature in 1892, 9 were planters, 7 were farmers, 1 was a lumber manufacturer, and 1 was a teacher. White, "Populism in Louisiana during the Nineties," p. 14. See also Woodward, *Origins of the New South,* pp. 245–46.

21. It would have been strange indeed had the American Federation of Labor, at this time, supported the Socialists, for the AFL was bitterly opposed to the syndicalism of the IWW and wanted nothing to do with socialism. During a period when the lumber workers of Louisiana were engaged in a desperate struggle with the lumber owners and the Socialists were appealing for united support, the AFL repudiated the lumber workers' cause and publicly thanked the Louisiana Senate for its allegedly fair treatment of the laboring man and his welfare. See *Baton Rouge New Advocate,* July 11, 1912. For evidence that members of the AFL supported Populism, see Woodward, *Origins of the New South,* pp. 253–54.

22. Caffery was the son of the conservative gold Democrat Senator Donelson Caffery, a man of substantial social and economic standing. On the Populist-Republican fusion, see White, "Populism in Louisiana during the Nineties," p. 17.

23. There is evidence that the small farmers of Louisiana continued to suffer after the collapse of Populism. There were, for example, more rented dwellings in Louisiana than in her neighboring states; the average number of persons living in a house was even greater than in Mississippi, a state notorious for its rural slums. Also the Louisiana cotton crop fell from 470,136 bales valued at $20,790,000 in 1908 to 245,646 bales valued at $17,180,000 in 1910, and corn production fell from 51,198,000 bushels in 1909 to

32,490,000 bushels three years later. *Statistical Abstract of the United States, 1916* (Washington, 1917), pp. 75, 76, 128, 140, 145. Naturally, the small farmers—hurt most by this loss in income—were resentful.

24. For an account of the strength of the lumber operators in Louisiana, see U.S. Department of Commerce, *The Lumber Industry* (Washington, 1913), pt. 2, pp. 132–54.

25. The large number of voters registered as "no party" or "independent" after 1900, coupled with the steady increase in Socialist votes in the upland parishes after 1904, tends to confirm this generalization. *Report of the Secretary of State . . . 1910*, pp. 145–67; *ibid., 1912*, pp. 101–4; *ibid., 1914*, pp. 154–61. For a good account of Socialist-Populist relations on the national level, see Howard H. Quint, *The Forging of American Socialism: Origins of the Modern Movement* (Columbia, S.C., 1953), pp. 210–46.

26. Personal interview with Covington Hall, New Orleans, January 29, 1951. Hall was at one time the leading radical writer and journalist in the South.

27. *Report of the Secretary of State . . . 1914*, pp. 162–63, opp. 226; *The Lumber Industry*, pt. 2, pp. 132–33.

28. *Report of the Secretary of State . . . 1905*, unnumbered folded page opposite xvi. There had been isolated groups of radicals in Louisiana before 1904, but they had never asserted themselves. Robert Owen visited New Orleans in 1828 but devoted most of his time to "baiting the clergy" rather than to setting up any more New Harmonies. Bernard Mueller founded a communitarian settlement at Grand Ecore in Natchitoches Parish in 1834, and in 1850 Wilhelm Weitling, a utopian communist, visited German friends in New Orleans and established a radical labor paper, which soon failed. Weitling also stopped over in Baton Rouge and learned that "a Hungarian society" was operating a communal boardinghouse there. But if there was extreme radical activity in Louisiana between 1850 and 1904, either it was successfully submerged during that troubled period or it found sufficient outlet in other movements. On Owen see *New Orleans Louisiana Advertiser*, January 29, 1828. Mueller's activities are covered in Arthur E. Bestor, Jr., *Backwoods Utopias: The Sectarian and Owenite Phases of Communitarian Socialism in America, 1663–1829* (Philadelphia, 1950), p. 35. On Weitling see Carl Wittke, *The Utopian Communist: A Biography of Wilhelm Weitling, Nineteenth-Century Reformer* (Baton Rouge, 1950), pp. 181–82.

29. The Socialist party (as an organization) and its membership contributed materially to IWW strikes and defense funds, and as important a figure as Eugene V. Debs helped establish the union. But a serious factional fight involving the fundamental ideology of American socialism followed the formation of the IWW; within the party conservative political-actionists were constantly at odds with the pro-Wobblie element led by William D. Haywood. For a recent account of this bitter struggle, which resulted in the repudiation of most of the IWW principles, see Ira Kipnis, *The American Socialist Movement, 1897–1912* (New York, 1953), esp. chaps. 7 and 8. See also Stow Persons and Donald Drew Egbert, eds., *Socialism and American Life* (Princeton, 1952), vol. 1, and Nathan Fine, *Labor and Farmer Parties in the United States, 1828–1912* (New York, 1928) on the Socialists. Paul F. Brissenden, *The I.W.W.: A Study of American Syndicalism* (New York, 1920) is still good on the Wobblies. On Debs see McAlister Coleman, *Eugene V. Debs, A Man Unafraid* (New York, 1930), and Ray Ginger, *The*

Bending Cross: A Biography of Eugene Victor Debs (New Brunswick, N.J., 1949). Quint's *Forging of American Socialism* is excellent, but does not go beyond 1901.

30. Covington Hall, "Labor Struggles in the Deep South" (typescript), Tulane University Library, New Orleans, pp. 54–55 (hereafter cited as Hall MS).

31. *Report of the Secretary of State . . . 1910*, p. 147. For the shift of Socialist strength, see *Report of the Secretary of State . . . 1905*, p. opp. xvi; *1910*, p. opp. 136; *1914*, p. opp. 226.

32. Myrtle and Eune Pollard to Editor, *Girard* (Kansas) *Appeal to Reason*, January 4, 1913.

33. *Appeal to Reason*, April 23, June 11, July 9, 1910, August 28, December 25, 1909; Hall MS, p. 175.

34. Glasscock interview; Hall interview.

35. *Appeal to Reason*, December 25, 1909; Glasscock interview.

36. Hall interview.

37. "Sparks from the National Convention," *International Socialist Review* 10 (1909–10):1128.

38. *Report of the Secretary of State . . . 1912*, pp. 101–2, 104.

39. George D. Brewer, "Awakening of Dixie," *Appeal to Reason*, March 18, 1911.

40. In Winn Parish, Jones got 143 votes, or 12.5 percent of the total; in Vernon, he got 252 votes, or 17.0 percent. *Baton Rouge New Advocate*, May 21, 1912.

41. *Ibid.*, May 4, 1912.

42. Hall interview. This is substantiated by the fact that the lumbering parishes showed the greatest increase in Socialist vote between the April and November 1912 elections. See *Report of the Secretary of State . . . 1914*, pp. 162–63, opp. 226, and *The Lumber Industry*, pt. 2, pp. 132–33.

43. John Spargo, ed., *Proceedings of the National Convention of the Socialist Party, 1912* (Chicago, 1912), pp. 100, 195; "The National Socialist Convention of 1912," *International Socialist Review* 12 (1911–12):822.

44. Spargo, ed., *Proceedings of the Socialist Party, 1912*, pp. 122–37.

45. *Ibid.*, pp. 137–43; "The National Socialist Convention of 1912," p. 828.

46. Spargo, ed., *Proceedings of the Socialist Party, 1912*, p. 100.

47. Woodward, *Origins of the New South*, pp. 114–20. See also *The Lumber Industry*, pt. 2, pp. 132–54.

48. *Thirteenth Census . . . Statistics for Louisiana*, p. 654.

49. Vernon H. Jensen, *Lumber and Labor* (New York, 1945), p. 5.

50. Glasscock interview. Glasscock was one of the hard-pressed farm owners who worked in the lumber industry.

51. William D. Haywood, "Timber Workers and Timber Wolves," *International Socialist Review* 13 (1912–13):105–10.

52. D. T. Hulse, "Employing and Handling Men in the Logging and Lumber Manufacturing Industry," *Bulletin of the Southern Logging Association* (New Orleans, 1925), p. 37.

53. Bob Shadrick, "Growing Worse in Dixie," *Appeal to Reason*, January 25, 1913.

54. William D. Haywood, *Bill Haywood's Book: The Autobiography of William D. Haywood* (New York, 1929), p. 243.

55. *Ibid.*

56. The town of Lutcher had the only Negro Socialist party local in Louisiana in 1905. Eraste Vidrine, "Negro Locals," *International Socialist Review* 5 (1904–1905):389.

57. *Second Biennial Report of the Bureau of Statistics of Labor for the State of Louisiana, 1902–1903* (Baton Rouge, 1903), p. 40.

58. Industrial Workers of the World, *The Lumber Industry and Its Workers* (Chicago, n.d.), p. 76.

59. Covington Hall, "Revolt of the Southern Timber Workers," *International Socialist Review* 13 (1912–13):52.

60. *New Orleans Times-Democrat*, July 20, 1911.

61. There is a difference of opinion as to the exact date of the founding of the Brotherhood of Timber Workers. In an unpublished work Covington Hall says it was in June 1910 that Emerson and Jay Smith gathered twenty-five lumberjacks and established the union. Hall MS, p. 124. But in a published article he states that the Brotherhood was founded by Emerson and Smith at Carson, Louisiana, on December 3, 1910. "I Am Here for Labor," *International Socialist Review* 13 (1912–13):223. Haywood says that Emerson founded the Brotherhood alone at Fullerton, Louisiana, in 1910, and later Smith joined him. "Timber Workers and Timber Wolves," p. 107. B. J. Glasscock only remembers the union starting in 1910.

62. Hall MS, p. 187.

63. Haywood, "Timber Workers and Timber Wolves," pp. 107–8; Hall, "I Am Here for Labor," p. 223.

64. Hall MS, p. 131; *New Orleans Times-Democrat*, May 17, 1911.

65. Haywood, "Timber Workers and Timber Wolves," p. 108; Hall, "I Am Here for Labor," p. 223.

66. *New Orleans Times-Democrat*, July 20, 1911.

67. Hall MS, p. 133.

68. Glasscock interview.

69. *New Orleans Times-Democrat*, July 20, 1911.

70. *Ibid.*, November 1, 1911.

71. IWW, *The Lumber Industry and Its Workers*, p. 77.

72. Hall MS, p. 139.

73. Brissenden, *The I.W.W.*, p. 267, citing Minutes of the Sixth IWW Convention held in Chicago, September 18–28, 1911; B. H. Williams, "Sixth I.W.W. Convention," *International Socialist Review* 12 (1911–12): 302.

74. Hall, "Revolt of the Southern Timber Workers," p. 51; Hall MS, p. 135.

75. Hall MS, pp. 136–38; Haywood, *Bill Haywood's Book*, pp. 241–42.

76. Hall MS, p. 149; Haywood, "Timber Workers and Timber Wolves," p. 107. Later the IWW denounced the farmers as exploiters of labor (Hall MS, p. 219).

77. P. Wagner to Editor, *Appeal to Reason*, January 16, 1909.

78. Hall MS, pp. 150–51.

79. *Ibid.*, pp. 152–53; *Baton Rouge New Advocate*, July 8, 10, September 27, 1912. Exactly what happened during the battle is unclear.

80. *Baton Rouge New Advocate*, July 8, 1912; Hall MS, p. 153.

81. *Baton Rouge New Advocate*, July 11, 24, 1912.

82. *Ibid.*, July 24, 1912.

83. *Ibid.*, July 11, 1912; *Appeal to Reason*, July 20, 1912; Hall MS, p. 156.

84. Hall MS, p. 149.
85. Covington Hall, "The Great Contest in Dixie," *Appeal to Reason,* July 20, 1912.
86. Kipnis, *The American Socialist Movement,* p. 411; Hall interview.
87. *New Orleans Times-Democrat,* September 14, 1912.
88. In September 1912 the Brotherhood of Timber Workers became part of the IWW. See J. P. Cannon, "The Seventh I.W.W. Convention," *International Socialist Review* 13 (1912–13):424. As an indication of just how radical a group of workers in the deep South had become, Covington Hall, the leader of the Louisiana lumberjacks, proposed that the Wobblies "recognize no title to machinery except that which vests its ownership in the users." See Brissenden, *The I.W.W.,* p. 296.
89. *New Orleans Times-Democrat,* October 9, 1912.
90. *Ibid.,* October 6, 1912.
91. Hall MS, pp. 169–73.
92. Mrs. Ira Dunn to Editor, *International Socialist Review* 13 (1912–13):439.
93. J. H. Helton to Editor, *International Socialist Review* 13 (1912–13):571.
94. For evidence that the lumber workers supported the Socialist in November, see *Report of the Secretary of State . . . 1914,* pp. 162–63, opp. 226, and *The Lumber Industry,* pt. 2, pp. 132–33.
95. *Report of the Secretary of State . . . 1917,* unnumbered folded page.
96. *Appeal to Reason,* August 9, 1912; June 8, 1913.
97. Hall MS, p. 219.
98. Jensen, *Lumber and Labor,* p. 91, citing Alexandria (La.) *Voice of the People,* January 1, 29, March 5, 1914.
99. Vidrine, "Negro Locals," p. 389; Kipnis, *The American Socialist Movement,* pp. 130 ff.
100. Edward Koeltgen, "I.W.W. Convention," *International Socialist Review* 14 (1913–14):275.
101. Phineas Eastman, "The Southern Negro and One Big Union," *International Socialist Review* 13 (1912–13):890–91.
102. Covington Hall, "Negroes Against Whites," *International Socialist Review* 13 (1912–13):349. Union men claimed that the strikebreakers were aided by so-called Good Citizen Leagues. Hall says that such a group attacked and destroyed a strikers' tent camp at Merryville on February 16, 1913. "With the Southern Timber Workers," *ibid.,* p. 805; Hall interview.
103. *Report of the Secretary of State . . . 1917,* p. 340.
104. *New Orleans Picayune,* November 7, 1912.

CHAPTER XII

Black History or Propaganda?

"We want black studies. We want black teachers," chanted a group of high school students during a meeting of the San Francisco Board of Education in December 1968. "We don't want any more meetings with anyone. Just meet our demands." [1]

Similar demands are being made and granted all over the country. New York and Detroit schools have adopted history booklets that elaborate the accomplishments of Negroes. A junior high school in Philadelphia has incorporated "black power" into all courses, including history. Even after black history courses had been instituted in Chicago high schools disorder occurred because Negro students objected to whites teaching the courses. In Nairobi (formerly East Palo Alto), California, Negro youngsters forced the resignation of their white principal and the adoption of courses in black history, Swahili, and "soul" music. The Black Student Union at Berkeley High School won even more extensive concessions. These included the establishment of a Black Curriculum Committee, consisting of four black students and three black teachers; student-initiated courses, including five additional courses exclusively for black students; more black literature in the school's library as well as African and "soul" food in the school's cafeteria and in food classes; the elimination of grouping students on the basis of their ability to learn; and the hiring of a black curriculum coordinator to recruit black teachers to teach black history. [2]

If none of this has happened in the schools in your area, do not despair. Wait until next week, or next month, or next year. A stampede is underway, and it is sure too reach them eventually.

Let me make it clear at the outset that I am wholeheartedly in favor of studying Negro history, or black history, or any other kind of history. As a professional historian, studying the past is both my job and my pleasure; it is an exciting activity. I welcome all who wish to undertake the study of any part of the past, but on one condition: their approach must be as scholarly, as honest, and as unbiased as possible. Otherwise, I believe, they are likely to mutilate and to misuse the past.

Many people demand that the historian become personally involved in current social and political controversies; they insist that it is the duty of the scholar to take a moral stand, to commit himself to some dogma. Once committed, he should use his knowledge to pass value judgments on the past and the present; to advocate this or that cause; to become, in fact, a missionary, a propagandist for some particular social or political tenet.

I suggest that a historian cannot be both a propagandist and a scholar; the two are incompatible. Where propaganda is apparent, scholarship is not. Historians need no additional commitments. Like most scholars, they already have enough unavoidable burdens—as citizens, wage earners, taxpayers, consumers, renters or home owners, spouses, and parents—to keep them from their scholarship. In his acknowledgment one author mentioned a young daughter without whose help, he confessed, his book would have been written years earlier.

The propagandist, certain that he has acquired truth, goes out to preach and to convert. He has no desire to understand the past, only to use it. He wants disciples, not students; he wants people to think as he does rather than to think for themselves. Often a glib lecturer with ready answers to even the most complex questions, he can have a profound influence upon impressionable youth. "Too many so-called historians are really 'hysterians,'" charged Thomas A. Bailey in his presidential address before the Organization of American Historians. "When their duties as citizens clash with their responsibilities as scholars, Clio frequently takes a back seat. How many of us can march in Mississippi one week and teach Negro history with reasonable objectivity the next? How many of us can be shining eggheads for Adlai Stevenson [or Eugene McCarthy] in the evening and sober spokesmen for scholarship the next morning? How many of us who are professional Southerners or New Englanders can deal fairly with other sections? How many of us can forget that we are white or black when writing about whites or

blacks? How many of us can avoid the academic homosexuality of falling in love with our own hero?" [3]

Even the most conscientious academics have certain prejudices and
are frequently guilty of subjectivity, but such sins are venial ones when
compared to the scholarly licentiousness of the propagandist. He looks
back at the past with a devout present-mindedness. His catechism is re-
plete with such jargon as "relevant," "meaningful," and "socially significant." To him history is only a means; he picks facts and distorts
events to suit his cause.

The historian, on the other hand, can never be sure that he has found
truth. His conclusions are always tentative. He must continually seek
new evidence as well as new ways of looking at old evidence; he is too
uncertain to become an advocate. Besides, advocacy would remove him
from his real area of competence—the past, which he studies and tries
to understand but cannot change. By definition, the historian cannot be
concerned with trying to influence the present or the future. His only legitimate function is to describe and to analyze a particular time or place
or event in the past. He tries to reconstruct what happened, to discover
how it occurred, and—if possible—why it happened. His role is to examine all those past human sayings, thoughts, deeds, and sufferings for
which records exist. Critics often claim that historians ask the wrong
questions or neglect important topics. The charge can be true, but only
if the evidence for the study of such topics exists. Without raw material
—letters, diaries, and other documents—no scholar can write extensively and confidently about any subject. For example, the absence of
sufficient and reliable evidence precludes a detailed analysis of poor
people in nineteenth-century America or of the thoughts of Negro
slaves.

Unfortunately, the advocate rarely lets the absence of reliable evidence stop him from proselytizing. Some people see black history primarily as a way of promoting black power, revolutionary doctrines, or
Negro self-respect. Such aims are evident in the demand that academic
standards and qualifications for blacks be determined exclusively by
blacks and that no whites or Negroes are qualified to teach black history. "The past is the source of our major interests, our rights, and our
duties," announces an editor of *Black Politics: A Journal of Liberation*.[4] A bookdealer who promotes black history says: "All of American history needs to be rewritten. . . . How can George Washington, a
slave owner, be presented as a hero?" [5] A spokesman for the Black Students Union at San Francisco State University admits that his group in-

tends to seize power in "all colleges, high schools and junior high schools." [6] Two Negro psychiatrists, assuming I suppose that color is more important than knowledge or training in the writing of history, have prepared materials for a "Black History" course that they hope "will instill a measure of pride in black audiences." This course consists of fifteen audio-visual presentations, each about twenty minutes in length. Some two thousand color slides and a taped narration trace the history of the black people in the context of worldwide economics, politics, and cultures. These doctors anticipate widespread use of their material in schools, adult education classes, community action groups, churches, and by corporations and foundations. [7] "One of our major battles is to root out corrupt Western values," argues Stokely Carmichael. "It is from our people's history . . . that we know our struggles. . . . We are working now to increase the consciousness of the African-American so it will extend internationally." "We must join those who are for armed struggle around the world." [8]

The major weakness of black history is not the subject but the aim of its practitioners. Too often it is being studied and taught for the wrong reasons. Too few people insist that the study of black history is worthwhile in itself; almost no one argues that knowledge of the Negro is important for its own sake. Instead, advocates want to use only those parts of the Negro's past that they believe will help bring about the social changes they desire. There has always been too much emphasis in history texts upon heroes and villains. To substitute black legends for white legends is no improvement. The "super-Negro" thesis is just as ridiculous, and just as dangerous, as the "inferior-Negro" thesis. "Overcompensation, in atonement for past omissions, is no more an example of good history textbooks than were the thoughtless books of the past," notes the president of Howard University. The Swedish social scientist who produced a monumental work on American race relations, Gunnar Myrdal, warns against the creation of a "black mythology." [9]

But, as the president of the Organization of American Historians announced in 1968, "the pressure is on to overstress Negro initiative in organizing revolts, in escaping from bondage, and in securing emancipation." [10] This use of history to promote a particular cause has been all too evident in works on the Negro, whether written by blacks or whites. The most extensive volume on Negro historians concludes: "some of the most outstanding of these historians have been influenced by the conception of Negro history as *a weapon in the fight for racial equality*. This orientation," admits the author, "has been . . . detrimental to their historiography." One reason why George Washington Williams, America's first serious Negro historian, wrote his *History of the Negro Race in America* was to "incite [Negroes] . . . to greater effort in the struggle of citizenship and manhood." W. E. B. Du Bois, the first Negro American to receive a Ph.D. degree in any of the social sciences, believed that the study of Negro history would help overcome racial prejudice; Carter G. Woodson, founder of the Association for the Study of Negro Life and History and the first editor of the *Journal of Negro History,* considered it the duty of Negro historians to prove that the race had a creditable past.[11]

Many of the new history books, especially those designed for use in the schools, mention only the achievements of Negroes. A volume entitled *The Negro in American History,* distributed to teachers by New York City's Board of Education, describes the black Africa of slave-trading days as generally being without written languages and having an agrarian economy. Nevertheless, it adds, "Negroes brought with them to the New World political experiences of every type and complexity." Slavery and the slave traffic among Africans themselves is considered somehow not so bad as that practiced in America. Another widely used text includes an admiring sketch of W. E. B. Du Bois but does not mention any of his activities—such as joining the Communist party or taking up residence in Ghana late in life—that some people would consider anti-American. *Eyewitness: The Negro in American History* allots ten pages to describing Negro exploits in World War II, but it fails to note the less than outstanding records of all-Negro divisions that fought in Italy and the South Pacific. Too many of the new black history texts are little more than lists of relatively obscure people whom the authors praise extravagantly. Among those usually acclaimed is Crispus Attucks, a rowdy killed in the so-called Boston Massacre of 1770. Actually, Attucks may have been an Indian rather than a Negro. But balance and qualification are not strong points in most of these texts. They never mention such men as the influential Negro legislator Robert Smalls of South Carolina, who was convicted of accepting a $5,000 bribe in 1877. As a rule, black history suffers from a one-sided presentation. A student magazine at the University of California at Berkeley devoted an entire issue to Black History Week, but included only laudatory articles by local militants on Du Bois and Malcolm X and poems by Imamu Amiri Baraka (LeRoi Jones). A nationally televised program on Negro history contained several inaccuracies, including the absurd statement that most slaves were branded.[12]

Recently I received an example of what is being presented to teachers and students. The volume to which I refer is a paperback of some 190 pages authoritatively entitled *Teachers' Guide to American Negro History,* which its publisher claims is a "basic handbook for schools and libraries." A casual examination of this book revealed far too many errors and distortions to be listed here, but a close look at one section is possible. Unit IV, "The South During Slavery," consists of eight and a half pages of text, illustrations, and bibliography. Only two and a half pages are actually text.[13] Within that limited amount of space the author manages to make no fewer than fourteen errors of fact or interpretation and to demonstrate that his understanding of antebellum southern history and of Negro slavery is shockingly scanty.

The first of these errors is the implication that most of the eight million white people who lived in the South in 1860 were poor whites.[14] If the work of Professor Frank L. Owsley and his students is accepted as reasonably correct, and it has never been systematically refuted, the overwhelming majority of the plain folk of the Old South were middle class; they belonged neither to the plantation economy nor to the destitute poor white class. Yeoman farmers composed the bulk of the South's population in 1860, and in the lower South between 80 and 85 percent of these people owned their own land.[15]

Errors number two, three, and four are contained in a single sentence, which reads in part: "the South had become a backward agricultural region devoid of industry, literature, and democracy."[16] The charge that the South was a "backward agricultural region" is questionable, but I have not counted this an error because in part it depends upon what one considers backward. Agricultural practices throughout antebellum America were backward. It should be remembered that some improvements in farming techniques were initiated in the South, and that it produced the overwhelming majority of antebellum America's exports.

The Old South was not "devoid of industry, literature, and democracy." Though far less industrialized than the North, the South experienced tremendous industrial growth in the twenty years before the Civil War. In 1860 goods manufactured in New England were worth $494,000,000; those manufactured in the South were worth $145,000,000. Respectable industrial activities developed in at least six southern cities before the Civil War, and by the end of the antebellum period the South, with only 39 percent of the nation's population, contained 34 percent of the nation's railroad mileage.[17]

Anyone familiar with the *Southern Review, Russell's Magazine,* or the *Southern Literary Messenger,* or with the works of William Gilmore Simms, Edgar Allan Poe, John Pendleton Kennedy, Augustus B. Longstreet, and George Washington Harris knows that the Old South produced some outstanding writers and literature. The most versatile man of letters was Simms—novelist, short-story writer, critic, journalist, and editor. Some authorities consider his historical novels to be notable achievements in American literature. Though Poe's work transcends region, some of it is set in the South, and Poe himself aspired to be a southern gentleman. A distinguished literary critic said of Kennedy: "Few Americans of his day were so generously gifted; none possessed a lighter touch. He has been somewhat carelessly forgotten even by our literary historians who can plead no excuse for so grave a blunder." [18] The humorists of the Old Southwest—such writers as Longstreet, Harris, Johnson J. Hooper, and Joseph G. Baldwin—were some of America's first realists. Ransy Sniffle, created by Longstreet, and Sut Lovingood, created by Harris, are worthy forerunners of characters portrayed a century later by Erskine Caldwell and William Faulkner.

Only by imposing the value system of the present upon the past and by ignoring the commonly accepted nineteenth-century definition of democracy can one argue that the Old South of the late antebellum period was undemocratic. At one time the older states of the Atlantic seaboard had been oligarchies run by county courts, but state constitutional conventions gradually swept away all aristocratic political privileges. By the 1850s every southern state except South Carolina had established white manhood suffrage and abolished property qualifications for office holding. In these states all officials were elected by popular vote; moreover, representation was apportioned on the basis of population rather than on wealth, with periodic reapportionment. The result of these changes was the rise of the self-made "common man" to political power in the South. Such "men of the people" as Alabama's W. R. W. Cobb, "friend of the poor against the rich," were unbeatable politicians. Of the eight governors of Virginia between 1841 and 1861, only one was born a gentleman; early in their careers two had worked as plowhands, and another, the son of a village butcher, as a tailor. At the close of the antebellum period there was as much democracy in the Old South as there was in the Old North. Of course, it was democracy for whites only; free Negroes lost their right to vote when white suffrage was extended, but this also happened in the North.[19]

One might even argue that there was more economic and social opportunity for whites in the Old South than in the Old North. Because more land was available in the South, in proportion to its population, than was available in the North, it was easier for Southerners to acquire good cheap land. Furthermore, the South's major crop, cotton, was extremely democratic. A major reason for the popularity of cotton was that it was less closely bound to slavery and to the plantation system than some of the other staple crops; it could be grown successfully by a plain farmer with no slaves, a little land, a few simple tools, and some seed. In this respect cotton was like tobacco, but unlike tobacco culture, cotton growing was simple enough to be satisfactorily performed by slave labor organized in large gangs. Thus, cotton offered a man with little capital a chance to begin, yet it placed no limits upon his desire to better himself. As Charles S. Sydnor noted: "A number of men mounted from log cabin to plantation mansion on a stairway of cotton bales, accumulating slaves as they climbed." [20]

The story of Henry Watson, who came to Alabama from Connecticut in 1834 to practice law, is instructive. At first he was critical of the state, complaining that the only crops raised were cotton and a little corn, and these with only a minimum effort. By 1836 Watson himself had caught the speculative fever. "Sell the Reed lot," he advised his father. "I wish every part of real estate belonging to me in Connecticut to be sold. . . . Sell for whatever the land may bring and not wait for good prices, and remit to me the proceeds. It will be worth fifty times as much to me here." Soon Watson became a cotton planter. At the beginning of 1839 he informed his father that his ambition was to own a plantation, despite his recent success in land speculation, money lending, and law. He believed nothing could equal cotton growing as a profession. "I think," he confessed, "it is the *most* reputable, the *most* healthy and the *most* honest, and in this country . . . the *most* safe and the *most* profitable."

Nineteen years later, on the eve of the Civil War, Watson was a wealthy man. He owned a summer home in Northhampton, Massachusetts; a town house in Greensboro, Alabama; a thousand-acre plantation at Newborn, Alabama; 110 slaves and securities valued at more than $150,000. His own estimate of the total value of his estate was $325,128.03. His income in 1860 was over $30,000 a year and increasing.[21]

Not all cotton farmers became Henry Watsons; indeed, many failed and failed again, never acquiring wealth. But there was considerable opportunity for white men of varied background in the Cotton Kingdom.

Error number five in the so-called *Teachers' Guide to American Negro History* is the statement "The slaveholders made the law and selected congressmen, teachers, ministers, editors, and sheriffs." [22] This could hardly have been possible except in a few areas. Slaveholding was not a requirement for officeholding or for voting in the late antebellum South. Nor is there any convincing proof that nonslaveholders were coerced or dictated to by slaveholders; in fact, there is considerable evidence to the contrary. The overwhelming majority of voters and citizens of the Old South were not slaveowners. In 1860 only 385,000 families owned slaves; 1,516,000 families did not own a single slave. As Kenneth M. Stampp noted: "Nearly three-fourths of all free Southerners had no connection with slavery through either family ties or direct ownership." [23]

Errors number six, seven, eight, and nine are all committed in a paragraph meant to characterize the institution of slavery as it existed in the antebellum South. Specifically, these errors are the unqualified assertions that slaves "had no rights any white person was bound to respect," that slaves ate a "poor" diet, were housed in "primitive" shelters, and were overworked. [24]

It is true that slaves had few rights, but every southern state adopted laws to protect them from cruel treatment and willful murder. And often social custom provided more protection for the slave than the law. Everywhere masters were required to maintain their slaves in full sustenance whether young or old, fit or incapacitated. Manumission of the disabled was nowhere permitted unless provision was made for the freedman's maintenance. In most states it was illegal to beat a slave without cause. And in Louisiana, under the *Code Noir*, it was illegal to sell slaves away from the lands on which they worked to settle a debt; neither husbands and wives nor mothers and young children could be sold separately under any circumstances, and all slaves were exempt from field work on Sundays and holidays. Though an owner was authorized to apply shackles and lashes for disciplinary purposes, the killing of slaves was declared criminal even to the degree of murder. [25]

The care and treatment of slaves varied according to such conditions as the size of the farm or plantation on which the slave lived; where and when the slave lived; the ratio of Negroes to whites in the region; the crops raised; the slave's job; and the social and economic position, background, sex, and age of the owner. Some authorities think that generally slaves were better treated on small farms, but no one can be certain. More suffering probably took place where slaves outnumbered whites; the average slave in Virginia worked harder in the colonial period, for example, than in the 1850s. Perhaps the most difficult life of all was to be a field hand in the rice or sugar regions. Artisans and house servants usually got on better.[26]

Few instances have been found where a master failed to provide sufficient food and shelter for his slaves. If slave dwellings were less than sumptuous, it should be recalled that about 40 percent of the American people lived in log houses in 1860. Bacon and corn meal were the staples of the slave diet. As a rule, slaves received the necessities of life, but rarely any luxuries. While at Charleston in 1855 Charles Eliot Norton wrote home to Boston: "The slaves do not go about looking unhappy. . . . Whips and chains, oaths and brutality, are as common . . . in the free as the slave states. We have come thus far . . . without seeing the first sign of Negro misery, or white tyranny." Another New Englander wrote of the slaves near Savannah: "They were well lodged and fed, and could have been worked no harder than was necessary for exercise and digestion." And a European remarked of the slaves he saw near New Orleans: "To say that they are underworked and overfed, and far happier than the labourers of Great Britain would hardly convey a sufficiently clear notion of their actual condition. They put me much more in mind of a community of grown-up children, spoiled by too much kindness, than a body of dependents, much less a company of slaves." [27]

Some slaves unquestionably were overworked and exploited mercilessly, yet here again it is difficult to generalize.[28] Most white laborers in the United States also worked from sunup to sunset during the antebellum period. One authority, who believes slaves were not often overworked, points out that "in plowing, mules which could not be hurried set the pace; in hoeing, haste would imperil the plants by enhancing the proportion of misdirected strokes; and in the harvest of tobacco, rice and cotton much perseverance but little strain was involved. The sugar harvest alone called for heavy exertion and for night work in the mill." [29] Yet William H. Russell was surprised to find that Louisiana sugar planters refused to use slaves for ditching—Irish gangs were hired for that dirty and exhausting job—and that slave children up to twelve years old were at play, "exempted from the cruel fate which befalls poor children of their age in the mining and manufacturing districts of England." [30] One way of attempting to determine how hard slaves worked is to compare what information is available on cotton picking. The extant sources suggest that the picking quota for the average slave was about 150 pounds a day. A skilled picker, however, could and often did pick between 200 and 300 pounds a day. On some large plantations each slave was given a task, an amount of work to be completed each day. This amount was determined by the age, strength, and sex of the slave. Visitors frequently reported slaves who had finished their day's tasks coming in from the fields as early as three or four o'clock in the afternoon. The task system was not always employed, of course, and some slaves were reportedly worked as much as eighteen hours a day. But as one of the most careful contemporary observers noted: "There was no rule." [31]

Occasionally a slave might be allowed to work for himself. It was not uncommon for slaves to have their own vegetable patches, and some were permitted to raise produce for sale. A visitor to the Fitzpatrick plantation in 1860 reported that Aham had a cotton patch and a nursery that consisted of several thousand peach and apple trees. He sold the fruit from these to neighboring plantations. During the previous year he had made $150 from his nursery and $159 more from his cotton patch. A good businessman, he had lent nearly a thousand dollars, including over $700 to two planters. Another slave, Simon Gray, was the captain of a river boat, which he operated for his owner. White crewmen often worked under Gray, who hired and fired them, kept their work records, paid their expenses, lent them money, and paid their wages.[32] If this appears strange, it should be remembered that slavery was a complex labor and social system that defies easy generalization; it was as varied and as difficult to characterize as capitalism.

Errors ten, eleven, and twelve all relate to the free Negroes of the Old South. The author of the *Teachers' Guide* describes them all as abolitionists, who offered "aid and comfort to their brothers in bondage. Their homes were often the 'stations' of the Southern branch of the Underground Railroad, and they forged the passes for the slave runaways." Much of this is pure romance. The author admits that four thousand free Negroes owned slaves, but he contends that these were "usually relatives they were allowed to buy but not liberate." [33]

No one would claim that life was easy for free Negroes living in the North or the South in the late antebellum period. They suffered various forms of restriction and discrimination. Laws impaired their freedom, and some southern states required them to choose white guardians.[34] Free Negroes in Alabama could not keep taverns or retail liquors, visit slaves without the owner's consent, or preach to slaves unless they were licensed by a church and unless five slaveowning whites were present.

Yet even in Alabama some free Negroes lived in integrated neighborhoods and held responsible jobs. Mobile's free Negro men, who engaged in twenty-two occupations, included barbers, bricklayers, shopkeepers, cigar manufacturers, coppersmiths, shoemakers, and carpenters. Only 12 of the city's 734 free Negroes were illiterate in 1850; 55 were attending public school.[35] Opportunities for the average free Negro appear to have been greater in New Orleans than in New York. In 1850 New York City had 4 Negro lawyers and 9 Negro doctors; New Orleans had no Negro lawyers and only 4 Negro doctors. But New Orleans had 4 Negro capitalists, 2 planters, 11 overseers, 9 brokers and 2 collectors, while New York had none of any of these. Moreover, New Orleans had 64 Negro merchants, 5 jewelers, and 61 clerks to New York's 3, 3, and 7 respectively, and 12 Negro teachers to 8. New York had thrice New Orleans' number of Negro barbers, and twice as many butchers, but the northern city's 12 carpenters and no masons were in sharp contrast to the 355 and 278 in these two trades in New Orleans. Indeed, one-third of all New York's Negro men were unskilled laborers and another quarter were domestic servants; only a tenth of New Orleans' free Negro males were unskilled and not one was a domestic.[36]

Some free persons of color unquestionably were abolitionists. How many is uncertain. Cyprien Ricard was not; in 1851 he bought an estate along with its ninety-one slaves for nearly a quarter of a million dollars. Nor were several substantial free Negro slaveholders in Virginia, South Carolina, and Louisiana. Some of Louisiana's "free colored" gentlemen announced in a New Orleans newspaper during the secession crisis that they "own slaves, . . . are dearly attached to their native land, . . . and are ready to shed their blood for her defence." They insisted that they "have no sympathy for abolitionism; no love for the North, but they have plenty for Louisiana. . . . They will fight for her in 1861 as they fought in 1814–15." [37]

One of the most remarkable of antebellum diaries was written by William Johnson, a free Negro barber and farmer of Natchez, Mississippi. Manumitted by his white father along with his mother and sister, Johnson was trained as a barber in New Orleans, and he eventually became the owner of the largest barber shop in Natchez. He was an industrious man who acquired considerable real estate and owned a number of slaves, none of whom was related to him. At the time of his death in 1851, he was worth over $40,000. In all respects Johnson aspired to be a gentleman. He never associated socially with slaves and scorned free Negroes who did; he followed many gentlemanly pursuits, with particular fondness for hunting and horse racing. He was a member of the Adams County Turf Club. Regularly he attended the theater; he subscribed to a large number of magazines, and for a time he had a French tutor. His home was in a white neighborhood, and he got along well with his neighbors without being an Uncle Tom. Though white Mississippians never acknowledged Johnson as their social equal, they did consider him a respectable and trusted member of society—the top of the free Negro caste. How typical Johnson was of successful free Negroes is impossible to determine. One point is certain: his diary reveals him as an intelligent and ambitious man who made a place for himself in a society he did not try to change. He had no interest in eliminating slavery. He whipped his slaves when they did not behave, and he did not acquire slaves out of benevolence or to liberate them.[38]

Errors thirteen and fourteen are relatively small matters—the militia is a state not a federal organization, and few rather than "many [antebellum] poor whites left the South seeking opportunities in the North" [39] —but they are indicative of the careless scholarship and propaganda found in too many works these days.

The trend in black history is all too apparent. Louis E. Lomax warns that Negro teachers are being intimidated into advocating black power.[40] So are white teachers. "The Negro . . . who does not become militant, who does not curse out white people, and who does not sanction the activities of the militants is in danger," charges the Negro pastor of a Los Angeles church.[41] When the acting chairman of the Black Studies Department at San Francisco State University was told he would not be rehired when his one-year appointment ended in June, he reportedly replied: "We are not accepting the fact I have been fired. . . . I have the backing of the black community to head the black studies department. The black students have said they will not accept anyone else. It'll take a way-out Uncle Tom to come here." [42] The director of the Race Relations Department at Fisk University admits: "many of the proponents of the study of Negro history hold concepts of the nature and purpose of history similar to those for which the textbook writers [of the past] have been so severely criticized. . . . These zealots, who . . . regard history as propaganda rather than inquiry, insist that Negro history can be taught only by a Negro because he alone can understand the black soul. This is sheer poppycock, which if followed to its logical conclusion would result in separate and isolated history for every ethnic, racial, and national group. . . . If this course is followed, it will result not only in a further distortion of history but also serve to reduce communication and lessen human understanding." [43]

Such warnings must be heeded. Scholars and teachers should not use books or courses to indoctrinate. The historian must realize that his duty is to try to understand and explain the past, but not to praise or damn it; he is neither a philosopher nor a theologian. The determination to serve a cause other than scholarship endangers free inquiry. It is hazardous to inject moral values into judgments of past events and times because moral values change. Who is to say that the conduct of Kwakiutl Indians, for example, was better or worse than that of New England Puritans? Historians should not forget the nationalist historians of nineteenth-century Germany, or the Fascist, Bolshevik, and Maoist historians of the twentieth century, who substituted ideology for accuracy. Propaganda has no legitimate place in the writing and teaching of history. Scholars and teachers should take six words of advice from the black militants: "tell it the way it was."

NOTES

1. *San Francisco Chronicle,* December 18, 1968.
2. *Time,* February 23, 1968, p. 48; *U.S. News & World Report,* November 4, 1968, pp. 69–70; *San Francisco Chronicle,* October 25, 31, 1968.
3. Thomas A. Bailey, "The Mythmakers of American History," *Journal of American History* 55 (1968):11.
4. Tom Sanders, "A Common Past of Greatness," *Black Politics: A Journal of Liberation* 1 (1968):22.
5. *This World,* June 2, 1968, p. 47.
6. *San Francisco Chronicle,* December 3, 1968.
7. *University Bulletin: A Weekly Bulletin for the Staff of the University of California* 17 (1968):13.
8. Stokely Carmichael, "Black Power and the Third World," *Black Politics: A Journal of Liberation* 1 (1968):11.
9. *U.S. News & World Report,* November 4, 1968, p. 71; *San Francisco Chronicle,* December 4, 1968.
10. Bailey, "The Mythmakers of American History," p. 8.
11. Earl E. Thorpe, *Negro Historians in the United States* (Baton Rouge, 1958), pp. 1–11.
12. *U.S. News & World Report,* November 4, 1968, p. 71; R. H. Woody, ed., "Behind the Scenes in the Reconstruction Legislature of South Carolina: Diary of Josephus Woodruff," *Journal of Southern History* 2 (1936):91, 235 n; *The Daily California Weekly Magazine,* January 21, 1968; "Of Black America," CBS-TV, August 13, 1968.
13. William Loren Katz, *Teachers' Guide to American Negro History* (Chicago, 1968), pp. 71–79.
14. *Ibid.,* p. 71.
15. Frank L. and Harriet C. Owsley, "The Economic Basis of Society in the Late Ante-Bellum South," *Journal of Southern History* 6

(1940):24–45; Blanche H. Clark, *The Tennessee Yeoman, 1840–1860* (Nashville, 1942); Harry L. Coles, "Some Notes on Slave Ownership and Land Ownership in Louisiana, 1850–1860," *Journal of Southern History* 9 (1943):381–93; Herbert Weaver, *Mississippi Farmers, 1850–1860* (Nashville, 1945); Frank L. Owsley, *Plain Folk of the Old South* (Baton Rouge, 1949).

16. Katz, *Teachers' Guide*, p. 71.

17. *Preliminary Report of the Eighth Census, 1860* (Washington, 1862), pp. 190, 195–210, 230; *Statistics of the United States in 1860* (Washington, 1866), pp. xviii–xix.

18. Vernon Louis Parrington, *Main Currents in American Thought* (New York, 1927–30), 2:56.

19. Fletcher M. Green, *Constitutional Development in the South Atlantic States, 1776–1860* (Chapel Hill, 1930), and "Democracy in the Old South," *Journal of Southern History* 12 (1946):3–23; Malcolm C. McMillan, *Constitutional Development in Alabama, 1798–1901* (Chapel Hill, 1955); W. Magruder Drake, "The Mississippi Constitutional Convention of 1832," *Journal of Southern History* 23 (1957):354–70; Edwin A. Miles, *Jacksonian Democracy in Mississippi* (Chapel Hill, 1960).

20. Charles S. Sydnor, *The Development of Southern Sectionalism, 1819–1848* (Baton Rouge, 1948), p. 14.

21. Robert Partin, ed., "A Connecticut Yankee's Letters from Conecuh County, Alabama," *Alabama Review* 4 (1951):52–54.

22. Katz, *Teachers' Guide*, p. 71.

23. Kenneth M. Stampp, *The Peculiar Institution: Slavery in the Ante-Bellum South* (New York, 1956), p. 30.

24. Katz, *Teachers' Guide*, p. 72.

25. Ulrich B. Phillips, *American Negro Slavery* (New York, 1918), pp. 493–94.

26. Besides the volumes by Stampp and Phillips, students should sample other works on slavery; for example, Stanley M. Elkins, *Slavery: A Problem in American Institutional and Intellectual Life* (New York, 1963); Eugene D. Genovese, *The Political Economy of Slavery* (New York, 1965); and Edward W. Phifer, "Slavery in Microcosm: Burke County, North Carolina," *Journal of Southern History* 28 (1962):137–65.

27. Charles Eliot Norton, *Letters* (London, 1913), 1:121; *Andover Review* 16:157; Louis F. Tasistro, *Random Shots and Southern Breezes* (New York, 1842), 2:13.

28. Stampp, *The Peculiar Institution*, pp. 73–85.

29. Phillips, *American Negro Slavery*, p. 384.

30. William H. Russell, *My Diary North and South* (London, 1863), 1:395–97.

31. Clement Eaton, *The Growth of Southern Civilization, 1790–1860* (New York, 1961), pp. 31, 57, 60, 83–84, 88–89, 108; John Hope Franklin, *From Slavery to Freedom: A History of American Negroes* (New York, 1956), p. 191; Katharine M. Jones, ed., *The Plantation South* (Indianapolis, 1957), p. 41; Frederick L. Olmsted, *The Cotton Kingdom: A Traveller's Observations on Cotton and Slavery in the American Slave States*, ed. Arthur M. Schlesinger (New York, 1953), pp. 8–11, 97–109, 372, 430–36, 451–52.

32. James B. Sellers, *Slavery in Alabama* (University, Ala., 1950), pp. 73–74; John H. Moore, "Simon Gray, Riverman: A Slave Who Was Almost Free," *Mississippi Valley Historical Review* 49 (1962):472–84.

33. Katz, *Teachers' Guide,* p. 72.

34. Franklin, *From Slavery to Freedom,* pp. 213–38. See also Charles S. Sydnor, "The Free Negro in Mississippi," *American Historical Review* 32 (1927):769–88; J. Merton England, "The Free Negro in Ante-Bellum Tennessee," *Journal of Southern History* 9 (1943):37–58; Leon F. Litwack, *North of Slavery: The Negro in the Free States, 1790–1860* (Chicago, 1961); Eugene H. Berwanger, *The Frontier against Slavery: Western Anti-Negro Prejudice and the Slavery Extension Controversy* (Urbana, 1967); and V. Jacque Voegeli, *Free but Not Equal: The Midwest and the Negro during the Civil War* (Chicago, 1968).

35. Sellers, *Slavery in Alabama,* pp. 361–98.

36. Phillips, *American Negro Slavery,* p. 438; James E. Winston, "The Free Negro in New Orleans, 1803–1860," *Louisiana Historical Quarterly* 21 (1938):1075–85. See also Roger A. Fischer, "Racial Segregation in Ante Bellum New Orleans," *American Historical Review* 74 (1969):926–37.

37. Stampp, *The Peculiar Institution,* p. 194; Phillips, *American Negro Slavery,* pp. 434–36.

38. William R. Hogan and Edwin A. Davis, eds., *William Johnson's Natchez* (Baton Rouge, 1951). See also Edwin A. Davis and William R. Hogan, *The Barber of Natchez* (Baton Rouge, 1954), a biography of Johnson.

39. Katz, *Teachers' Guide,* p. 74.

40. *Chicago's American,* March 17, 1968.

41. *Oakland Tribune,* November 27, 1968.

42. *San Francisco Chronicle,* March 1, 1969.

43. Clifton H. Johnson, "A New History: An Essential Alternative to Narrow, White Mythology," *Journal* 7 (1969):8–11.

INDEX